T0095670

Other books by the author

I Must Decrease
The Elder Shall Serve the Younger
Holiness, the Joyful Pursuit

Jesus, The Book

Understanding the Word of God

by

William Moore

authorHOUSE®

AuthorHouse™
1663 Liberty Drive
Bloomington, IN 47403
www.authorhouse.com
Phone: 1 (800) 839-8640

© *2013 William Moore. All rights reserved.*

No part of this book may be reproduced, stored in a retrieval system, or transmitted by any means without the written permission of the author.

Published by AuthorHouse 06/11/2019

ISBN: 978-1-4918-4381-9 (sc)
ISBN: 978-1-4918-4380-2 (e)

Library of Congress Control Number: 2013923081

Print information available on the last page.

Any people depicted in stock imagery provided by Getty Images are models, and such images are being used for illustrative purposes only.
Certain stock imagery © Getty Images.

This book is printed on acid-free paper.

Because of the dynamic nature of the Internet, any web addresses or links contained in this book may have changed since publication and may no longer be valid. The views expressed in this work are solely those of the author and do not necessarily reflect the views of the publisher, and the publisher hereby disclaims any responsibility for them.

Contents

Foreword

My first major lesson to a church occurred when I was nineteen years old. Moments into my lesson, a minister shouted his disagreement from the back of the church, not once, but twice. After requesting a full hearing of the lesson, I continued. At the end of the service that minister was the first person I encountered. He shook my hand and told me how much he enjoyed the lesson. On another occasion, following a "prayer" meeting, a lady in the group asked a question, "Where is Heaven?" When I alluded to an answer, a minister became threateningly indignant and declared that no man knew the answer to that question as he moved quickly toward me with his arms thrashing menacingly. An initial reaction of disagreement or lack of understanding is not unusual. To avoid a scene and being pounded into a small pulp, I stopped any attempt to finish my response. Agreement, however, is not my primary goal. My primary goal is to share my understanding of the Scriptures. With or without agreement in every point, hopefully there will be enough agreeable material to make reading of this book worthwhile. Incidentally, the verse in question was "And if I go and prepare a place for you, I will come again and receive you to Myself; that where I am, there you may be also. Joh 14:3" It seems amazing that I remember the verse being questioned, and yes, I did and do know the answer to the question. It is simple! Heaven is wherever God is, and God is everywhere. The complication is in dimensionality, but that could be another book. Indeed, there are 57 references to dimensions in this book. There may be more before it is complete.

Examples of subjects in this book include the significance of name in Scriptures; for example, what does it mean to have a new name which no one knows except the person receiving it? We will examine the importance of numbers, especially through the number forty.[1] We will discuss the importance of spiritual principles; for example, The Elder Shall Serve the Younger. The Bible is emphatic that the bones of Jesus[2] could not be broken. We will also discuss why Moses, as great a prophet as he was, could not lead Israel into the Promised Land. Why is baptism important? Other subjects include redemptive and non-redemptive temples.

It is my prayer that this book is worth your reading. In any event, may you find some new understanding of the greatest book ever compiled, the Word of God.

Unless specified to the otherwise, all biblical references are to the New King James Version.

---

[1] Pages 16 432

[2] Page 108

Spiritual Principles

Before we delve into mysteries, we should become familiar with principles and their importance. Principles are truths revealed through use and consistency. Once a subject is mentioned in book, chapter, and verse it is established as a principle through persistent demonstration. What appears as a simple, mundane observance is revealed as a major principle. In this chapter we will look at the phrase "The elder shall serve the younger," repetition and number meanings. For meanings found in numbers, we will restrict ourselves to the number forty and a few others. Let us begin our study of principles with "the elder shall serve the younger." (Moore, The Elder Shall Serve The Younger, 2007)

The Elder shall serve the younger

And the LORD said to her: "Two nations are in your womb, Two peoples shall be separated from your body; One people shall be stronger than the other, And the older shall serve the younger." (Gen 25:23)

This is again quoted by Paul in Romans 9:12 in another context. Other verses reveal its significance as a spiritual principle in unexpected ways. We will revisit that shortly, but first we will look at the most obvious confirmations

1

There are also celestial bodies and terrestrial bodies; but the glory of the celestial is one, and the glory of the terrestrial is another. There is one glory of the sun, another glory of the moon, and another glory of the stars; for one star differs from another star in glory. So also is the resurrection of the dead. The body is sown in corruption, it is raised in incorruption. It is sown in dishonor, it is raised in glory. It is sown in weakness, it is raised in power. It is sown a natural body, it is raised a spiritual body. There is a natural body, and there is a spiritual body. And so it is written, "The first man Adam became a living being." The last Adam became a life-giving spirit. However, the spiritual is not first, but the natural, and afterward the spiritual. The first man was of the earth, made of dust; the second Man is the Lord from heaven.[3]

This passage demonstrates the spiritual significance of the principle of the ruling authority of the last over the first. Christ, the second Adam, was greater than Adam of the Garden of Eden. Paul also tells us that our glorified body will be greater than our current body. This body is corruptible, but our resurrection body will be everlasting. It is incorruptible.

Behold, I tell you a mystery: We shall not all sleep, but we shall all be changed--in a moment, in the twinkling of an eye, at the last trumpet. For the trumpet will sound, and the dead will be raised incorruptible, and we shall be changed. For this corruptible must put on incorruption, and this mortal must put on immortality. (1Co 15:51-53)

---

[3]   1Co 15:40-47

"Now I saw a new heaven and a new earth, for the first heaven and the first earth had passed away. Also there was no more sea." (Rev 21:1)

Even the universe as we know it will be changed. The first heaven and earth where we live today will be replaced by a better existence. Understand that by "no more sea" we are also being told that there will be no more troubles.[4] Peter confirms the words of the apostle John.

But the day of the Lord will come as a thief in the night, in which the heavens will pass away with a great noise, and the elements will melt with fervent heat; both the earth and the works that are in it will be burned up. Therefore, since all these things will be dissolved, what manner of persons ought you to be in holy conduct and godliness, looking for and hastening the coming of the day of God, because of which the heavens will be dissolved, being on fire, and the elements will melt with fervent heat? Nevertheless we, according to His promise, look for new heavens and a new earth in which righteousness dwells.[5]

Even David added support to this principle when he said, The LORD said to my Lord, "Sit at My right hand, Till I make Your enemies Your footstool." (Psa. 110:1) David recognized here that, as great a king as God had made him, his son of subsequent generations was greater than he. The elder shall serve the younger.

This principle was repeated in the next generation after being introduced through the birth of Jacob. The firstborn of Judah, Jacob's firstborn, was Er. His second son was Onan. Er was evil so God slew him. Onan, the

---

[4]   See Baptism

[5]   2Pe 3:10-13

second son, refused to raise a family to Er, so he too was killed. The story takes strange twists from here which I do not fully understand, but Perez was the second son born to Judah through his daughter-in-law, Tamar. Zerah put his arm forth first and a ribbon was tied to it to show him as the firstborn, but Perez was first to fully emerge from the womb. His name indicates a problem he created in Israel. The heritage would have been named through Zerah, but this birth caused a breach, so Tamar named him Perez or Breach. Following the birth chronology of Jesus, we see in Matthew 1:3 that Jesus was born through the linage of Perez. As Jacob stole the blessing of Esau, Perez stole the blessing of Zerah. Again, the elder serves the younger.

We have also seen in the Scriptures we have cited that this principle extends beyond the physical men and women living on the earth. It applies to the very universe. Our first reference to this principle was from the middle of Genesis, but its first appearance is in the first chapter of Genesis.

Then God said, "Let there be light"; and there was light. And God saw the light, that it was good; and God divided the light from the darkness. God called the light Day, and the darkness He called Night. So the evening and the morning were the first day. (Gen 1:3-5)

That evening precedes day, it is the elder. The day is greater than the night. This is affirmed through verse sixteen.

Then God made two great lights: the greater light to rule the day, and the lesser light to rule the night. He made the stars also. (Gen 1:16)

Two other great lights that God made were the dispensations of Law and of Grace. We may cite whole chapters that demonstrate the preference of Grace to the Law, but we will restrict ourselves to the following. The light from the moon is also only a poor reflection of the light of the sun, as the Law is an inadequate reflection of grace through Christ.

"But when the fullness of the time had come, God sent forth His Son, born of a woman, born under the law, to redeem those who were under the law, that we might receive the adoption as sons. And because you are sons, God has sent forth the Spirit of His Son into your hearts, crying out, "Abba, Father!" Therefore you are no longer a slave but a son, and if a son, then an heir of God through Christ." (Gal 4:4-7)

The Law had no power to make us sons. Grace, through faith in Christ, gives us adoption as children of God.

Repetition

Principles are, to my awareness, always repetitious. We have already seen this in the principle that the elder serves the younger, so we will spend very little time here, but one more example is worth pointing out. There is, however, much more to glean from this principle. A quick example is that this principle was demonstrated six times in the first chapter of Genesis in the phrase, "The evening and the morning."

Another example of repetition is seen when Pharaoh had a dream and sought for understanding of the dream. The dream had two parts. The magicians and wise men of Egypt could not interpret his dream. Pharaoh's chief butler remembered that while in prison Joseph correctly interpreted dreams of both him and the chief baker. Pharaoh inquired of Joseph the meaning of his dream.

'Then Joseph said to Pharaoh, "The dreams of Pharaoh are one; God has shown Pharaoh what He is about to do. . . And the dream was repeated to Pharaoh twice because the thing is established by God, and God will shortly bring it to pass."' (Gen 41:25, 32)

By repeating the dream, it was established. It would occur as Joseph had interpreted. Repetition is a method God has used to establish principles. We will see this very firmly established in other studies.

Forty

Numbers are another way God presents truths. Where translators change the unit of measure camouflages the important NUMBERS revealed there. Translators have taken the liberty to change cubit measurements into ones we are familiar with. To make the Bible more understandable to us is a good goal, but in so doing, they have adjusted the numbers to reflect those measurements. One example of this is in the measurements of Noah's ark. The original numbers carry significance that is erased by such a change. Other changes to render God's word gender neutral also change the meaning. While it may not always be detrimental to understanding the simple plan of salvation, it does present the Bible as an interpretation instead of a translation. The New King James Version also takes this liberty: for example, interpreting firkins as gallons. (John 2:6) I guess that any translation from the original language may be similarly detrimental in determining the deepest meanings behind the Scriptures, but we will understand enough to be saved.

Before this discussion is concluded, we will make an assertion based on the number principle. This assertion will not affect anyone's understanding of Scriptures. If correct, it will merely add to what is presented concerning the potential importance of numbers and principles.

The Flood

For after seven more days I will cause it to rain on the earth forty days and forty nights, and I will destroy from the face of the earth all living things that I have made." (Gen 7:4)

The earth was filled with evil, and God was determined to destroy evil from the earth, so He caused this great flood. He purged the earth. He baptized the earth! This removed outside temptations. It is like being baptized in the Word of God and understanding what is expected of us. They could not ascribe their subsequent failures to others. Likewise, being buried in God's Word identifies those things we should avoid and often provide insight in how to overcome.

Unbelief

Shortly after Israel began their journey from Egypt, twelve Israelites were chosen to see the lay of the land. This was to be their homeland. These men studied the land for forty days, after which, they reported back to Moses and the people. It should have been forty days of seeing what God was going to deliver into their hands. Instead, ten of them saw the problems they would face, and the people accepted the negative report instead of the encouragement of Joshua and Caleb.

Israel was guilty of unbelief in that they did not believe God would conquer the promised land through them. The land was full of giants. Even though the land was a horticulturalist's paradise, they feared they would be destroyed by the land's inhabitants. Only Caleb and Joshua believed they could conquer the land, and the people believed the report of the ten. Because of their unbelief, God declared that none of that generation except for Caleb and Joshua would enter the land. They were forced to stay in the wilderness forty years or until all that generation had died. In this case, forty years was to teach them the penalty of unbelief and to purge Israel of that generation of unbelievers. During this time, they would learn to trust God.

They were ridded of that source and threat of unbelief. As Pharaoh's army (threat of destruction) was destroyed at the crossing of the Red Sea, here we see the destruction of the unbelief in the heart of Israel. That unbelief would have been as dangerous to Israel as Pharaoh's army.

They would mature in their faith. Also, by the things they would endure, they would learn how God would provide for them in every situation. The next time they prepared to cross Jordan, they were eager to go. The giants, while still present, were no longer a threat to them.[6]

This is the effect of baptism. Baptism cleanses us from the power of sin. The blood redeemed us from the penalty for our sins. Baptism is the symbolic washing of water by the Word-to a point. Baptism is symbolic of the effect of studying the Word of God: hence, the washing of water by the word.

Fasting

The sight of the glory of the LORD was like a consuming fire on the top of the mountain in the eyes of the children of Israel. So Moses went into the midst of the cloud and went up into the mountain. And Moses was on the mountain forty days and forty nights. (Exo 24:17-18)

So he was there with the LORD forty days and forty nights; he neither ate bread nor drank water. And He wrote on the tablets the words of the covenant, the Ten Commandments. (Exo 34:28)

Again, we see the principle of repetition at work. During these periods of time, God was teaching Moses. During the forty days, God burned the Ten Commandments into the stones. Of course, these stones represent the heart of God's people. The laws of God are written on our hearts. We have two lessons here that we will touch on.

---

[6]   We know giants were still there, since Goliath was killed years later by David.

First, for whatever reason, God wrote the laws in stone twice. From the principle of repetition, it is assured. God will write His laws in our hearts. We have this assurance also from the prophet Ezekiel.

For I will take you from among the nations, gather you out of all countries, and bring you into your own land. Then I will sprinkle clean water on you, and you shall be clean; I will cleanse you from all your filthiness and from all your idols. I will give you a new heart and put a new spirit within you; I will take the heart of stone out of your flesh and give you a heart of flesh. I will put My Spirit within you and cause you to walk in My statutes, and you will keep My judgments and do them. (Eze 36:24-27)

Notice that Ezekiel does not mince words with uncertainty. This is only a subset of the promises God made to His people in this chapter, but He uses the phrase "I will" five times. He uses the phrase 'you will' once when He affirms that we will keep God's judgments.

These things are not accidents. God is purposeful. He doesn't make mistakes. The instructions given to Moses about the Tabernacle are explicit. Was Moses allowed any latitude in diverting from what God had told him? I think not!

According to all that I show you, that is, the pattern of the tabernacle and the pattern of all its furnishings, just so you shall make it. (Exo 25:9)

And see to it that you make them according to the pattern which was shown you on the mountain. (Exo 25:40)

And you shall raise up the tabernacle according to its pattern which you were shown on the mountain. (Exo 26:30)

Every item, every material, every design, every number is meaningful. Translations that alter the numbers by using a different unit of measure have lost a significance of the message.

Until this time, Moses was the redeemer, the promised one that led them to freedom. He saved them from death through the blood of the lamb. Now, he begins to minister to the people. He has provided them with the commandments, the rules for their lives. Now, He is telling them how to please God. They now have the Ten Commandments, and he instructs them in how they will live before God. His full ministry began after the forty days of fasting. Moses has had the power of God in his life before this, but now, the anointing of God is so strong that the people cannot look on his face. For forty days twice, he has been prepared to lead the people. It was in the mount that God gave him the design for the Tabernacle, the center of their religious worship. It was during this period that God gave him the rules they must follow.

We see the same forty days before Jesus officially begins His ministry. He fasted forty days and was tempted of the devil. It was a period of trial, learning, and humbling Himself before the Father.

Jesus continued this pattern after His resurrection. He taught His disciples for forty days before His ascension. They had been with him for several years, and now He is speaking clearly to them things that they may not have understood prior to His resurrection from the dead. Now, however, even Thomas addressed Him as "my Lord and my God." (John 20:28) The veil is gone. Now, as much as humanly possible, he has seen the Father.

Other examples of forty include the terms of the rules of the three kings of <u>united</u> Israel. Each of them reigned forty years. After Solomon, the kingdom was divided, and there was no king over all Israel.

There were three divisions in the life of Moses. His first forty years was spent in learning the wisdom of the teachers of Egypt. His next forty years was spent in the wilderness where he was prepared (hardened, in this case) for ministry. His last forty years was dedicated to ministry in leading the people of Israel to the Promised Land.

It appears that forty is a number denoting preparation (studying), hardening (experience), and ministry.

Israel spent four hundred years in slavery and forty years inuring in the wilderness. I have not studied their subsequent history relative to the number forty.

Excuse me for another aside? Moses led them from Egypt after their salvation from death through the blood of the children of Egypt, which was also retribution for the slaying of innocents when Moses was born. The salvation of Israel at the Exodus was accomplished through the death (blood) of the Egyptian innocents. At the Red Sea, Israel began their baptismal experience when they entered the wilderness. This was their place of preparation for the Promised Land. Their baptism lasted through forty years of hardening in the Wilderness. It was a place of learning trust and obedience in preparation for entering the Promised Land.

Note also, that Moses could not lead them into the Promised Land. His ministry was baptism, teaching, preparing. This is washing of water by the Word. Moses ministry began with leading Israel into the Red Sea and ended when he brought them to the river Jordan that they might now enter the promised land, a place he could not take them in to.

A new leader was necessary to enter the Promised Land and that leader was Joshua, which is Hebrew for Jesus (Yeshua).

In the foregoing discussion, we see that forty is associated with teaching, maturing, and spiritual growth. It was also the duration of the ministry of Moses after receiving the Ten Commandments. We have not exhausted the study of the significance of this number, but I feel confident that we have seen enough to ask other questions. At the start of this lesson, I referred to a broad assertion that I would make. It is pointing out a possibility more than an assertion.

If forty is so important in the lengths of ministries and preparation for ministries, does it not seem odd that Jesus is thought to have been crucified in His mid-thirties? My wife and I were discussing the number forty on the drive to church one day, when I brought this question up. A few days later I dug into it more. I knew that the birth of Jesus had been placed at 4BC. In my studies, I learned that the year of the crucifixion is placed between 30 and 36AD. Granted that there is no definite proof, but it appears possible that Jesus may have walked the earth for forty years. That forty years would have been His preparation for His future responsibilities as well as bringing redemption of the world. What is the significance if it is true? It does nothing but add an element of certainty to the significance of the number and the importance of principles in understanding Scriptures. It also helps us determine a VERY close approximation as to His return. To me, Jesus is the ultimate illustrator and illustration of truth, so I firmly believe He lived forty years on earth. We shall return to and repeat some of this material in the Final Chapter.[7]

In a later chapter we shall discuss balance, but it seems appropriate now to introduce the fact that balance is a principle of God. We have seen that forty is a number significant of learning and maturing. The following Scriptural reference demonstrate that it is also associated with peace or blessings.

So the land had rest for forty years. Then Othniel the son of Kenaz died. (Jdg 3:11)

"Thus let all Your enemies perish, O LORD! But let those who love Him be like the sun When it comes out in full strength." So the land had rest for forty years. (Jdg 5:31)

David was thirty years old when he began to reign, and he reigned forty years. (2Sa 5:4)

The period that David reigned over Israel was forty years; seven years he reigned in Hebron, and in Jerusalem he reigned thirty-three years. (1Ki 2:11)

And the period that Solomon reigned in Jerusalem over all Israel was forty years. (1Ki 11:42)

Even Saul's period of rule over Israel was forty years.

And afterward they asked for a king; so God gave them Saul the son of Kish, a man of the tribe of Benjamin, for forty years. (Act 13:21)

---

[7]   Page 429

The Temple

This discussion will be a very limited look into the Temple. We will only look at the Temple as it relates to Jesus from limited aspects.

Solomon's prayer of dedication for the Temple is so inspiring that it is tempting to include the entire prayer here. Due to its length, however, we will use excerpts instead of the entire text. It is doubtful that Solomon, with all his wisdom, realized the prophetic nature of the Temple or the prayer he prayed on this day. Simply stated, Solomon prophesied of the coming Messiah and His office.

"But will God indeed dwell on the earth? Behold, heaven and the heaven of heavens cannot contain You. How much less this temple which I have built!" (1 Kg. 8:27)

Likewise, when Jesus walked on the earth as the tabernacle of the Living God, could all of God be contained in a single body? Of course not! Even Jesus said, "...My Father is greater than I." (John 14:28) However, Jesus was and is (through the Holy Spirit baptism) the focal point of God's communication with man, so Solomon asked God to hear the prayers of those who prayed toward this temple.

"that Your eyes may be open toward this temple night and day, toward the place of which You said, 'My name shall be there,' that You may hear the prayer which Your servant makes toward this place. And may You hear the supplication of Your servant and of Your people

Israel, when they pray toward this place. Hear in heaven Your dwelling place; and when You hear, forgive." (1 Kg. 8:29, 30)

God had said that His name would be there. When the angel announced to Mary that she would bring forth a son, he also told her to call His name Jesus. (Mat.1:21) Why? Because He was to save His people from their sin. Jesus means "salvation of Jehovah." The Israelites were to look toward the Temple, as we are to look to Jesus. We call upon Jesus for salvation, healings, helps, and anything we need. He is our advocate with the Father. He presents our defense in heaven. (1 John 2:1)

The Father has respect to the Son. Whatever we ask in His name[8] (His nature) with faith is granted. God had respect to this Temple, so anything prayed toward this Temple was as if one were praying to Jesus.

"When there is famine in the land, pestilence or blight or mildew, locusts or grasshoppers; when their enemy besieges them in the land of their cities; whatever plague or whatever sickness there is; whatever prayer, whatever supplication is made by anyone, or by all Your people Israel, when each one knows the plague of his own heart, and spreads out his hands toward this temple: then hear in heaven Your dwelling place, and forgive, and act, and give to everyone according to all his ways, whose heart You know (for You alone know the hearts of all the sons of men), that they may fear You all the days that they live in the land which You gave to our fathers. (1Ki 8:37-40)

How emphatic the message! We may have been plagued with insects, enemies, or other disasters because of

---

[8]   9 See the section "What's in a name?"

our sins, but we look toward this Temple with outstretched arms and repentant hearts. Hear us, oh Lord, and forgive. This temple was a type of Christ to whom we call upon with outstretched arms for forgiveness, and we are heard. Solomon's prayer even made accommodation for those of us who have been adopted into the family of God with salvation for the gentiles.

"Moreover, concerning a foreigner, who is not of Your people Israel, but has come from a far country for Your name's sake (for they will hear of Your great name and Your strong hand and Your outstretched arm), when he comes and prays toward this temple, hear in heaven Your dwelling place, and do according to all for which the foreigner calls to You, that all peoples of the earth may know Your name and fear You, as do Your people Israel, and that they may know that this temple which I have built is called by Your name. (1Ki 8:41-43)

Solomon's Temple was, however, a teacher of something greater—pointing toward true redemption; therefore, it does have some shortfalls. God acknowledged Solomon's prayer concerning the Temple. He told Solomon that He heard His prayer and would establish his throne, but the throne was only established if Solomon and his sons continued to serve God. With Jesus, there is no such warning. The throne of Christ is firmly established forever; yet, while Jesus continues, the Temple has been ground to nothingness and waits, I feel, for one last resurrection before His return. My prayers are with the Temple Mount Faithful in Israel that God will bless their efforts in the reconstruction of the Temple.

This brings us to another point. We have mentioned only the Temple. We have spoken of Solomon only as someone who prayed concerning the Temple. Solomon was also a lesson of Christ. Solomon could build this Temple because he was a man of peace.

"You know how my father David could not build a house for the name of the LORD his God because of the wars which were fought against him on every side, until the LORD put his foes under the soles of his feet." (1 Kings 5:3)

Solomon was a king of peace, as his name suggests, and Jesus is the Prince of Peace. (Is.9:6) The family of Solomon was to last forever, not Solomon himself. Solomon was a type of the spiritual side of Christ. While the king followed the commands of God, there was fellowship between God and Israel. The implication and reality were that if the king obeyed God, the people would also follow God. The Temple was a demonstration of the fellowship between the people of Israel and God. When the fellowship between God and the people of Israel was broken, the Temple, the physical symbol of that fellowship, was destroyed.

In this, we see the shortcomings of physical symbols for spiritual truths. Christ never fails. He is forever one with the Father. Christ is both the Temple and the King, and we are spiritual Israel.

We have just been studying levels by seeing the Temple as a type of Christ; yet, Christ is eternal, but the Temple of Israel is temporal. There are other differences in our schoolmaster, the Temple, and its reality, Christ. First, worship at the Temple required sacrifices of the blood of bulls and goats. Again, these are parts of the schoolmaster that point to Christ. They do not actually take away sin.

"Therefore the law was our tutor to bring us to Christ, that we might be justified by faith." (Gal. 3:24)

"And every priest stands ministering daily and offering repeatedly the same sacrifices, which can never take away sins. But this Man, after He had offered one sacrifice for sins forever, sat down at the right hand of God. . ." (Heb 10:11-12)

It becomes clear that God does not accept the life of animals as an appropriate sacrifice for sin. The sacrifice must be something pure and offered of its own will. The only sacrifice pure enough was Jesus, He that was born of God. He had no sin, yet He gave His life as an offering for our sins. Now, if we accept the sacrifice of Jesus for us and commit our lives to Him, our sins are covered by His offering, and we are no longer under the penalty of death; we are clean. Yes, we will die to the flesh, but we will live forever. Later in our studies, we will answer the question, "Was it imperative that Jesus die and if so, why?" We will also return to the Temple for further insights.[9] We have seen numerous references to the Name, but before we address the significance of His name, we will touch on baptism.

---

[9]   See Temple revisited

Baptism

I have heard ministers say that they do not know if baptism is necessary, and there is evidence that it may not always be required. Jesus told the thief on the cross that he would be with Him that day in paradise, implying that the penitent thief would be saved even without baptism. Deathbed repentance may be such that any form of baptism is impossible, but I have no doubt to the mercy of Christ toward the penitent. So, why do we baptize? Following are four reasons for baptism: a testimony of commitment, testimony of obedience, testimony of humility, and destruction of the power of sin in our lives.

Testimony of Commitment

It is first a testimony of commitment to Him whom we have trusted for salvation. How important is this? Among non-Christian peoples, baptism is the outward symbol of Christianity. In this sense, baptism also acts as a testimony to the World of that commitment to Christ. Islamic communities will sometimes ignore a profession of faith in Christ by another Muslim, perhaps expecting that the individual is going through a phase, and this rebellion will wear off. Baptism is, however, a testimony of commitment that will not be ignored.

Bilquis Sheikh (Sheik, 1999) was so emphatic about being baptized and being baptized by immersion that on the day she was to be baptized she acted to make sure her wishes could not be halted by disapproving relatives. She was concerned that Muslim relatives would try to prevent her from being baptized. It began to appear that her plans for baptism would not work out, so she filled a bathtub with water and baptized herself. She still desired to be baptized by a minister of the Gospel, so she followed through on her plans. Her baptism by a Christian minister was successfully carried out later that day, but she was glad that she went to the trouble of baptizing herself. The Christian minister who baptized her did not immerse her in water but merely sprinkled water on her head. After that day, her relationship with other Muslims became more and more strained, and she ultimately escaped death by leaving the country where she was born. There was also another cause for the straining of her relationship with Muslims and her leaving the country. She became too successful in gaining new converts from Islam to Christ. Baptism played a pivotal role in that once baptized, she was considered hopelessly Christian. (Sheik, 1999, pp. 66-75)

Another story deals with a young man that had trained to be an imam, a Muslim priest. Jesus began dealing with him in dreams, and after several dreams, he gave his life to Christ. His father was furious and commanded the family to ignore him. For a time, he was treated with contempt and isolation. Then his father changed tactics and began to show him love, thinking that what ostracism had not accomplished, love might. When the young man was baptized, however, his father hired someone to kill him. That demonstrates again the effect of baptism, but I must relate the rest of this story. He was shot with a poison dart by the hired assassin and almost died. Sometime later, the father became ill and asked for his son. He apologized to his son for his treatment of him and asked for his forgiveness. When his son assured him that he had forgiven him years earlier, his father asked "Why? I never asked you to forgive me." He explained that Jesus is love and teaches him to forgive his enemies. That evening, his father died after giving his heart to Jesus. Like the thief on the cross, it does not appear that there was opportunity for his father to be baptized. I am inclined to believe I will meet him some day. (Producers@morethandreams.org, 2006) Likewise, the thief on the cross was not baptized, but Jesus assured him that he would be with him in paradise that day. (Luke 23,43)

Testimony of Obedience

Secondly, baptism is a testimony of obedience. After being commanded by God to destroy all the people and animals of the Amalekites, Saul took the king prisoner and took as loot all the animals that were good. He destroyed only animals that were not good. He then offered some of the animals as sacrifice to God.

Samuel's response to Saul's excuses for keeping the good animals was, ". . . Has the LORD as great delight in burnt offerings and sacrifices, As in obeying the voice of the LORD? Behold, to obey is better than sacrifice, And to heed than the fat of rams. For rebellion is as the sin of witchcraft, And stubbornness is as iniquity and idolatry. Because you have rejected the word of the LORD, He also has rejected you from being king." (1Sa 15:22-23)

One act of disobedience cost Saul the blessing of God, and the kingdom that should have gone to his descendants was transferred to the house of David.

Jesus, himself was baptized. (Mat. 3, Mark 1, Luke 3) In answer to the resistance to His baptism by John the Baptist, Jesus responded, "Permit it to be so now, for thus it is fitting for us to fulfill all righteousness." (Mat. 3:15) In what is called the Great Commission, Jesus commanded his disciples to baptize all nations. (Mat. 29:19) If they were given instructions to baptize, there was an expectation for obedience by believers to be baptized.

On the day of Pentecost, when the people asked the disciples what they should do, Peter instructed them to repent and be baptized.[10] Three thousand believers were baptized that day. Other examples followed in Acts 8, 9 and 16. In Acts 10, receiving the Holy Spirit and speaking in tongues did not obviate baptism. Peter ordered them to be baptized in the name of Jesus Christ. In Acts 19, we see Apollos preaching Christ to the Corinthians. Upon hearing that Apollos had been baptized by John the Baptist, Paul taught Apollos about baptism in the name of Jesus, and he was baptized in His name and received the Holy Spirit. He knew he had received the Holy Spirit because he spoke in tongues.

Testimony of Humility

The meaning of the word baptize is to be completely wet. No matter what argument is used; to be baptized is to

---

[10]   Acts 2:38

be wholly submersed. Again, it is not in my hand to judge those who have been sprinkled as opposed to baptized. It is my responsibility to present God's word for what it says. It is every believer's responsibility to act nobly in their obedience to His commands, as they understand them AND as they are able.

I will ask you to search your heart. If you have not been baptized as it was practiced in the early church and in accordance with the intent of the word "baptize", what hinders you? If you are completely satisfied, well. If you think it is simply not necessary, that you see no need to be buried, is it from pride? Jesus said, "Assuredly, I say to you, unless you are converted and become as little children, you will by no means enter the kingdom of heaven. Therefore whoever humbles himself as this little child is the greatest in the kingdom of heaven." (Mat 18:3-4)

Baptism, especially by immersion, requires humility. When baptized, an individual places himself or herself completely in the hand of the baptizer.

Baptism many times results in great spiritual blessings. I have heard of numerous baptisms where people came out of the water speaking in tongues. I have witnessed this experience. One young woman recently baptized was so blessed spiritually that she seemed to be in a state of ecstasy for weeks.

Blessings such as these are rewards for humility, but even the most humble and holy may feel nothing but wet after baptism, but God will not fail to bless us for obedience. It will become evident later in this text that God, without personal intervention, has established our accountability for a lack of obedience and humility. He has also established the surety of blessings for obedience and humility. This is covered in the chapter, The Bones of Jesus.

Removal of Sins

Peter spoke of baptism saying, "This water symbolizes baptism that now saves you also—not the removal of dirt from the body but the pledge of a good conscience toward God. It saves you by the resurrection of Jesus Christ. . ." (1 Peter 3:21)

Again "There is also an antitype which now saves us—baptism" are the key words here. We who believe are baptized in obedience to the behest of Jesus.

Are we lost if we are not baptized? Again, that is judgment best left with God. According to the Scriptures, baptism is a requirement—not merely an inconvenient rite of obedience. We are not given many rules by which to live. We do not kill animals to show our repentance. We do not concern ourselves with grain offerings and drink offerings. Jesus told us to love, and if we love, we have fulfilled all the laws of Moses. (Mat. 22:40) Baptism is not a Law of Moses. We were commanded to be baptized by the resurrected Savior.

We may get a more perfect understanding from the exodus of Israel from Egypt. Israel was saved from the curse of death that plagued the homes of the Egyptians by putting blood of a sacrificial lamb on the doorpost and lintel of the entrance to each home. When the destroying angel went through Egypt, he passed over each home that was protected by the blood.[11] Pharaoh then allowed Israel to go into the wilderness to worship, but when he realized that Israel had escaped, he led his army against Israel. Israel crossed the Red Sea in a type of baptism. When the army of pharaoh chased into the sea after them, the waters returned and drowned them. Until this time, Israel was in danger of being returned to the service of pharaoh.[12] If they had not passed through the water, Pharaoh would have destroyed them.

What baptism did for us here was to break the power of pharaoh over Israel. They were now free from the oppression of Egypt. Likewise, baptism frees us from the oppression of Satan. We are no longer subject to him. We shall return to this discussion later.[13] We shall also revisit the Exodus later to compare it to the Temple. I emphasize the fact that it is baptism in the Word of God that breaks the bondage of sin, not merely getting dipped in water. Purely ritual or not, let us be obedient to the commands of our savior.

How to be Baptized

Baptism should not be a subject of argument among serious believers in the gospel of Jesus; however, it is worthy of discussion. For this reason, I present here reasons to baptize in the name of Jesus. This is a time for unity, not doctrinal debate. Here, I merely explain my viewpoint

---

[11]   Ex. 12
[12]   Ex. 14
[13]   Page 409

on baptism, but I have fellowshipped for years with good Christians who do not baptize in Jesus name. Before we begin the presentation, let me offer this observation. When we discuss baptism in His name in the next chapter, we will see why the words spoken at Baptism are, from one perspective, "almost" inconsequential.

I was attending a Sunday afternoon singing with a close friend, and it had been a wonderful singing. Everyone was enjoying the blessings of God. As in most charismatic services, this Pentecostal people was singing, clapping hands, and dancing before the Lord. When leaving the service, I commented to my friend about how good the service was. His reply almost floored me. He said, "Yes, if only they were baptized in Jesus' name." I understand what he meant. When you believe in something so strongly, you desire to see others agreeing with you. However, my immediate thought was that God did not seem to mind that they were baptized differently, and we certainly enjoyed our fellowship with Christians from a slightly different school of thought. So let us not create rifts in the church by unnecessarily arguing doctrine divisively but let us present our views objectively and with the love of Christ.

Another experience, after visiting this same church for another singing service with two other friends, demonstrated God's work through our worship that afternoon. My two friends and I were driving down the street returning from the service. The memory is still vivid, sixty years later. I remember our location and that we had just crossed the street after the light turned green. We had been quiet for a while. Suddenly, we all began singing—at exactly the same time. We began singing the same song.

We started at exactly the same place in the middle of the song, and we all sang in the same key. We sang only briefly as we stopped and looked in amazement at one another. An hour after leaving the church, we were all still enjoying the Spirit from the service. By the way, the name of the song was "It's Springing, Springing Up."

The difference in baptisms appears to be the result of Mat. 28:19 and Acts 2:38. We will add these additional references to the discussion: Acts 8:16, Acts 10:48, Acts 19:5, and Gal. 3:27. Most of these Scriptures refer directly to being baptized in the name of the Lord Jesus.

The words father and son are not names in this usage but adjectives describing a relationship. Except in a very narrow discussion, no name is associated with them.

In other uses, the Holy Spirit or Holy Ghost identifies a very specific personification. There is only one Holy Spirit. When we think of the Holy Spirit, we think of the Pentecostal experience described in chapter two of Acts where those that had been praying for seven days were baptized with the Holy Spirit. So, one could feel "reasonably" correct that "Holy Ghost" or "Holy Spirit" is a name. The same logic can be applied to the use of "Father."

Jesus, in Mat. 28:19, instructed us to teach all nations and baptize them in the name of the Father, the Son, and the Holy Ghost. If one will argue that they will obey the command of Jesus instead of the command of His disciples, the fact is missed that the disciples were there when Jesus gave the command; and they surely did not disobey His command as their first act after being baptized with the Holy Spirit. They understood that the name Jesus was all-inclusive or recognized the fullness of the Godhead.

Jesus said this very thing explicitly when He said, "But the Comforter, which is the Holy Ghost, whom the Father will send in my name . . ." (John 14:26 KJV) The Holy Ghost comes in Jesus name. In John 5:43 Jesus states clearly, "I am come in my Father's name . . ." Again, "He who has seen Me has seen the Father . . ." (John 14:9) Finally, Paul lays the matter to rest. "For in Him dwells all the fullness of the Godhead bodily." (Col. 2:9)

Even when we pray and ask God's blessings on our food, many will close with "in the name of the Father, Son, and Holy Ghost." Yet Jesus said, "And whatever you ask in My name, that I will do. . ." (John 14:13) The evidence appears overwhelming that we should do things in the name, Jesus! Paul spoke plainly when he said, "And whatever you do in word or deed, do all in the name of the Lord Jesus, giving thanks to God the Father through Him." (Col. 3:17) Why then, are those that do things in Jesus name ridiculed by other Christians? Why must we be so careful not to offend other Christians by carefully choosing our words? Some will say, "I baptize you in the name of the Father, Son, and Holy Spirit; and that name is Jesus." They do this to make sure everyone is happy with the baptismal rite. I do not baptize in this way, but they are to me, correct.

Did the apostles err when they acted in the name of Jesus? I have heard it said that it is better to obey the Lord than the apostles. Were the apostles not taught of the Lord? Did they not spend several years listening to His teachings? Were those that built up the church by the Holy Ghost in the name of Jesus so dull witted that they could not fathom what Jesus was saying to them. The Scriptures are convincing that the apostles knew exactly what Jesus was telling them, and they were obedient. Assuredly, they baptized in Jesus name, they cast out devils in Jesus name, they healed people in Jesus name, and they blessed their food in Jesus name.

Peter surely did not miss God when he spoke to the lame man at the gate of the temple when he said, "In the name of Jesus Christ of Nazareth rise up and walk." The man leaped up and praised God. All those who knew the lame man believed God had performed a miracle, and 5000 souls were added to the church.[14] I am bewildered! The Scriptures awesomely assert that we are to do "all" things in the name of the Lord Jesus, yet we do not mention Him by name. Even if it were correct to use the words "Father, Son, and Holy Spirit" in baptism because of Mat. 28:19, there is nothing anywhere in Scriptures that tells us to use anything other than the name of Jesus in prayer.

Let us take a quick step back to acknowledge that Christians bless their food and close that blessing in great humility, respect, and adoration with reference to the trinity of God. God honors those prayers. He looks on our hearts. When we bless our food or when we are baptized, we do so out of heartfelt commitment to Christ. Christ honors that commitment above the words we use. But why do we not speak the name of the Lord who sacrificed his life, honor, and position on the cross? Baptizing other than in Jesus' name predated the association with Jesus-only or "oneness" teachings.

---

[14]   Acts 4:4

The only reason that seems likely for introducing into the church the practice of not speaking the name of Jesus at baptism is to avoid persecution. One may be able to be baptized without mentioning Jesus and, thus, not be immediately associated with the Christian faith. This could have been a serious consideration in the early church, but we (I) do not know that this is the cause of the change.

Regardless of the cause, it seems important today to speak the name of Jesus—to let the world know about Jesus and our association to Him. "Therefore I take pleasure in infirmities, in reproaches, in needs, in persecutions, in distresses, for Christ's sake. For when I am weak, then I am strong." (2 Cor:12:10) "Yes, and all who desire to live godly in Christ Jesus will suffer persecution." (2 Tim. 3:12) Jesus, instructing Ananias to pray for Paul, desired to encourage Paul in His service. "For I will show him how many things he must suffer for My name's sake." (Acts 9:16) When Jesus got Paul's attention, He did not say "I am the Father, Son, and Holy Ghost whom you are persecuting. . ." He said, "I am Jesus, whom you are persecuting." (Acts 9:5) After Peter and John had been arrested for healing the lame man at the temple and were subsequently released, "they departed from the presence of the council, rejoicing that they were counted worthy to suffer shame for his name." (Acts 5:41)

My pastor for over thirty years, good friend, and laborer in Christ said, "Jesus is the name by which God is doing business in this dispensation." This same friend baptized in the name of the Father, Son, and Holy Spirit. The name Jesus itself recognizes the Father, as it means JEHOVAH is Salvation. By focusing on the name Jesus, we do not deny the Father and the Holy Spirit, but, at this time, the fullness of the Godhead works through the name of Jesus. It is through the suffering of Jesus that we enjoy this salvation, and it is for the name of Jesus that we will be persecuted. This will take on additional meaning in the next chapter.

The apostles rejoiced for the blessing of suffering for His name. They were grateful that they were considered worthy to suffer for His name. Other Scriptures referenced earlier include the following. "who, when they had come down, prayed for them that they might receive the Holy Spirit. For as yet He had fallen upon none of them. They had only been baptized in the name of the Lord Jesus." (Acts 8:15,16) Another reference says, "When they heard this, they were baptized in the name of the Lord Jesus." (Acts 19:5) For as many of you as were baptized into Christ have put on Christ. (Gal. 3:27)

One thing may not be clear. I have not explicitly stated that there is not a single example of baptism after the resurrection of Christ other than in the name of Jesus. Let me state that now. Look through your concordance or search with your electronic Bible for every occurrence of baptism. In every case, the disciples baptized in the name of Jesus.

I wonder, however, if the apostles spoke any words at all when they were baptizing 3,000 to 5,000 in a day. Perhaps, it was simply understood. In the day that I baptize 3,000 people, we will see if my voice will last long enough to utter that wondrous name 3,000 times.

I have acknowledged that God accepts prayers and baptisms in the name of the Father, Son, and Holy Spirit.

Many, who are better Christians than I, have different views from mine. There are those with greater love, more humility, more wisdom, and are more righteous. Yet, I love that name enough that I want to hear it, speak it, and praise it.

This said, we will look further at the significance of baptism and the significance of His name in the next chapter.[15]

---

[15] If you have been able to endure to this point, I Praise the Lord. There will be additional challenges ahead.

What's in a name?

Then Manoah said to the Angel of the LORD, "What is Your name, that when Your words come to pass we may honor You?" And the Angel of the LORD said to him, "Why do you ask My name, seeing it is wonderful?"

Jdgs. 13:17-18

Beyond understanding? Wonderful? A name? How can a name be so wonderful as to be beyond understanding? This was merely the name of the angel promising the birth of Samson and his name (*the angel's*) was too much for the man to understand. If the name of the angel was so exalted, what is said about the name of Jesus?

"Therefore God also has highly exalted Him and given Him the name which is above every name, that at the name of Jesus every knee should bow, of those in heaven, and of those on earth, and of those under the earth, and that every tongue should confess that Jesus Christ is Lord, to the glory of God the Father."

Php 2:9-11

The name of the angel was so marvelous, so beyond understanding that he would not divulge his name. Yet, the name of Jesus has been revealed, at least so we know what to call Him; but is that all it is? No! It is far more than just a word. There is something so wonderful about the name of Jesus that every knee will bow in His honor. Yes, it means Salvation of JEHOVAH or JEHOVAH Saves, but names have greater significance than simple identification.

Naomi, the name for the mother in law of Ruth, means pleasant. When she returned from Moab after the famine in Israel, she told her neighbors to call her Mara, which means bitter. She explained that the Lord had dealt bitterly with her.[16]

Jacob's name was changed after he successfully wrestled with an angel. The angel told him he would be called Israel, because he struggled with God and men and overcame.[17] Israel means to rule as God.

Conversely, the name change of Saul does not appear to carry great significance, as Paul is the Greek for the Hebrew name Saul. If there is significance, it is that Saul became identified by his Greek name. Saul may have taken the Greek name Paul as a testimony of his conversion to Christianity. It is his Christian name.

There are numerous examples in the Old Testament of parents giving names to their children that held meaning to the parents. When Rachel was dying in childbirth with Benjamin, she named him Ben-Oni, which means "son of my sorrow." Jacob changed it to Benjamin, Son of the right hand.

After Abel was murdered, Eve named her next son Seth; because God gave her another son in place of Abel. Seth means substitution.[18]

Some names identify the craft of a person's ancestry. The name Miller identifies the family's profession as a grinder of meal. Sawyers cut wood, and so forth.

---

[16] Ruth 1:20

[17] Gen. 32:28

[18] Gen. 4:25

When there is significance to the name, name is synonymous with nature. The Bible speaks of making a name for one's self.[19] We often speak of gaining a good reputation by making a name for ourselves. The name speaks of personal qualities or characteristics. Jesus said that He came in His father's name, so He came in His father's nature.[20] The Holy Spirit is sent in Jesus' name, so the Holy Spirit comes in the name or nature of the Father and the Son.[21]

Baptism

When we understand more fully what is meant by baptism in His name, the suitability of sprinkling or immersion becomes clear. In our last discussion, we saw that name is synonymous with nature. Simply saying a name while we are dipped in or sprinkled with water does not complete the baptism. Baptism in water, as wonderful and important as it is, is symbolic of a more meaningful baptism. We are commanded to be buried in the nature of Jesus—the nature of the Father, Son, and Holy Spirit. Praise God!

Now, how do we do that? It is simple. We crucify our flesh. Whoops! Did I call that simple?

When life on earth had reached deplorable standards, God took notice of Noah. He told Noah that He was going to baptize the earth and wash away all sin. There

---

[19]   2 Sam. 7:23

[20]   John 5:43

[21]   John 14:26

was not much left after he washed away all sin. God sent a devastating deluge on the earth to destroy all that were ungodly.

Likewise, sin had come to rule in our bodies. We were self-willed, self-seeking individuals. The blood of Jesus saved us from eternal death, and we were new creatures. Yet, we still carried a lot of baggage. We did not become perfect at the altar of repentance.

Remember the Israelites when they left Egypt, which we discussed earlier.[22] The angel of death visited Egypt to kill the firstborn in every household. Israelites were saved from death by the blood of the sacrificial lamb that was smeared around the door, but they were still in Egypt. They moved to escape the bondage of Egypt. They ran for the wilderness, and their final goal was to "return" to Canaan.

The army of Egypt was hot on their heels. A mistake was made. They freed the cheap labor they had enjoyed for four hundred years.[23] In their escape, Israel ran headlong into the Red Sea. They could not walk across the sea, but it was necessary that they pass through the sea. God

---

[22] Page 407

[23] Actually, they were essentially in Egypt for four hundred and thirty years and the years were not contiguous. They were not in bondage that entire time. God had told them they would be in bondage for four hundred years. When they first arrived, they were guests of the Pharaoh for the sake of Joseph. If they were not in bondage that first thirty years, the last four hundred was their time in bondage. The significance is the multiple of forty— the number of testing. Also, the four hundred years appears to include the multiple sojourns to Egypt before Israel moved there permanently.

made a dry path through the sea, and Israel was baptized by passing through the sea. When the Egyptians chased after Israel, they were drowned. The bondage of Egypt was destroyed.

Baptism washed away the sin that had oppressed Israel. Now, let us look at this from another view.

To Satan it was said, "And I will put enmity Between you and the woman, and between your seed and her Seed; He shall bruise your head, And you shall bruise His heel." (Gen. 3:15) The blood of the sacrificial lamb symbolized the heel of the woman's seed. For an explanation of the woman's seed, refer to More Than a Carpenter. (McDowell, 2005, pp. 100, 101) Baptism is the means of crushing or bruising the serpent's head. The "power" of the serpent, Egypt, was destroyed at the Red Sea.

Ah, but we are still tempted. Four hundred years living under the domination of Egypt had a lasting effect on Israel. This is terrible! We keep saying, "The devil made me do it," but the power of the devil was broken at baptism. Just as many in Israel longed to return to Egypt, we have clung to some of the things of Egypt. Yes, it was bondage, but we had plenty to eat. Our bellies were full, and our flesh still desires to be full. The fullness can even be of forbidden fruit.

Even though the power of our enemy was overwhelmed at baptism, we have been growing (hopefully). We did not suddenly become perfect. Our growth is the destruction of the habits we raised while we were in Egypt, the generation that had to be destroyed in the wilderness.

Jesus said, "Blessed are those who hunger and thirst for righteousness, for they shall be filled." (Mat. 5:6)

Ever since we started this race, we have been seeking righteousness. It has been elusive. We pray, but we seem plagued by the desires of the flesh. At some point, it seems that something happens. Paul confessed to his failures and explained their causes.

For I know that in me (that is, in my flesh) nothing good dwells; for to will is present with me, but how to perform what is good I do not find. For the good that I will to do, I do not do; but the evil I will not to do, that I practice[24]. Now if I do what I will not to do, it is no longer I who do it, but sin that dwells in me. I find then a law, that evil is present with me, the one who wills to do good. For I delight in the law of God according to the inward man. But I see another law in my members, warring against the law of my mind, and bringing me into captivity to the law of sin which is in my members. Romans 7:18-23

Paul admitted to doing what he would not do, but he could understand that it was the lusts of the flesh—sin that lived within him. So are we all. We are spiritual beings housed in this structure of flesh. Paul does not condone sin. He recognizes that we sometimes do what we would not do, but he continues, "For those who live according to the flesh set their minds on the things of the flesh, but those who live according to the Spirit, the things of the Spirit. For to be carnally minded is death, but to be spiritually minded is life and peace. Because the carnal mind is enmity against God; for it is not subject to the law of God, nor indeed can be. So then, those who are in the flesh cannot please God."

Rom 8:5-8

---

[24] Oh, me!

For if you live according to the flesh you will die; but if by the Spirit you put to death the deeds of the body, you will live. Rom 8:13

When Paul was nearing the end of his life in the flesh, he had this testimony.

I have fought the good fight, I have finished the race, I have kept the faith. 2Ti 4:7

Therefore, we continue to seek righteousness. We seek to be able to say as Paul, "I have fought a good fight. I have kept the faith." We are destroying the deeds of the flesh. We are being baptized in His name; buried in His nature. As we are baptized, the power of the flesh loses control over us. Eventually, if we are diligent, we become overcomers. That does not mean we become perfect. Holiness is more than we can imagine. With the power of the enemy removed, we are now truly prepared for war.

And what of the next baptism? Huh? What next baptism? Good brothers and sisters, we have fought and perhaps we have had to say that we have not prevailed. Israel walked through the wilderness for forty years until the lusts of the flesh that came out of Egypt died. God would not allow this sinful people to enter His rest. (Heb. 3:7-11) The wilderness was a baptism of forty years of spiritual growth.

What kind of rest did they desire to enter? Was it not Canaan? Of twelve Israeli spies who searched out the land of Canaan, only two, Joshua and Caleb, wanted to enter the land at the first opportunity. The other ten concentrated on those formidable giants in the land and discouraged Israel from claiming their inheritance. The people wanted to return to Egypt rather than face the giants of Canaan. They had no faith that the God who delivered them from Egypt by marvelous miracles would deliver to them the land He promised.[25] After forty years in the wilderness however, Israel was ready to fight the giants.

Wait a minute! What fight? This is His rest? We are going to fight the giants!? Yes, our faith has grown over the years, and we are ready to overcome our greatest weaknesses. God will go before us and conquer those enemies that have kept us from His blessings. Yes, those enemies are in the Promised Land, but it is a fertile land. We must enter this land and destroy the inhabitants of the land, the children of Anak, the giant. Then we will fully enjoy the rest available through Christ. We thought we were doing pretty good. We matured over forty years, but we are just now ready to face our greatest foes. What could they be?

Now, we can learn to love our enemies. Now, perhaps we can learn to be humble. Now, we can realize what Christ meant when He said, "he who is greatest among you shall be your servant." (Mat. 23:11)

Before we can go into the Promised Land, though, we need new leadership. As great as Moses was, he is not the one to lead us into Canaan. We have been under the condemnation of the law, the Thou Shalt Nots. We have tormented ourselves with guilt for our failures. Now, it is time to truly believe in our savior. We must be led by Joshua, Hebrew (Jehoshua) for Jesus.

Why could Moses not take us into the promised land? Moses was the ministry of baptism. Even his name

---

[25] Num. 13-14

suggests this. Its meaning is "drawn from water."[26] His name is derived from Egyptian where it means birth or "drawn out" in the sense of birth. (Brier, 1999) The Bible gives as a reason for Moses not being allowed to lead Israel into Canaan—his transgression at the waters of Meribah (strife).

Lack of faith almost kept all of Israel from entering Canaan. Because of disbelief, Israel wandered in the wilderness for forty years, until that generation had died. It was only Joshua and Caleb who had enough faith to enter Canaan immediately. Then Moses failed to trust God at Meribah.

Waters are a symbol of trials[27], and it is through trials that we learn to trust Jesus. It is through trials that His nature is brought forth in us. Jesus is cited in two of the Gospels as asking the disciples if they could be baptized with the baptism He would be baptized, referring to His crucifixion.[28] This was the ultimate test of the perfection of His nature. Could the only begotten Son of the Living God demonstrate such total humility as to allow those who hated Him to curse Him, spit on Him, and finally, crucify Him? Every trial we endure is a new depth in our baptism into His nature. When we prove ourselves worthy, we will enter the Promised Land.

Moses takes us up to this point, but we need the Jesus (Joshua) nature to take us to the next level. This is not

---

[26] For a complete treatment of the stages of spiritual growth, see I Must Decrease. (Moore, I Must Decrease, 1999)

[27] Water also represents the cleansing Word of God and nature, depending on usage.

[28] Mat 20:22, Mark 10:38

the heavenly kingdom of eternal bliss. The Promised Land is a land filled with giants. We get to fight the enemies of Christ on a completely new level—a level we could not have endured before. Once we have conquered these enemies, we can live in peace.

We should look at these two experiences of passing through the water as one. We enter the wilderness of spiritual growth at the Red Sea, but we remain immersed in this growth period until we finally emerge from the wilderness with a new mind, a new leader. We spent forty years in this baptism. Taking on a new name, a new nature, does not happen overnight.

From these examples, it should be clear that taking on the name of Jesus requires suffering—enduring. The nature of Jesus includes suffering. If this is true, how does the Holy Spirit exemplify suffering?

Before we proceed further, allow me a side note. Jesus suffered an agonizing death on the cross. At the time of his death, the sky darkened. This was a demonstration of the sadness of the Father at the death of His Son. It did not stop there. On Pentecost, the Holy Spirit took an abode in (on) the cross of our individual beings where He suffers for every sin we commit. But that did not end it. On the day that we gave our lives to Christ, we volunteered, perhaps more willingly than if we had greater understanding, to join Christ in His suffering on our behalf. We suffer the trials of hanging between heaven and hell on the cross of our flesh.

We are baptized with the indwelling Spirit of the Most High, Most Holy God. The Holy Spirit must endure our failings as He leads us to holiness. What about the

Father? Excuse me for speaking of God in His individual manifestations as though He is divisible, but it seems needful to fully demonstrate the oneness of the Father, Son, and Holy Spirit. God is in every way enduring the sinfulness of mankind: through their sinfulness, through the suffering of His Son, and through the suffering of His Holy Spirit. Realizing that the name (nature) of Jesus includes suffering, how does this apply in eternity?

Realizing that suffering is part of baptism in His name should perhaps make us more accepting of the bad things that happen to us in this life. Everyone suffers. Continuing faithfully in His service with praise and thanksgiving will keep us in such contact with Him that the suffering is tolerable. Paul said that he could do all things through Christ who strengthens him.[29] Permit me to address suffering specifically with a slight paraphrase of this verse. I can endure all things through Christ who strengthens me.

He who overcomes, I will make him a pillar in the temple of My God, and he shall go out no more. I will write on him the name of My God and the name of the city of My God, the New Jerusalem, which comes down out of heaven from My God. And I will write on him My **NEW** name. (Rev 3:12)

So, in eternity, Jesus will have a new name (nature) that does not include suffering. Also, having His new name written on us indicates that we who have followed Him in life will no longer endure suffering in eternity. Notice that in Rev. 21:1, there was no more sea. There are no sufferings. There are no more baptisms. It is stated more clearly a few verses further.

---

[29] Php. 4:13

And God will wipe away every tear from their eyes; there shall be no more death, nor sorrow, nor crying. There shall be no more pain, for the former things have passed away." Then He who sat on the throne said, "Behold, I make all things new." And He said to me, "Write, for these words are true and faithful." (Rev 21:4-5)

We have discussed Joshua, but we should not forget Caleb. Caleb was ready to fight the giants forty years before the rest of Israel. Likewise, a few people seem so in tune to the will of God that they grow quickly in holiness and the nature of Christ. These are the Calebs of Christ. Ah, to have been one of them!

Is there any other significance to these two people who had a positive testimony after spying out the Promised Land and seeing the giants? The reference to the lineage of Joshua is interesting. He is often referred to as the son of Nun. His lineage is not traced before Nun. Joshua is as mysterious in this regard as Melchizedek who had no history. Nun means perpetuity. Joshua is known throughout the Scriptures as the son of Nun, the son of perpetuity. Synonyms of perpetuity are time without end or eternity. Joshua was a type of Him who is eternal, Jesus. He was a type of the Son of God. Only He can lead us into Canaan and to victory.

At the beginning of this chapter, I said that understanding the significance of baptism by sprinkling or immersion would become greater. Baptism is a symbol of our commitment to Christ, to becoming like Him. Is it our desire to be sprinkled with a little of His nature, or is our desire to be buried in His nature?

In the last chapter I said that we would see in this section why the words spoken in baptism are from one perspective inconsequential—Jesus or Father, Son, and Holy Spirit. In this chapter, we have clearly seen that baptism in His name is to be baptized in His nature. Jesus said that He came in His Father's name (nature), and the Holy Spirit would come in His name (nature). Regardless of the words spoken in baptism, the heart of the participants is what is most important. We are baptized in love: the love of both the baptizer and the baptized for our King.

I will continue to baptize in Jesus' name, because to me, it is a declaration of my association to Him. I was baptized in His name for the same reason. We are persecuted for His name, and now it is clear that we are persecuted for His nature in us.

We can say we believe in God and be reasonably safe. In Afghanistan, one young Muslim made it a point to greet me every morning with "Praise God," and I responded in kind. He felt that this was common to both of our religions. Likewise, if I mention Jesus as Lord, I am recognized as a Christian. In this case, the spoken name of Jesus is a source of persecution. However, to tell someone you have been baptized will suffice to identify you as a Christian, regardless of the name spoken.

Jesus instructed us in more than simply being baptized in His name. In the next section, we will discuss praying in His name.

Praying in Jesus Name

Christians pray for things that never happen and this when they have been praying in His name, or were they? We have been ending our prayers by saying "in Jesus' name." Did that not make our prayer in His name, or are we trying to convince God that we are praying properly?

"And whatever you ask in My name (nature), that I will do, that the Father may be glorified in the Son." (John 14:13)

Some people are praying to win the lottery, and they are ending their prayers with "in Jesus' name." Saying these words does not make our prayers in His name. For our prayers to be in His name, they must be in His nature and will. When we ask for something through greed, we are not in His will: We are not in His nature: We are not in His name.

I have heard of people vengefully praying for someone to die. Regardless of what name they speak, the true nature of such prayer is likely in the name of our common enemy, our tempter. God is love, and Jesus came in the nature of that love.

How can we be sure that we are praying in Jesus' name? Unless you have perfect communication with Christ, I am unaware of any foolproof way to know His will concerning the target of your prayer. There are some things indicative of His nature. If you are praying in love, selflessly and humbly, you are much surer of being in His name than if you are praying to win the lottery. However, it may be His will that you win the lottery, so praying for this may be in His will. Ask yourself the question if praying for lottery wining. What will you do if you win? Who will benefit? Remember that we are taught to give, and a full tenth belongs to God, minimally.

Sometimes, it is very difficult to understand His will in our lives. We may be going through a very difficult period, and we desperately seek relief, but no relief is in sight. Is this trial necessary? The Hebrew writer pointed out that no trial is pleasant at the time, but in due time we will prosper from them.[30]

Our prayers must be seasoned with humility. We may pray for spiritual gifts, but why do we seek the gifts? Do we long to see souls added to the Kingdom of God through our ministry, or do we desire to be elevated in the eyes of others by the power of God in our lives? Praying that we might be exalted in the eyes of others is pride, and it certainly is not in the nature or name of Jesus.

Of course, a spiritual gift may exalt you in the eyes of others, but that should not be the main desire. Anytime God uses us puts us in a position to be exalted in pride. Surely, we feel honored to be used of God. Three times in the sixth chapter of Matthew, the translators of the King James version use the phrase "reward you openly." We were told to pray in secret. Hypocrites put on a show of their prayers. We are not to do so. We are instructed to pray in secret, and then God will reward us mightily or openly.

Balancing the Word of truth, do not fear to pray publicly. Sometimes praying publicly is a testimony and may draw persecution instead of praise. Many times, you may be asked to lead in prayer. It is what is in your heart

---

[30] Heb. 12:11

that is important, not whether you pray publicly or not. It may, indeed, be an act of humility to pray publicly.

Are we able to do anything without some element of pride? After all, we are flesh. It warms our souls when God honors us in the presence of others. Perhaps even our humility is slightly tainted with pride. Perhaps the honor that God shows us warms us, yet it embarrasses us. Maybe we will be able to be blessed of God without tainting our humility. Paul recognized the potential for pride through God's grace in our lives.

And lest I should be exalted above measure by the abundance of the revelations, a thorn in the flesh was given to me, a messenger of Satan to buffet me, lest I be exalted above measure. Concerning this thing I pleaded with the Lord three times that it might depart from me. And He said to me, "My grace is sufficient for you, for My strength is made perfect in weakness." Therefore most gladly I will rather boast in my infirmities, that the power of Christ may rest upon me."

2Co 12:7-9

Paul was so blessed with revelations that God gave him a thorn in the flesh to keep him humble. If one of God's apostles can become proud through the blessings of God, anyone can. We have seen examples that I will not enumerate, where ministers of Christ have been lifted in pride after developing prosperous, well-known ministries. Thank God, that some of them humbled themselves before God and continued their ministries.

Baptism in His nature is the surest way of praying in the name of Jesus: buried in humility, servitude, and love. As it is said, "It is all about Him." After being reminded of her own self-love, Saint Bernadette drew a circle in the sand and said, "Let the one who has no self-love put her finger there." (Trochu, 1985, p. 276) Yet, her desire was to serve Jesus to the greatest limit, even (in her words) "to annihilation." (Trochu, 1985, p. 316) This is a reasonable desire for the servant of God. When we become nonexistent, as it were, God completely takes over.[31] Then we can say with Paul, "I have been crucified with Christ; it is no longer I who live, but Christ lives in me. . ." (Gal. 2:20)

I will suggest one more level of measurement to discern God's working in you. Do you desire to be a leader? A program is being developed. Do you wish to manage the program, or are you happy, perhaps even preferring, to serve invisibly? If you want to manage the program, examine your motives. It may be what God wants, too; but manage with humility.

Being baptized in His name (nature), we learn how to approach all things. Recall the verse, "Therefore God also has highly exalted Him and given Him the name which is above every name, that at the name of Jesus every knee should bow, of those in heaven, and of those on earth, and of those under the earth, and that every tongue should confess that Jesus Christ is Lord, to the glory of God the Father." (Php 2:9-10)

---

[31] The animal sacrifices in Leviticus require the killing of the animals. Only when they are dead are they placed on the altar of burnt offerings where they provide a pleasing fragrance to God. When our carnal nature can no longer present itself in our offerings to God, they will provide a perfectly pleasing fragrance to our Lord. (Rom. 12:1)

Every knee shall bow to this name. The will of every creature will one day subject themselves to the will of God. Bowing our knees to the name is to recognize its honor and power. It is difficult to comprehend that humility can be so powerful. People seek power with authority. Mother Teresa had no authority, but people around the world listened to her words and emulate her life. Ghandi had no authority, but he brought independence to India in the face of the British empire. Martin Luther King had no authority, but he changed attitudes in America. Saint Francis of Assisi had no authority, yet he is perhaps the most universally loved Christian in the world: honored even among Muslims.

I heard a sermon preached that compared the apostle Paul to Nero. Nero was the emperor of the most powerful nation on earth. Paul was a simple preacher that had to work to pay for his ministry. Nero had Paul imprisoned and subsequently had him beheaded. How many monuments are built with the name of Nero? Yet, there are churches throughout the world named for the apostle Paul. The pastor's sermon expressed, much more eloquently and powerfully than I, the power of humility and anointing of God over all the power of leaders of great nations, especially despotic leaders.

We will discuss one more aspect of the nature of Christ and, by extension, the mature Christian in the section "Christ In You."

Who is Jesus?

A coworker on a mission trip to Russia looked at me with unbelief when I referred to Jesus as God. He is a student of the Godhead and somehow felt that I had missed the mark. I never was sure how he thought I missed the mark, but it was not an opportune time to discuss such an extensive subject. I have heard too many arguments and vitriolic sermons on the Godhead. Some offend people by saying Jesus is God. Others are offended by preaching about the Trinity as if it is a doctrine of three Gods. I feel that most people are essentially saying the same things from different vantage points. Trinitarians believe in one God, and Jesus-only ministers believe in the Father, Son, and Holy Spirit. I think much of the confusion arises from a lack of understanding of the other's viewpoint.

We have cited this verse earlier, but it is appropriate to remember Paul's summarization of the subject in Col. 2:9, "For in Him dwells all the fullness of the Godhead bodily.

My goal in this chapter is not to try to formulate a complete picture of God. That would be an ostentatious goal, and I am confident that no one is capable of doing such. It is not that God is hiding things from us: It is simply that He is too magnificent to be comprehended in a lifetime. There are attributes of Jesus that are knowable, and even the least of these attributes is mind blowing.

Only Begotten

No one has seen God at any time. The only begotten Son, who is in the bosom of the Father, He has declared Him. (John 1:18)

As the only begotten, Jesus is the only son born of God. No other person has ever been born of woman through divine fertilization. Oh, the carnality of man!

Some (not Christians) assert that God supposedly fertilized Mary as men fertilize their wives. Some Muslims tried to tell me that the angel Gabriel is the Holy Spirit and he was the father of Jesus.

"'But while he thought about these things, behold, an angel of the Lord appeared to him in a dream, saying,' Joseph, son of David, do not be afraid to take to you Mary your wife, for that which is conceived in her is of the Holy Spirit'". Mat 1:20

Jesus was not a son by adoption. He was a son by birth. That He was the only son by birth is stated in five verses in the New Testament.[32] He was spiritually conceived. If He were conceived through normal means, I think the Scriptures would not say that a "virgin" was with child.[33]

Friend and Firstborn among Many

For whom He foreknew, He also predestined to be conformed to the image of His Son, that He might be the firstborn among many brethren.

Rom 8:29

While Jesus was born a son or the Son, we enter sonship through the spirit of adoption.

"For you did not receive the spirit of bondage again to fear, but you received the Spirit of adoption by whom we cry out, "Abba, Father." (Romans 8:15)

"But when the fullness of the time had come, God sent forth His Son, born of a woman, born under the law,

---

[32] John 1:14, 1:18, 3:16, 3:18, 1 John 4:9

[33] Mat. 1:23

to redeem those who were under the law, that we might receive the adoption as sons. And because you are sons, God has sent forth the Spirit of His Son into your hearts, crying out, 'Abba, Father!'" (Gal. 4:4-6)

We are not beggars. As sons and daughters, we have a right to ask of God. It is our right through the Spirit of adoption. "Let us therefore come boldly to the throne of grace, that we may obtain mercy and find grace to help in time of need." (Hebrews 4:16)

"You are My friends if you do whatever I command you. No longer do I call you servants, for a servant does not know what his master is doing; but I have called you friends, for all things that I heard from My Father I have made known to you."

Joh 15:14-15

Head of the Body

"And He is the head of the body, the church, who is the beginning, the firstborn from the dead, that in all things He may have the preeminence.

Col 1:18

He it is who gives us life and direction. Christ fits the body together to work as a unified entity, though we members of the body number in the millions.

". . . and not holding fast to the Head, from whom all the body, nourished and knit together by joints and ligaments, grows with the increase that is from God. Col 2:19

As members of the same body, we should care for others as we care for our own body. ". . . but, speaking the truth in love, may grow up in all things into Him who is the head—Christ—from whom the whole body, joined and knit together by what every joint supplies, according to the effective working by which every part does its share, causes growth of the body for the edifying of itself in love." (Eph. 4:15, 16)

Paul prefaced these words in verse 13 of Eph. 4 with, "till we all come to the unity of the faith." As the body of Christ, we are to care for the entire body. We are to work for unity, forgiving others for faults.

We have all pointed at others and called them "different," But to others we are different. We are different members of the same body. The toe does not have the same function as a finger, regardless of their anatomical similarities. The glue that makes this disparate world of personalities one body is love. The central message of Christ was love.

When Christ was suffering the agony of the cross, He prayed "Father, forgive them." God help us to love one another. As we have been forgiven, help us to forgive. Let us, the body of Christ, be unified in love.

The great difference between us as Christians and those of other religions is that we are taught by Scriptures to love our enemies and to do good to them who misuse us. We can learn from the examples of many Christians that have gone before us, but the first example was Jesus. He that created all things allowed His creations to abuse Him and crucify Him and could even love them so much as to pray for their forgiveness.

As the head of the body, another aspect of Christ is introduced in that we are the bride of Christ. From this aspect, too, Jesus is our head.[34] In every aspect, He has preeminence. At no point do we now or shall we in the future become equal to Christ, although we shall be coheirs with Him. This is clear from Paul's statement, "He is the head of the body, the church, who is the beginning, the firstborn from the dead, that in all things He may have the preeminence. (Col. 1:18)

Preexistent

"He was in the beginning with God." (John 1:2)

He is the image of the invisible God, the firstborn over all creation. For by Him all things were created that are in heaven and that are on earth, visible and invisible, whether thrones or dominions or principalities or powers. All things were created through Him and for Him.

(Col 1:15-16)

Jesus himself said, "And now, O Father, glorify Me together with Yourself, with the glory which I had with You before the world was." (John 17:5)

"Jesus answered, 'If I honor Myself, My honor is nothing. It is My Father who honors Me, of whom you say that He is your God. Yet you have not known Him, but I know Him. And if I say, 'I do not know Him,' I shall be a liar like you; but I do know Him and keep His word. Your father Abraham rejoiced to see My day, and he saw it and was glad.' Then the Jews said to Him, 'You are not yet fifty years old, and have You seen Abraham?' Jesus said to them,

---

[34] 1 Cor. 11:3, Eph. 1:22-23 4:15 5:23, Col 1:18 2:10

'Most assuredly, I say to you, before Abraham was, I AM.'"
(John 8:53-58)

These words, particularly the last two, stirred the Jews to anger. They would have stoned Him. These words are particularly emphatic, meaning "I exist." He was essentially referring to Himself as the God that spoke to Moses on Sinai when He said, "I am that I am."

"And God said to Moses, 'I AM WHO I AM.' And He said, 'Thus you shall say to the children of Israel, 'I AM has sent me to you.'" (Ex. 3:14)

The "I am" in these verses are also emphatic, so Jesus was explicitly identifying Himself with the Father. Soon, the prayer He prayed for the restoration of the unity He had with the Father would be fulfilled.

Beginning of Creation of God

"And to the angel of the church of the Laodiceans write, 'These things says the Amen, the Faithful and True Witness, the Beginning of the creation of God: . . .'" (Rev. 3:14)

These characteristics of Christ begin unfolding mysteries of Jesus Christ. We see that Jesus is the only Son of God. He is preeminent among many brothers and sisters, and He is the head of the church. He was also preexistent, and did not simply appear at birth. Look at the very telling verse of John 17:5, "And now, O Father, glorify Me together with Yourself, with the glory which I had with You before the world was.

Joh 17:5

"He is the image of the invisible God, the firstborn over all creation."

Col 1:15

The word in Rev. 3:14 translated creation, may also be rendered ordinance and is rendered so in 1 Peter 2:13. That Christ is the beginning of the ordinance of God is paramount in importance. The verse could be translated to "the beginning of the Law of God." The relevance will become evident in the next chapter.

Wisdom

The queen of the South will rise up in the judgment with this generation and condemn it, for she came from the ends of the earth to hear the wisdom of Solomon; and indeed a greater than Solomon is here. Mat 12:42

Here Jesus declares His wisdom as greater than the Wisdom of Solomon. What do the scriptures say of Solomon's wisdom?

"behold, I have done according to your words; see, I have given you a wise and understanding heart, so that there has not been anyone like you before you, nor shall any like you arise after you." (1 Kings 3:12)

Solomon prayed for wisdom and God granted him wisdom so great that people travelled great distances to hear him speak; yet, the wisdom of Christ greatly exceeded that of Solomon. That should surprise no one, considering that Jesus is the personification of Wisdom.

In the beginning was the Word, and the Word was with God, and the Word was God. He was in the beginning with God. All things were made through Him, and without Him nothing was made that was made.

Joh 1:1-3

The word Logos, translated from Greek as Word, is said to have no direct English equivalent; however, after shaking it out, the nearest English word appears to be Wisdom. Logos is translated in various verses with such words as "cause," "saying," and even "word" in its traditional context—a word spoken.

When we speak of wisdom in these verses, we are not referring to the horse sense that it would be nice if we all possessed. We are referring to the very essence of life itself. John, the beloved, says it clearly.

"In him was life; and the life was the light of men." (John 1:4)

This life is fire or vibrancy, the essence of all that is. This Wisdom formed the universe. It is the Wisdom that formed living cells so small that seventy trillion are required to form the average human body. This Wisdom transcends every element of the universe and every living being.

This life vibrancy permeates our existence, especially as Christians. Literally, the first understanding of the opening verses relates to Jesus. Spiritually, they relate to every individual professing Christ as his/her savior. The Word was made flesh and dwelt among us. The Word dwells in me, in you, and in every other Christian.

"And the Word became flesh and dwelt among us, and we beheld His glory, the glory as of the only begotten of the Father, full of grace and truth." (John 1:14)

There are other aspects of these verses that, however wonderful, would only obscure our current study; but we shall return to them in the chapter on the Bones of Jesus. This much should be obvious: Christ was the incarnate manifestation of Wisdom, and we have received of His grace as the Scriptures affirm. We have a spark of that omniscient Wisdom.

"And of His fullness we have all received, and grace for grace." (John 1:16)

Without Christ, we are restrained in our approach to the Spiritual Wisdom ultimately available to us. Angels were given charge over the tree of life, brandishing flaming swords to keep us from reaching it. Wisdom is the tree of life.[35] There is no indication that the protection for the Tree of Life was ever removed. (Moore, The Elder Shall Serve The Younger, 2007, pp. 58-65) To access that wisdom, we must go through the flaming sword. It will cut us backward and forward. It will reveal to us our failures and our accomplishments. By this we will attain wisdom.

We have looked superficially at a few attributes of Christ. In our next chapter, we will delve further into His authority.

---

[35]   Prov. 3:18

Bones of Jesus

Scriptures seem to make an important point of the fact that His bones were not broken on the cross. It was prophesied in the Psalms.

"He guards all his bones; Not one of them is broken." (Ps. 34:20)

Then John reminds us of this prophecy.

"For these things were done that the Scripture should be fulfilled, 'Not one of his bones shall be broken'" (John 19:36)

In Exodus, it says of the Passover, "In one house it shall be eaten; you shall not carry any of the flesh outside the house, nor shall you break one of its bones." (Ex. 12:46)

What is the significance of His bones? Why can they not be broken? We will not initially refer to numerous Scriptures for an explanation; rather, we will look at the purpose of bones and support our conclusion with Scriptures.

Without bones, we are unable to stand. We would be without form beyond a gelatin-like mass of skin and muscle. To get anywhere, we would somehow slither around on the ground with less dignity than a snail. Similarly, people without rules are not societies: They are mobs. They have neither form nor honor.

Following the overthrow of a government, chaos prevails. Sometimes the army will step in to restore order. The order that is restored is based on laws, regardless of how ad-hoc these laws are. They bring some sense of stability. I must point out, however, that even a lawless mob has some rules; for example, do not disagree with the mob. Looting, killing, and raping may be allowed, encouraged, or uncontrollable, but do not oppose the mob. The bones that give form and order to the Christian, the body of Christ, and indeed to all of society are the laws of God.

Laws of God

Laws are required to provide stability for a society or to qualify as a society—a civilization. The fact that the bones of Christ could not be broken demonstrates the irresistibility of God's laws. It is impossible to break the laws of God. To break the laws in this sense would be to nullify them or somehow exist beyond the scope of the laws.

Everyone acts contrary to the commandments, the laws; but that is only half of the law. If we act one way toward the law of God, the law of God acts to bring things back into balance.

'If a man causes disfigurement of his neighbor, as he has done, so shall it be done to him--fracture for fracture, eye for eye, tooth for tooth; as he has caused disfigurement of a man, so shall it be done to him.

Lev 24:19-20

Of course, we know that not every injury to an eye or a tooth by another person necessarily results in a similar injury to the offender, but the offense is repaid by a response of equal severity. When weighing a pound of meat in a meat market, the counterbalance is not likely to be meat. It must simply weigh the same.

It may also seem that this law requires the injury to be intentional, but I think not. The injury is inflicted and must have equal retribution. Laws of God possess a quality of degrees of crime similar, to America's civil laws. Our laws include first- and second-degree murder, first-degree burglary, etc. Punishments for the crimes decrease with the lowering degree of the crime.

Under the Old Testament, if a person kills another person by accident, a way out was provided for the offender. He or she could run to a city of refuge, and if the death was deemed accidental, he was not subject to the death penalty. The avenger of blood who was to take the life of the offender could not enter the city of refuge to avenge blood, but if the guilty party left the city, the avenger of blood could take his life.

"Speak to the children of Israel, and say to them: 'When you cross the Jordan into the land of Canaan, then you shall appoint cities to be cities of refuge for you, that the manslayer who kills any person accidentally may flee there. They shall be cities of refuge for you from the avenger, that the manslayer may not die until he stands before the congregation in judgment. Num 35:10-12

It could be argued that this is not equal retribution for the loss of a life, but here we encounter the degree aspect of the crime. This could be like the offence of accidental manslaughter. Although the death was accidental, the guilty party is essentially imprisoned in the city of refuge for the life of the high priest. If he leaves the city of refuge, he has broken the rule of his confinement and may be killed by the avenger of blood.[36] Also, the emotional

---

[36] Num. 35:22-27

suffering for having taken a life could be enormous, depending on the personality of the individual. This isolation and confinement together with whatever other discomforts the individual must tolerate are sufficient. Why I state this so adamantly should become clear as we proceed.

"Your own wickedness will correct you. And your backslidings will rebuke you. . ." (Jer. 2:19)

God does not have to intervene. Our actions cause reactions that will judge us and, hopefully, provoke us to correct our actions. He has set the law in place, and they enforce themselves. They are part of our everyday life.

The fact that Christ had to suffer death for our redemption is evidence of the firmness of God's laws. The sins of any individual are such that we are worthy of death, and we are not capable of self-redemption. Nothing we do will erase our guilt. Our guilt required repayment by an untainted atonement. None of us is untainted, and as good as many people are, they err. Even Paul, who had rebuked Peter for behaving one way when around Jews and another way around gentiles, confessed faults.[37] In the book of Romans as elsewhere Paul confesses his humanity.[38]

For you put up with it if one brings you into bondage, if one devours you, if one takes from you, if one exalts himself, if one strikes you on the face. To our shame I say that we were too weak for that! But in whatever anyone is bold--I speak foolishly--I am bold also.

2Co 11:20-21

---

[37] Gal. 2:11, 12
[38] Rom. 7:8-11, 15-24

Tradition tells us that Paul was eventually beheaded for the name of Jesus, but that act of martyrdom was not adequate to save his soul. Our inability to save ourselves through works, meditation, or other methods is why Christ had to die. The Laws of God require retribution for sin. We were cast out of God's presence in the Garden of Eden.

Only the sacrifice of Jesus Christ is adequate to restore our acceptable relationship with the Father. Not only must the sacrifice be untainted, but it also must be holy enough and great enough to account for all the sins of the world. Not even the sacrifice of angels of heaven will suffice for such a magnificent atonement.

Jesus, the Wisdom of God, submitted Himself to the death of the cross. Such a sacrifice, on such a grand scale, is adequate to atone for the sins of the world. There is no other atonement sufficient to cover the sins of every human who has ever lived. To ignore such a sacrifice, failing to come to Christ, may add His death to our guilt. Remember, there must be a perfect balance between the offense and the retribution. We will revisit the crucifixion in the chapter, "Did Jesus Have to Die?"

It becomes clear that the laws of God are not mere rules that may be followed or not. Not to follow the laws of God requires balance: retribution. His laws are not like the laws of man.

Man passes a law and we may choose to ignore it. It is frequently said that something is only illegal if you are caught; that is, you are only penalized for breaking the law if you are caught. Notice how many people do not abide by speed limits regardless of enforcement levels. The difference is that we are always caught when we break God's laws.

The blood of Jesus Christ saved us from the penalty of death. As unacceptable as it may be to many Christians, intentional sin still requires recompense on our part.[39] We can provide recompense for such sins through agape (selfless) love.[40]

There is a verbal agreement, I think, among every Christian Church that we are no longer under the Law, but Grace. This is substantiated by Paul in Romans 6:14 when he said, "For sin shall not have dominion over you: for you are not under the law, but under grace." We are not under the law, in that we do not have to offer bulls and goats for our sins. We do not have to recognize the feasts and fasts of the Old Testament, but holiness is still expected of us. We are also expected to abide by the Ten Commandments - all of them.

"Do not think that I came to destroy the Law or the Prophets. I did not come to destroy but to fulfill. For assuredly, I say to you, till heaven and earth pass away, **one jot or one tittle will by no means pass from the law till all is fulfilled.** Whoever therefore breaks one of the least of these commandments, and teaches men so, shall be called least in the kingdom of heaven;[41] but whoever does and teaches them, he shall be called great in the kingdom

---

[39] Heb. 12:5-11

[40] 1 Peter 4:8

[41] The kingdom of heaven is only mentioned in Matthew. The other Gospels, in parallel passages, refer to this as the Kingdom of God. As the Kingdom of God, it relates to a New Covenant experience.

of heaven. For I say to you, that unless your righteousness exceeds the righteousness of the scribes and Pharisees, you will by no means enter the kingdom of heaven. You have heard that it was said to those of old, 'you shall not murder, and whoever murders will be in danger of the judgment.' But I say to you that whoever is angry with his brother without a cause shall be in danger of the judgment. And whoever says to his brother, 'Raca!'[42] shall be in danger of the council. But whoever says, 'You fool!' shall be in danger of hell fire." (Mat. 5:17-22)

We are expected to abide by the commandments of God, but Jesus showed us the more perfect way when He explained to the lawyer which commandment was the greatest.[43] That commandment is love. Love will not bear false witness. Love will not covet the belongings of another: material goods, position, or spouse. Love will not put possessions before God. Love will honor father and mother. If we love, we do not have to concern ourselves with rules. The rules are there, but we obey them by default through selfless love. We behave counter to the laws through ignorance or weakness. An excellent description of love's characteristics is found in 1Cor. 13:4-7. This love does not describe the relationship between a man and a woman. This passage describes selfless, holy love.

While we are not under the Law, we tend to put the burden of the Law on our shoulders. New converts to Christ are often instructed in what is expected of them, and the shine is off salvation before they leave the altar. Rules must be obeyed. Skirts must be a specific length.

---

[42]   Empty one or worthless one

[43]   Mat. 22:35-40

Long sleeves are required. Men's hair must be cut in military style. Women must not cut their hair. Tattoos are not allowed in heaven. Beards, heaven help me, are of the devil. These are examples of men's definitions of God's laws.

There are standards to which we must live. Too much flesh showing does not show Christian concern for others. Smoking makes one stink and may someday cause death, but the individual must decide that it is wrong for him or her. For me, it is wrong. For others, it may not be. Paul instructed us to work out our own soul salvation with fear and trembling.[44] We have sometimes changed that to working out everyone's salvation with pomposity and determination. My daughter recently told me of a young woman that was put out of a church because she refused to give up her cell phone. Evidently, a pastor was convicted of everyone else's cell phones and declared them sinful. He, in such case, is working out his congregation's salvation. Much more could be said about this issue, but this is enough. Let us be led by the Laws of God through love; and when we see someone with a fault, let us offer correction in a spirit of meekness, considering the soul of the individual in error. Sometimes, it is better to make allowances for sin than to drive a hopeless wedge between a would-be saint and God. Deal lovingly. I wish I could be more definitive, but I cannot.

Thus far, we have dealt with the spiritual side of these laws of God. We have seen that they are uncompromising. Now we will observe parallels of the domain of the laws of God that stretches beyond spiritual considerations.

---

[44] Phil. 2:12

On a summer trip to teach English in Russia, a student told me, "I don't believe in God. I believe in physics." I told him that I too believe in physics. I also believe physics was created by God. We cited a verse from Revelations earlier[45] that refers to Jesus as the beginning of the creation of God. The word translated to creation, ktisis from the Greek, can also be translated to ordinance and is, for example, in First Peter 2:13. Of course, an ordinance is a law. In 1st Cor. 1:24, Jesus is called the Wisdom of God. It is no stretch that the wisdom of God is also the law of God. Jesus, then, is the beginning of the law of God.

It was Wisdom, the eternal Christ, who formed the universe. Christ established the rules by which the cosmos is controlled. The laws of physics are His laws. If you can break a law of God, you can break a law of physics.[46]

Scientists have labored for centuries to understand the laws by which the universe is governed, and they keep closing in on a complete understanding. Of course, many, Christians and non-Christians, say they will never understand it all because it is a mystery of God. Real scientists, in my opinion, do not believe in unknowable mysteries. They believe there are simply things that they do not yet understand. While there are some things we are not allowed to know[47], to acknowledge something as unknowable closes off many things that, in time, would

---

[45] Rev. 3:14

[46] The laws of physics are continuously evolving. Newton's laws were perfect in Newton's perspectives, but Einstein's laws of relativity made Newton's laws conditional. Laws of God are not conditional.

[47] Rev. 10:4

be known. If we recognize something as an unknowable mystery, we will not search deeper when it may truly be knowable.

We should remember the Tower of Babel[48] where the technologists of the day were building a tower to heaven. When God took notice of what they were doing, He acknowledged that they could indeed, build a tower to heaven. Instead of using stones and mud, they were using the technology of the day, bricks and mortar. Today, technologists are building a tower to heaven—a technological tower. God acknowledged that if that first tower had been completed, there would have been nothing impossible to them.[49] Without His intervention, the tower would have been built. This tower is being built again, but this time He will not intervene as quickly. These builders have singleness of purpose. They have an international language of technology through computer technology. They also have a universal language in the worldwide use of English as the language of commerce.

One of the best-known laws of physics is Newton's third law of motion. "To every action there is always opposed an equal reaction, or, the mutual actions of two bodies upon each other are always equal and directed to contrary parts." (Translated from the Principia's Latin) It is stated more familiarly, if not correctly, that "for every action, there is an equal and opposite reaction."[50]

This law correlates to the preceding discussion of the laws of God. We affirmed earlier that for every action in

---

[48] Page 131

[49] Gen. 11

[50] It may be more accurate to say "force" instead of action.

opposition to God's laws there is a commensurate reaction. Unfortunately, my focus was on trespassing against the laws. Actions against the laws of God provoke action against the transgressor. However, actions supporting the laws of God cause blessings to the person supporting those laws.

The Peace Prayer of St. Francis demonstrates this truth when he says, "... for it is in giving that we receive, and it is in pardoning that we are pardoned." Covering both types of actions relative to God's laws results in either positive or negative responses. Positive actions result in positive responses. Negative actions result in negative responses.

Recently, I had my first encounter with a pressure washer. It sprayed water with 2500 pounds of pressure. A measure of respect for Newton's laws of motion and the pressure washer was evoked when, standing on a ladder and leaning out from the ladder with the wand, I activated the spray. The water sprayed onto the house with its 2500 pounds of pressure, and the pressure of the wand suddenly pushing back against me made me aware of my need for stability on the ladder.

We see in either spiritual or physical applications of these laws only a small number of basic laws with incomprehensible effects. The Bible lists ten commands or basic laws in one chapter and repeats them in a second chapter,[51] but most of three books of the Bible (Leviticus, Numbers, and Deuteronomy) contain further instruction on how to interpret these laws in differing circumstances.

Society has laws against the taking of a life. Prosecutors, instead of treating all cases alike, may

---

[51]   Ex. 20, Deu. 5

prosecute as first-degree, second-degree, or third-degree levels of severity. Additionally, they may choose to call the crime manslaughter or self-defense. The charge is further complicated based on whose life was taken. What special circumstances surround the case? Was it particularly brutal? Was the crime against a child, or was it committed by a child? For the punishment to be fair, the action against the offender depends on the severity of the offense.

I need to emphasize one point about the laws of God. We try to justify ourselves by earning our way to heaven. It does not work that way. As shown on page 55, There must be an action so magnificent that it can be the atonement to all sin ever committed. That occurred when Jesus gave His life on the cross.

Misunderstood?

"He who believes in Him is not condemned; but he who does not believe is condemned already, because he has not believed in the name of the only begotten Son of God."
Joh 3:18

Those among us who are born of God follow the leading of the Spirit and often do not follow conventional wisdom. They make decisions that are contrary to common sense. They do things that seem eccentric. Their actions do not always please their families and friends.

My wife, for example, makes unilateral decisions that blows me away. I do not know about them in advance and when she tells me about them, I am speechless. They seem extreme, but her blessings in these decisions are also extreme. You cannot out-give God!!!!

Not all such actions are Spirit led, but if we follow the Spirit, we shall indeed seem eccentric to society at times. Even other Christians or family members will not understand your actions when you are led by the Spirit; and the closer you come to the Father, the more eccentric you may seem to become.

My wife has not expressed an opinion about my recent announcement to her that I would observe the Sabbath on Saturday, from sunset Friday to sunset on Saturday. She expressed no opinion then or since. Worship any day or every day of the week, but the ten commandments were not obviated at the cross; only the ritualistic Levitical laws. I may extend the intent of the Scriptures about pulling animals out of a ditch on the Sabbath, however.

One of my favorite Scriptures is Rev. 2:17. It says in part, "To him who overcomes I will give some of the hidden manna to eat. And I will give him a white stone, and on the stone a new name written which no one knows except him who receives it."

This new name is the name or nature of your personality merged (married) to the nature of Christ. The reason no one else will know this name is that only you and Jesus know all that goes on between Him and you. No one else will understand how Jesus uses you. As the song by Tom T. Hall says, "Me and Jesus have our own thing going." This should not be used as a license to do things that are obviously in opposition to the laws of God, but now you may understand better why you may sometimes do strange things that have positive results. If we are doing things differently because of pride in being different, the actions are not of the Holy Spirit.

Understand the concept of marriage of our personalities to the personality or nature of Christ. Christ is not trying to change our personalities, at least not in most cases. He really desires to change our focus. The apostle Paul is an excellent example. Before conversion, Paul was a Jew laboring zealously in the persecution of Christians.[52] After conversion, Paul worked diligently to bring souls to Christ.[53] Paul was a tireless laborer before and after conversion, but his focus was changed. Instead of destroying the church, he built it.

We were born with qualities that are not inherently bad. We merely use them wrong. After combining our qualities with the name of Jesus, we are a new creature: one whom no one completely understands, including ourselves.

The Power of Babel

I had been pondering prayer and the promises of God's Word. "Why Lord," I asked, "are prayers sometimes not answered?" Yes, I have received many answers to prayers, but sometimes, it seems answers evade us. I knew my life had been blessed by the grace of God, however little I have deserved those blessings; but some things I have sought diligently only to feel a complete absence of God's awareness to my prayers. And, I am not alone!

"But seek first the kingdom of God and His righteousness, and all these things shall be added to you." (Mat 6:33)

---

[52] Acts 22:3, 4
[53] 1 Cor. 15:9, 10

Many times, the answer is as simple as we have not sought the face of God. We go to church, but we are passive Christians. We only pray when we want something. We do not advance the cause of Christ in any capacity. Seeking the face of God would be the first place to start finding answers to prayers.

I am aware of all the quick answers. Sometimes He says, "Yes." Sometimes He says, "No." Sometimes He says, "Wait a while." People say you are asking amiss, or it is not time, or you are not asking in faith. Sometimes these are reasonable answers; sometimes they are put-offs because others have no better answer than we do. It appears "wait a while" is the most realistic of the listed choices. The souls under the altar in the sixth chapter of Revelations are told "rest a little while longer." We have already discussed another reason for unanswered prayer, like asking amiss; that is, not asking in His name, in His nature. Questioning why, however, should be secondary to pondering the promises of God's Word.

"Ask, and it will be given to you; seek, and you will find; knock, and it will be opened to you. For everyone who asks receives, and he who seeks finds, and to him who knocks it will be opened. If you then, being evil, know how to give good gifts to your children, how much more will your Father who is in heaven give good things to those who ask Him!" (Matt. 7:7, 8, 11)

"And whatever things you ask in prayer, believing, you will receive." (Matt. 21:22)

"And whatever you ask in My name, that I will do, that the Father may be glorified in the Son. If you ask anything in My name, I will do it." (John 14:13, 14)

When doing something in Jesus' name is to do it in His "nature."

These scriptures represent only a few of many similar promises. Yet, we are given reasons for why God does not answer—sometimes seemingly unsound reasons. Believing that many answers are merely put-offs, we may become disillusioned, disheartened, disappointed, and angry.

We have discussed earlier that many of our prayers are not in His name, regardless of how many times we say, "in Jesus name."[54] We are told to trust God, but we thought that was what we were doing. We were told to believe, but we thought we were believing. We think we do not understand faith and seek understanding. We read the scripture in Hebrews, "Now faith is . . ."[55] It tells us what faith is, but not in a way that greatly helps our understanding of how to believe.

Surely, there are many reasons for prayers not to be answered; and surely, the fault is ours; but I am a believer that God will not fail His people. I will not be denied! I have asked; and God is faithful to answer; so, I prayed and meditated for weeks, seeking a better understanding of prayer.

Gradually, things began to come together. Little by little, I was concluding that there was a single element, perhaps more important than, or as important as faith, missing from my prayers.

Then one July morning in 1994, it became gloriously apparent. I sat, meditating on what I was seeing. Its power was such that I trembled with excitement. Is the missing

---

[54] Page 84
[55] Hebrews 11:1

element really this powerful? I had never anticipated such power in the spirits of men; yet that is what I was seeing: unlimited power through prayer with the missing catalyst. Unfortunately, the missing element is not a simple achievement. What is the missing catalyst that will unleash the power of prayer? There is an answer in the Scriptures. It lies in the Tower of Babel.

Why Now?

The simple answer to "Why now?" is because it is time. The end of an age is near. The day of the Lord is approaching. See "The Final Chapter."

"But you, Daniel, shut up the words, and seal the book until the time of the end; many shall run to and fro, and knowledge shall increase." (Dan 12:4)

Because of the gulf separating heavenly knowledge from earthly knowledge, we are seeing through dark glasses. Scientists are telling us that there are eleven dimensions instead of four. Concerning seven of the eleven dimensions, physicists have said that although they were present during the big bang, they are now inaccessible: like rain clouds to a carp.[56] Similarly, heavenly knowledge has been inaccessible to us. We are on this side of a great gulf.

The words have been shut up. The book has been sealed until this time. Daniel was told clearly that many

---

[56] This seems to be a favorite analogy to scientists, so I will use it here. Much is going on that this fish cannot see from his vantage point. Likewise, things that existed in the past may not be visible to us.

would run back and forth. Look at it from different angles and it remains true.

If you think Dan. 12:4 is referring to physical travel, so be it. If you think it is talking about people being in confusion, so be it. If it sounds like people working themselves to death to make money, so be it; but the fact is, people are running here and there physically, mentally, emotionally, and spiritually. The world is confused with wars here and there, famines in Africa and Asia, and crime in the streets of America. Modern communication technology enables us to lobby our legislators to the point of madness for the most mundane causes; and simultaneously, divide peoples over those causes. We want the highest priority to go to our cause.

We have already discussed the increase in knowledge. Natural knowledge is increasing at a pace impossible to maintain as individuals. A few years ago, a person could feel comfortable with the idea that a chosen profession would carry him or her throughout life. Today, a profession may be history in just a few short years.

The computer industry, as young as it is compared to others, required keypunch operators a few years ago. A new professional in the computer industry today may not know what a keypunch was, finding one only in a museum. Computer operations are becoming an endangered profession as computers are becoming virtually self-sufficient. Many computers operate unattended.

Anyone running a personal computer has encountered an error where the operating system offered to diagnose the problem and attempt to repair it. There are security devices that notify the police when it appears a home or office is being broken into. I have personally experienced the appearance of the sheriff at a cabin my wife and I were renting in the Smoky Mountains after disconnecting a television from the cable outlet, so I could hook up a VCR and watch a rental tape. Other devices turn in an alarm to the fire department when they detect smoke. Inserting a microchip in a pet's ear makes it easily locatable when it strays or is stolen.

Compared to time travel and holes in the universe, these are tame topics. Knowledge is surely increasing as never before, and God has treasures for us to enjoy in this life that we have never dreamed possible.

Babel

"Now the whole earth had one language and one speech. And it came to pass, as they journeyed from the east, that they found a plain in the land of Shinar, and they dwelt there. Then they said to one another, 'Come, let us make bricks and bake them thoroughly.' They had brick for stone, and they had asphalt for mortar. And they said, 'Come, let us build ourselves a city, and a tower whose top is in the heavens; let us make a name for ourselves, lest we be scattered abroad over the face of the whole earth.' But the LORD came down to see the city and the tower which the sons of men had built. And the LORD said, 'Indeed the people are one and they all have one language, and this is what they begin to do; now nothing that they propose to do will be withheld from them. Come, let Us go down and there confuse their language, that they may not understand one another's speech.' So the LORD scattered them abroad from there over the face of all the earth, and they ceased building the city. Therefore its name is called Babel, because there the LORD confused the language of all the earth; and from there the LORD scattered them abroad over the face of all the earth.[57]

Notice the prevailing conditions. All the people had one language and were in one place. That they were in one place was less important than all the people in the place were of one mind. Here they were in one city, but if they were in one state or dominion, and everyone in that state or dominion were of the same mind, the conditions would be identical.

They decided as one people to do a thing: build a tower to heaven.[58] God saw what they intended and did not treat it lightly. He was upset enough that He disbursed them throughout the world and confused their languages, so they could not communicate. He noted that if they were not stopped, **nothing** would be impossible to them. I am sure that, like me, you have read this passage before. You saw the words. Nothing would be impossible for them that they have imagined, but think about it. If they were permitted to continue, "nothing they imagined" would be impossible.

Many of us have said man would not be allowed to go to the moon or other planets. God said nothing was

---

[57] Gen 11:1-9

[58] It is interesting to speculate about a tower whose top may reach heaven. What would it take to build a tower to heaven? How high would that be? Yet it seemed plausible, because it was a concern to God. Was the tower merely another pyramidal shaped structure, or could it have been symbolic of an intellectual tower?

impossible to them. Jesus pointed out that people would enter the fold without going through the door and referred to them as thieves.

"Most assuredly, I say to you, he who does not enter the sheepfold by the door, but climbs up some other way, the same is a thief and a robber." (John 10:1)

It appears there may be other ways to enter God's blessings, but it does not appear that it is possible to remain there. Another parable tells of those at the wedding feast without the wedding garment who were subsequently thrown out.[59] The New Age movement may indeed have understanding that will enable them to enter God's treasures. Other religions may usurp God's blessings, but in the end, only those whose lives are hidden with Christ in God will be allowed to remain in His blessings. Even the antichrist has the power to perform deceptive wonders.[60] Similarly, nothing is restrained from man if he approaches it the right way.

We should take notice that they were building this tower in Shinar or Babylon. Babylon is a constant Scriptural reference to the seat of devils. Although prophesies of the fall of Babylon have been fulfilled, there remain others yet unrealized.

What does Babel have to do with us and prayer? It becomes evident: fellowship, love and respect for one another, a common goal, unity! This is the missing catalyst for our prayers: unity. We must be unified in our goals.

Charles Morris (Morris, 1993, p. 15) said of scientific endeavors, "Psychology, like all science, is a communal

---

[59] Matt. 22:14

[60] Rev. 13:13, 16:14

enterprise." Scientists work together, building on the discoveries of others. Christians must also work together, building on the name or nature of Jesus and encouraging one another.

The world is moving toward a potential single world government. It is being achieved through commerce with free trade and mutual trade agreements; for example, the unification of Europe is not intended to be merely an economic union. Since World War II, Europe has been moving toward a political union forming the United States of Europe. The economic part of the unification is merely the easiest to achieve. These efforts at unification, however, have been derailed.

The Americas have NAFTA and Southeast Asia has SEATO. They have a single goal: free trade or open markets.

Mankind no longer populates one city in a corner of the world. We now populate the entire world. English has become the universal language of commerce between people. Serving to further the cause of Christ through the teaching of English for a month each year in Russia t, I was told that if the college where I was teaching could afford it, they would support these programs on a year-round basis. The demand for this universal language is in that great demand. This same demand exists throughout the world. There are other languages used to talk through and to computers. Communications are more open and universal than at any other time in history. There is no more disbursing of the population around the world. The population is disbursed, and it is still united. It still has one goal. They are building a scientific or technological tower to heaven; and nothing will be impossible to mankind. Let me repeat and emphasize, NOTHING will be impossible to mankind. The goal is to build a heaven on earth. We wish to wipe out disease, poverty, and every form of discomfort, and there is surely nothing wrong in such goals.

Realize, however, that what happens in the natural merely mirrors what is happening spiritually. Man is building a tower to heaven and nothing is impossible to him. The problem with man's tower is also revealed in these verses. They were constructing the tower of brick instead of stone.[61] Their tower is being constructed on the works of man and using man's technology. In Exodus, God warns against making an altar with stones that have been touched by the technology of man. Man's technology pollutes the altar. At Babel, man was constructing an altar, a tower that would reach to heaven. The body of Christ is building a tower to heaven and nothing will be impossible to that body. This tower is being built to the name of Jesus and is being constructed according to Scriptures.[62]

I am not talking about something that may happen. It will happen! It is happening. The only question is, "Will we be part of it?" There is a resurgence of Spiritual revival in the world right now, and we can be part of it.

Christians must unite, not as one denomination, but as one people. The people within the church must become

---

[61] Exodus 20:25

[62] (Moore, I Must Decrease, 1999), 1st Books, 2003

[We] are following the pattern laid down in Acts 2:38. We are giving our hearts to Christ and being buried in His nature. Then, He fills us with the Kingdom of God.

one family. Begin praying together and begin praying for the same things. The greatest events in Christendom have occurred through communal prayer. A group of people praying together began the Pentecostal movement of the 19th century. Catholics praying together began the Catholic Pentecostal movement. Christians from various denominations are working together in mission efforts, and the church is growing in these places.

The concept of power through unity is found in the commission to the apostles when Jesus sent them out, not alone, but in pairs.[63] We are also told that while five have the power through God to put a hundred to flight, a hundred will put ten thousand to flight.[64] Unity is much more powerful than solitary power. Even the witnesses in Revelations are not sent as one; there are two.[65]

Perhaps the greatest example of the power of unity and communal prayer is found at Pentecost. One hundred twenty people praying for seven days resulted in the Pentecostal experience.[66] They were in one place, but they were not immediately in one mind with one focus. When after seven days they became of one mind, seeking the same thing, flames of fire set upon each of them and they began to speak in other languages.

Compare this to Babel. At Pentecost, they spoke in one or more languages; and, while at Babel their languages were confused so they could not understand one another, at Pentecost everyone heard these people

---

[63] Mark 6:7

[64] Lev. 26:8

[65] Rev. 11:3

[66] Acts 2:1-11

speaking in their own language and could understand it. At Babel, they likely spoke in one language, yet they could not understand; but at Pentecost, everyone understood whatever language(s) was/were spoken.

This was the complete reverse of Babel. The intent of the tower builders was to build a tower to heaven, and God disallowed it because there would be no limit to their power if they had been successful. Great power was released to God's people at Pentecost, because they achieved what the tower builders did not: a tower that reached heaven.

We are yet living on the experience of Pentecost, but the power released was also manifested in the wonders God performed through His people. God performed special miracles at the hands of Paul; Peter healed the cripple at the gate called Beautiful; Philip traveled from place to place instantly.[67] Yet, I expect the things we read about in the scriptures to be dwarfed by the things God will do in this day.

It sounds too simple, doesn't it! All it takes is a people unified in seeking God. Well, there is a little more to it. Communal prayer implies a communal spirit where people love one another; that is, they are one people.

You may have noticed that you are not blessed while you are judging others. While you are thinking that God could not bless someone else because of the terrible things they have done, you are losing your blessing. At the same time, the other person is rejoicing in the blessings of God.

We should learn to forgive one another and put our petty differences behind us. We must stop judging other

---

[67] Acts 3:1-10, 8:39-40, 19:11

denominations because they fail to agree with us in every area. If God is blessing them, although they believe some things differently than we do, should we not accept them also and vice versa?

Paul said whoever calls on the name of Jesus would be saved. He did not specify Catholic or Protestant denominations. Christianity is the only true religion: not Catholicism, Mormonism, Charismatic or any other; and the Catholic Church is not the Antichrist. First John 2:18-23 tells us the Antichrist spirit is that spirit that says Christ is not come in the flesh. This is most definitely not the Catholic Church. In fact, for much of fifteen hundred years, the Catholic Church was the principle vehicle for the ministry of Christ. It is time for the body of Christ to begin caring for itself instead of biting at its own flesh.

What can you expect if you make such a magnanimous sacrifice as accepting other Christians? Everything! Nothing will be restrained to you that you imagine doing.

Philip traveled from place to place instantly. Why should anything be impossible to the church of Christ?

The scientific community has returned to Babel, and nothing will be impossible to them. This time they will not be disbursed throughout the earth. This time God will likely allow mankind to accomplish much of its ideas culminating it with the fall of Babylon the Great. Christians can also attain the power desired at Babel by building a tower to the name (nature) of Jesus; and like the scientific community, nothing will be impossible to us. However, Christ will get the glory from the tower He enables us to construct.

We began our discussion about the problem of unanswered prayer, and I have forsaken the discussion of faith for the discussion of unity. I truly believe unity to be as powerful as faith. I have cited examples where God has used pairs of witnesses and will use pairs in the future. He sent the disciples out in teams of two, and He promised that He would be amid a gathering of two or three. If two or three would agree, God would agree also.[68]

When Peter was in prison, the church was praying for him, and he was freed. When he went to the house where they were praying, however, they said that it must be Peter's ghost, because Peter was in prison. They could not even believe the physical result of their prayers standing before them.

This does not mean that faith is unimportant. My pastor[69] explained this phenomenon in this manner. No single individual had sufficient faith to believe for Peter's release, but the combined faith of each person in unified prayer was sufficient to free Peter. While our faith may not be strong enough by itself to yield the desired results, through our little bits of united faith, God moves. Faith yields the results, but unity is the catalyst that gives our faith its working power.

Unified prayer efforts have been initiated throughout the world. Annually, in America, we have a National Day of Prayer. Annually, there is a global day of prayer with topics selected for focus. We can pray in unity for these needs and add additional requests in local groups.

---

[68]   Mat. 18:19,20
[69]   Tom Flewellen of Eldorado, IL

Babel Summary

Christianity will experience a spiritual resurgence through cooperation. I am confident that this will occur even in the face of a falling away.

"Those who do wickedly against the covenant he shall corrupt with flattery; but the people who know their God shall be strong and carry out great exploits." (Dan 11:32)

It benefits Christians of all faiths to lay differences aside for our mutual benefit, the body of Christ, and the glory of His name. It is not necessary to deny our beliefs to accept others with different views. If we cannot get beyond that, we will have difficulty partaking of the blessings available to us.

Jesus tried to teach the disciples tolerance when John wanted to forbid others from teaching in Jesus' name because they were not members of their congregation. [70] Today, we see Christians of various denominations working together harmoniously.

Diversity in Christian denominations provided an opportunity to witness to a woman in Russia. Several of us from different church backgrounds were teaching there during the summer, and this woman asked how Christianity could be true and have so many denominations. I was able to point out to her that each of us was from a different denomination and had some different views, but we all agreed on the essentials. We agreed that we are saved by the sacrifice of Jesus on the cross and baptism.

---

[70]   Mark 9:38-40

If we can relegate doctrinal differences to second place and seek the common goals of Christianity, there is no limit to what the body of Christ will see and do. At the very least, let us concentrate on the similarities instead of the differences. Let us be peacemakers wherever possible. Let us find fellowship with all we can.

The central point is that mankind will do great things (miraculous in the eyes of the church), and God will have a people through whom He will do great things. It is incontrovertible! God will have this people. What is left to us is to elect to be part of this people: a people who will build a tower to heaven, a tower of His name.

"The name of the LORD (Jesus) is a strong tower; The righteous run to it and are safe." (Prov. 18:10)

Liberalism

There is a tendency to relativize the Bible to the modern culture, instead of modifying modern culture to adhere to the teachings of the Bible. Christ reproved liberalism that had been allowed by priests of the Judaic law, insisting on adherence to the written Word of God.

"For God commanded, saying, 'HONOR YOUR FATHER AND YOUR MOTHER'; and, 'HE WHO CURSES FATHER OR MOTHER, LET HIM BE PUT TO DEATH.' But you say, 'Whoever says to his father or mother, "Whatever profit you might have received from me is a gift to God"--then he need not honor his father or mother.' Thus you have made the commandment of God of no effect by your tradition." Mat 15:4-6

The Levitical priesthood applied this escape clause to the fifth commandment to eliminate the necessity of caring for parents by the children. They sought to liberalize the law so that it would fit the liberal, self-serving greed of the culture. Jesus did not liberalize the law: He made it even more rigid.

"You have heard that it was said to those of old, 'YOU SHALL NOT COMMIT ADULTERY.' But I say to you that whoever looks at a woman to lust for her has already committed adultery with her in his heart.

Mat 5:27-28

Before, adultery was thought of as a physical act. Simply contemplating adultery was probably considered a part of human nature, but Jesus revealed that part of human nature as evil and unacceptable. Contemplating adultery was like committing the act. That does not necessarily make the offenses equal! Jesus said, "Brood of vipers! How can you, being evil, speak good things? For out of the abundance of the heart the mouth speaks." (Mat. 12:34)

The opposite of this is that from the abundance of the heart the mouth is silent. In this case, the individual does not act on the temptation, showing love for God by overcoming (somewhat).

"Whoever therefore breaks one of the least of these commandments, and teaches men so, shall be called least in the kingdom of heaven; but whoever does and teaches them, he shall be called great in the kingdom of heaven. For I say to you, that unless your righteousness exceeds the righteousness of the scribes and Pharisees, you will by no means enter the kingdom of heaven."

Mat 5:19-20

These words must not be construed as applying only to the Jews, simply because they were spoken to Jews under the law. Jesus insisted on righteousness and compliance to the laws of God to enter the kingdom of heaven. The kingdom of heaven was ushered in at Pentecost, the church, so the law applies as aptly to the church as it did to the Jews.

The rituals of the law, the schoolmaster that taught us of Christ, are not part of the universal laws of God. They were imperfect symbols of the truths to be revealed through Jesus. So we are not suggesting here that you should kill animals as sacrifices. Paul summed up our relationship to the law in his statement to the Galatians,

"But if you are led by the Spirit, you are not under the law."
Gal 5:18

When we are led by the Spirit of Love, no law is
necessary.

Adjust the relevance of the Scriptures to the current
culture? God forbid! God and His laws are not adaptable
to mankind. The culture in the Garden of Eden was to
educate ourselves in the knowledge of good and evil.
To do so was to make us like God. It appears that God
disapproved of liberalism in Eden. What makes the current
culture different from that culture? As Adam and Eve did
not believe they would die, because the serpent told them
they would not die, we are guilty of faithlessness. We do
not believe the Word of God. We may do as we wish. Of
course, I am referring to the liberal "we." As surely as the
liberal Adam and Eve were introduced to death because
they believed the liberal teaching of the serpent, so shall
those who justify their moral liberalism in this day.

The laws of God were interpreted more rigidly by
Christ to the culture of His day-not more liberally.
However, he did teach us a better way. Instead of trying
to remember the laws and walk a tightrope trying to
obey them, He left us with two simple rules, which if we
follow, we will not disobey any of God's laws. These two
rules were love: love for God first, and then love for one
another.[71]

One of the current areas of liberalization is marriage.
There are several areas where God's displeasure has
been rigorously demonstrated. His actions to Sodom

---

[71] Mat. 22:37, Mark 12:30, Luke 10:27

and Gomorrah[72] displayed His feelings towards homosexuality.[73] Paul, the author of the letter to the Galatians, where he stated that we are not under the law if we are led by the Spirit, also wrote, "'honor your father and mother,' which is the first commandment with promise: 'that it may be well with you and you may live long on the earth.'" (Eph. 6:2,3) Malachi cites God's feeling toward divorce, an offense that has become rampant among Christians in America. The bluntness of Malachi's words should drive the point home to any soul with an honest heart before God. "the LORD God of Israel says That He hates divorce

. . ." (Mal. 2:16)

Ah, but Malachi's words are from the Old Testament, so they no longer apply. Not so! When Jesus preached concerning marriage, He closed the loopholes.[74] Except for adultery, divorce is not acceptable. When Christ speaks of loving God and loving one another, it is not a carnal love. It is a spiritual love that will not do anything to harm another. To marry a person divorced for reasons other than adultery makes one an adulterer. The lawful spouse of another person has been coveted and stolen. Paul expounds further on divorce and addresses the issue of an unbelieving spouse divorcing the believer in 1st Cor. 7.

The love Christ taught was a selfless love; giving without expecting the love given to be returned. Of course,

---

[72] Gen. 19:1-25

[73] God's hatred of homosexuality does not imply hatred of homosexuals. This is a temptation that must be overcome. Rom. 1:26, 27

[74] Mark 10:2-12

the love will be returned, but it may not be returned by those to whom it was given. If we offer selfless love, God will assure through the laws He has created that the love will return. Selfless love is an acceptable sacrifice to God.

Perhaps a few words of the writer of Hebrews will help put our obligations into perspective. We do not hear these words quoted very often.

"For if we sin willfully after we have received the knowledge of the truth, there no longer remains a sacrifice for sins, but a certain fearful expectation of judgment, and fiery indignation which will devour the adversaries. Anyone who has rejected Moses' law dies without mercy on the testimony of two or three witnesses. Of how much worse punishment, do you suppose, will he be thought worthy who has trampled the Son of God underfoot, counted the blood of the covenant by which he was sanctified a common thing, and insulted the Spirit of grace?"

Heb 10:26-29

The sacrifice of Christ at Calvary removed the sentence of death for anyone who would accept His saving power and continue in His service. No work of any man could save from that penalty except the Son of God. Having saved us from that penalty, he expects us to lead holy lives. We will fail from time to time. We will say the wrong thing at the wrong time. We forget to meet someone for an appointment. We feel a little unjustified hostility at other drivers. These are unintentional sins. They were atoned for at the cross, but intentional sins after committing our lives to Christ requires recompense on our part. We will receive stripes for these sins. Receiving stripes is not the same as losing our souls. We do not need to walk a tightrope to serve Christ. He is not trying to trick us. That was not the purpose of His sacrifice on Calvary.

"And that servant who knew his master's will, and did not prepare himself or do according to his will, shall be beaten with many stripes. But he who did not know, yet committed things deserving of stripes, shall be beaten with few. For everyone to whom much is given, from him much will be required; and to whom much has been committed, of him they will ask the more." Luke 12:47-48

"But if you are without chastening, of which all have become partakers, then you are illegitimate and not sons." (Heb. 12:8)

Discipline is required by the inviolable laws that God has established. There must be a tooth for a tooth, a reaction to an action. The cross covers all past sins and all unintentional sins, but each person must atone for subsequent intentional sins.

We saw earlier that not to act on our temptations was overcoming, or at least, somewhat overcoming. If a temptation enters our minds and we put it out of our minds, or try, we are overcoming. When we meditate on the temptation and feed it, we are failing. We are yielding to temptation. Any time we take willful pleasure in the allure of sin, we are failing.

"I beseech you therefore, brethren, by the mercies of God, that you present your bodies a living sacrifice, holy, acceptable to God, which is your reasonable service. And do not be conformed to this world, but be transformed by the renewing of your mind, that you may prove what is that good and acceptable and perfect will of God." (Rom. 12: 1, 2)

Here, Paul exhorts us to be holy physically, but also mentally through the renewing of our minds. The renewed mind needs to be continually disciplined to pure thought.

"Finally, brethren, whatever things are true, whatever things are noble, whatever things are just, whatever things are pure, whatever things are lovely, whatever things are of good report, if there is any virtue and if there is anything praiseworthy—meditate on these things." (Phlp 4:7)

Paul acknowledges his own humanity in this same epistle and is an example to us of our need for continually reaching out to holiness. "Not that I have already attained, or am already perfected; but I press on, that I may lay hold of that for which Christ Jesus has also laid hold of me." (Phlp. 3:12)

While Jesus and the apostles laid a straight course for us, liberalism allows all things, declaring that there is no sin. Whatever is not in agreement with the laws and principles of God is sin. If there is no sin, then everything is pure or holy. If everything is holy, then the exhortation to, "Pursue peace with all people, and holiness, without which no one will see the Lord," (Heb. 12:14) is meaningless, but nothing in the Scriptures is meaningless. This Jesus, whom we serve, is not morally liberal. He insists on adherence to the principles of righteousness that were established at the beginning. He has never conformed to the culture of society, and He never will.

Jesus Christ is the same yesterday, today, and forever. (Heb 13:8)

Before continuing to the next subject, let me add one more thing. Each morning, I do my devotions. The beginning of those devotions is communion, spiritual communion. I do not have bread and wine. I meditate on the cross, on the sacrifice of Christ for me. I thank Him for that sacrifice, for His suffering. I recognize that He died for my sins, and He has forgiven me. This is my acknowledgment of sin and need for His forgiveness. It is the best "minute" of my day.

Predestination

This has been a disturbing subject for me. I hate to think of people as being predestined to damnation. There remain areas of the subject about which I am not completely comfortable; however, predestination is a reality.

"Blessed be the God and Father of our Lord Jesus Christ, who has blessed us with every spiritual blessing in the heavenly places in Christ, just as He chose us in Him before the foundation of the world, that we should be holy and without blame before Him in love, having predestined us to adoption as sons by Jesus Christ to Himself, according to the good pleasure of His will, to the praise of the glory of His grace, by which He made us accepted in the Beloved. Eph 1:3-6

Notice, however, that this verse speaks of being predestined to life. We assume that others are irrevocably predestined to death, but that is an assumption on our part. There are specific examples where this seems absolute; for example, Judas Iscariot.

That sounds pretty straightforward. We are predestined to serve Him or not, or not!

"Therefore, brethren, be even more diligent to make your call and election sure, for if you do these things you will never stumble..." 2Pe 1:10

From this verse, it appears that we may be lost regardless of being predestined. Predestined or not, we may be saved, or we may be lost. We have said of others that they were born to do thus or so. They were especially suited to certain actions in life. God forbid that Pavarotti never sang. Thank God, that Dotty Rambo composed the music she heard in her soul. How many people's lives have been extended and healthy because Pasteur studied medicine? On the flip side, we have bemoaned wasted lives. They could have accomplished this or that. People seem specifically talented in certain areas, but sometimes they show no interest in applying that talent for whatever reason.

We like to believe we are free to choose, and though these Scriptures indicate that our destinies are chosen before our birth, other Scriptures are specific about our freedom of choice.

"And if it seems evil to you to serve the LORD, choose for yourselves this day whom you will serve, whether the gods which your fathers served that were on the other side of the River, or the gods of the Amorites, in whose land you dwell. But as for me and my house, we will serve the LORD." (Josh. 24:15)

Of course, one will say, each one chose as he or she was predestined to choose. So, does freewill really exist? I am aware that this is a purely spiritual question; nevertheless, is there insight into this question in the scientific laws of God?

Brian Greene, in his book, The Elegant Universe, states the following about free will.

"The rigid lock-step view of the unfolding of the universe raises all sorts of perplexing philosophical dilemmas surrounding the question of free will, but its import was substantially diminished by the discovery of quantum mechanics. We have seen that Heisenberg's uncertainty principle undercuts Laplacian[75] determinism because we fundamentally cannot know the precise positions and velocities of the constituents of the universe. Instead, these classical properties are replaced by quantum wave functions, which tell us only the probability that any given particle is here or there, or that it has this or that velocity." (Greene, The Elegant Universe, 2003, p. 341)

"The probabilistic aspect of quantum mechanics significantly softens Laplacian determinism by shifting inevitability from outcomes to outcome-likelihoods. . ." (Greene, The Elegant Universe, 2003, pp. 341-342)

Laplacian determinism theorized that if we could know all things at any point in time, we could accurately foretell every subsequent event. In other words, everything that has already happened determines everything that will be done. Heisenberg's uncertainty principle tells us that there is a limit to what can be known for certain. The simple act of attempting to measure aspects of subatomic particles changes the particles. Attempts to determine position alters the precision in measuring velocity. Therefore, at these microcosmic levels, it becomes impossible to know some things for certain.

Again theoretically, according to Laplace, if everything fully measurable about every minute particle in the universe was known, science could predetermine what will transpire at any location at any point in time. The uncertainty principle sets a finite limit that implies a limit

---

[75] Pierre Simon de Laplace (Analytical Theory of Probabilities, 1812) and Philosophical Essay on Probabilities (1814; trans. 1905).

to the certainty of predestination, as even the Scriptures seem to support.

Jerald Schroeder in a chapter on The Science of Free Will says this in a different way, but still referring to Heisenberg's uncertainty principle.

"According to this theory, which forms much of the basis for quantum mechanics, objects in the universe have extended, fuzzy boundaries. Being fuzzy, there are no exact edges to measure. Recent experimental data indicate that the fuzziness is real."

(Schroeder G. L., 1997, p. 149)

This statement reemphasizes the fact that there is some miniscule potential for change. Another observation by Dr. Schroeder adds further emphasis.

"Quantum mechanics teaches that while the general path of a reaction may be predictable, the exact path is not." (Schroeder G., 2001, p. 40)

Again, we are faced with probabilities, not certainties. We also gain insight and support for a subject covered earlier relative to action-reaction, tooth for a tooth. In that discussion, we stated that the reaction for an action may not be identical but would exert an equal force. That is, if one person knocks another person's tooth out, it may not result in the first person's tooth being knocked out. The reactive path, as shown here, may be different. Instead of losing a tooth, the individual may be somehow otherwise scarred. The resultant injury would be equal to the injury inflicted but not necessarily the same injury.

What I feel we have seen here is that there is no conflict between predestination and free will. Regardless of what destinies were planned for us (or we chose?) from the foundation of the worlds, we "usually" have the ability to choose other destinies.

"but to sit on My right hand and on My left is not Mine to give, but it is for those for whom it is prepared." Mar 10:40

God set a plan in order from the beginning, and His purpose will stand. However, it is not His will that any should perish; so, everyone is given an opportunity to accept salvation through the blood of Jesus Christ. He desires that everyone would come to repentance.[76] There is an implication here that everyone made a choice before we entered this life, and we shall look at this further.[77] While we may all be predestined to life or death, we have a chance to change that destiny. In 2 Peter 1:10, we are told to make our calling and election sure. We have elected, perhaps through predestination, to accept Jesus as our Lord, but Peter urges us to continue in the faith. To reinforce the concept that predestination is not necessarily final, let us refer to a few Scriptures from Revelation.

"He who overcomes shall be clothed in white garments, and I will not blot out his name from the Book of Life; but I will confess his name before My Father and before His angels." (Rev 3:5)

Here is a promise to not blot a name from the Book of Life. This suggests that one predestined for salvation can be lost.

"and if anyone takes away from the words of the book of this prophecy, God shall take away his part from the

---

[76] 2 Pet. 3:9

[77] Page 284

Book of Life, from the holy city, and from the things which are written in this book." (Rev 22:19)

Again, we see a reason for being removed from the Book of Life. I am confident that it is difficult to be removed from the Book of Life but not impossible. Yes, it is impossible for man to fully determine anything. God, however, can and has fully determined the destiny of certain men.

But indeed for this purpose I have raised you up, that I may show My power in you, and that My name may be declared in all the earth." (Exo 9:16)

God had a specific purpose that Pharaoh was to fulfill. There was no alternative. In this case, there is no assurance that Pharaoh was lost. There is historical evidence which states that after losing his army in the Red Sea that he became a man of peace. (Brier, 1999)

One obvious subject of predestination is the apostle Paul.

"Now there was a certain disciple at Damascus named Ananias; and to him the Lord said in a vision, "Ananias." And he said, "Here I am, Lord." So the Lord said to him, "Arise and go to the street called Straight, and inquire at the house of Judas for one called Saul of Tarsus, for behold, he is praying. And in a vision he has seen a man named Ananias coming in and putting his hand on him, so that he might receive his sight." Then Ananias answered, "Lord, I have heard from many about this man, how much harm he has done to Your saints in Jerusalem. And here he has authority from the chief priests to bind all who call on Your name." But the Lord said to him, "Go, for he is a chosen vessel of Mine to bear My name before Gentiles, kings, and the children of Israel. For I will show him how many things he must suffer for My name's sake."

Act 9:10-16

We have already seen that Judas committed suicide and that he had no recourse. To attain balance, when the Christ was crucified, the antichrist also had to die. Both were made curses by hanging on a tree: Jesus, at the hands of His crucifiers, Judas by his own hand. Remember Peter's admonishment to make your calling and election sure.

In the next chapter, we will discuss balance, *a principle that was demonstrated when Judas committed suicide.*

Balance

Tooth for a tooth, mountains and valleys: The Bible is filled with lessons on balance. The Sword of the Spirit cuts two ways. It reveals to us our failures and shows us our achievements. The fire of the Spirit will convict us for our errors or cause our hearts to dance. We feed the body, but we must also provide adequately for the soul.

Humility and exaltation must be balanced. The opposite of humility is pride but pride itself is an offense to God. This introduces an added dimension when dealing with humility. One aspect of pride is taking pleasure in one's own accomplishments as though we are somehow above others in ability. We should enjoy doing things well but eliminate self-absorption. Remember Bernadette![78]

"So on a set day Herod, arrayed in royal apparel, sat on his throne and gave an oration to them. And the people kept shouting, "The voice of a god and not of a man!" Then immediately an angel of the Lord struck him, because he did not give glory to God. And he was eaten by worms and died." Act 12:21-23

Through a God-given ability to oration, Herod was exalted in the eyes of the people. How great an experience, yet Herod forgot humility! He accepted praise from men for a gift from God. Humility would have given praise to God for such a gift, for such an experience. He would still have enjoyed the honor afforded him through his gift.

---

[78]   Page 89

Nowhere in the Scriptures is there any positive mention of pride; Instead, it is one of the things God hates. Three times in the sixth chapter of Matthew, we are told to do things quietly or secretly. These things could earn us honor in the eyes of men, yet we are told to use modesty in doing good deeds. In each case, God will reward us openly. God blessed Herod openly, but Herod internalized the praise he received. He could have walked away in awe at the blessing God had given him, but he chose to take full credit for his great oratory.

Humility and pride are opposites in righteousness and sin. Humility is good, and pride is sin. The only balance between the two is that pride is to be eliminated. It is to be replaced by exaltation, which God grants to each soul in a measure equal to the level of humility. One should not confuse self-respect for pride.

Mother Teresa made no name for herself. She walked humbly before God and man. Her interest was in her hospital and serving the people of India. Yet, she became a figure known and honored throughout the world.

Saint Francis of Assisi died thinking his life was a failure. He lived in obscurity and poverty; his only apparent desire to be a servant to God. He sought humility when he could have been a wealthy merchant. He chose to serve lepers. It is hard to imagine that this beggar would be known and honored by millions throughout the centuries. We should all be such failures. These are only two examples of many. Many other examples of Christians that have eschewed glory in this life are recorded in writing.[79]

---

[79] To list a few references: (Talk, Jesus Freaks, 1999) (Talk, Jesus Freaks Vol II, 2003) (Foxe, 2001)

Contemporaries, and there are many, are documented in monthly periodicals such as Voice of Martyrs.

God's balance is illustrated through a couple of lines in the Peace Prayer of St. Francis. "It is in giving that we receive. It is in pardoning that we are pardoned." We give, and God sees to it that we receive. As a tooth for a tooth does not mean that the same thing will happen to both people involved, neither does giving money mean that the return will be in money.

"Give, and it will be given to you: good measure, pressed down, shaken together, and running over will be put into your bosom. For with the same measure that you use, it will be measured back to you." (luke 6:38)

The "same measure" in this verse means liberality, not a nickel for nickel exchange. When you give liberally, you will receive liberally, and yes, it can be financial. We give of our abundance, however scant that might be; then God gives of His abundance, which has no limit. Then there is the sword.

"All who take the sword will perish by the sword." (Mat. 26:52)

In this verse, we see that those who live violently will die violently or in some equally undesirable manner. Does all this mean that humility never takes a stand, but allows people to walk on them? Not exactly! Jesus did teach us to be peaceful when He instructed His disciples to turn the other cheek.[80] People are missing the lesson when they hint at a violent response after being hit on both cheeks. Consider the second cheek to be the first. Now turn the other cheek. Of course, this is not easy. I have not

---

[80] Mat. 5:39

experienced this temptation, but it is a natural tendency to return violence for violence. Supporting Scripture to forgiveness is found in Mat. 18:21-22. Note also in these verses that forgiveness is not dependent on repentance.

Are we supposed to let people walk on us: to spit in our face? Jesus did! For our sakes, He submitted to people smacking him and spitting on him. Then He allowed them to beat Him and humiliate Him publicly. He allowed them to mock Him. Finally, for our sakes, He permitted them to crucify Him.

He asked His disciples if they could drink the same cup He was to drink or to be baptized with the same baptism He was to endure. They said they could, and after years of evangelizing for His name, they did. Only a few are believed to have died a natural death, and there is some doubt that John suffered death, at all. I am one of those who doubt he suffered death.

Before being martyred for Jesus, Paul evidently demonstrated his humanity in what we said about turning the cheek. We repeat the Scripture where speaking to the Corinthians, he said, "For you put up with it if one brings you into bondage, if one devours you, if one takes from you, if one exalts himself, if one strikes you on the face. To our shame I say that we were too weak for that! But in whatever anyone is bold--I speak foolishly--I am bold also.

2Co 11:20-21

Paul admits to missing God in this example but remember that Paul later faced martyrdom for the name of Jesus.

Jesus demonstrated the ideal, and we do our best to follow His example, but we do not make excuses for ourselves. Furthermore, there is a time to take a stand and act with boldness. In the fifth chapter of Acts, Peter and John were beaten and ordered not to preach the name of Jesus. When ordered to stop preaching Jesus, these men of God told the authorities that they would not obey them, but God. Then they rejoiced that they were considered worthy to be persecuted for His name.

After many days of being adulated by a woman with a spirit of divination, Paul became so grieved that he turned to her and rebuked the spirit.[81] There is a time for humility and a time for boldness. There was nothing meek in the message Stephen delivered to the Jews before they stoned him.[82] I leave this phase of our discussion with the admonition of Jesus.

"Behold, I send you out as sheep in the midst of wolves. Therefore be wise as serpents and harmless as doves." (Mat. 10:16)

An excellent reference on balance is Eccl. 3:1-8.

Our purpose in this book has been to explain the significance embodied in the name of Jesus. To that end, we looked to the laws of God, the bones of Jesus that cannot be broken. A discussion of balance is not separate from a discussion about the laws of God and, by extension, the laws of physics. Something that seems to enthrall Physicists is the smoothness, the balance, and the symmetry of the universe.

Dr. Gerald Schroeder explains the importance of balance in the formation of our universe in the first three

---

[81]   Acts 16:13-18
[82]   Acts 6, 7

minutes following the big bang. Elements began forming during this time.

"But none of it would have, had it not been for the extraordinary balance of power played out among the strong nuclear force, the weak nuclear force, and the electromagnetic force. These meshed in just correct proportions so that protons and neutrons drew together and bonded, thus forming the nuclei of atoms." (Schroeder G. L., 1997, p. 183)

Brian Greene speaks of balance through particle opposites.

"Each of these particles has an antiparticle partner-a particle of identical mass but opposite in certain other respects such as its electric charge (as well as its charges with respect to other forces. . ." (Greene, The Elegant Universe, 2003, p. 8)

There existed matter and antimatter, but that coexistence was brief. Matter and antimatter destroy one another.

Mr. Greene is conclusive in the following quotation. "Although I haven't covered it explicitly in the text, note that every known particle has an antiparticle-a particle with the same mass but opposite force charges (like the opposite sign of electric charge). The electron's antiparticle is the positron: up-quark's antiparticle is, not surprisingly, the anti-up-quark; and so on." (Greene, 2005, p. 528)

Throughout these texts, there are affirmations of opposites that balance each other out in the form of a particle of one type and an antiparticle of the same type. It would be repetitive to cite the numerous references to these opposites. The text I would suggest immersing oneself is a study of these balances is Greene's The Elegant Universe. His books are not casual reading for us nonscientists. Even without the math, many of the concepts are very abstract. If you are like me, you may have to reread much of his writings.

I mentioned an anomaly relative to matter and antimatter. At the big bang, identical quantities of both matter and antimatter formed and should have annihilated both types of matter, yet we see that matter exists.

". . . for each 10,000,000,000 antiparticles, 10,000,000,001 particles formed. As the particles and antiparticles annihilated one another, that one extra particle in ten billion remained. From those rare 'extras,' every galaxy, star, and human is composed." (Schroeder G. L., 1997, p. 181)

This is another slight argument against determinism. Had the particles done what they would be expected to do, there would be no universe, as we know it. There would be no earth, and there would be no humans. This slight imbalance is reflected in our current existence. Beyond an example of the nth degree of uncertainty in predestination, I am not sure of the implications of such an anomaly on spiritual understanding.

It is interesting to note the smoothness, consistency, and agreement between the Bible and scientific discoveries. One would expect such agreements in the Word of God and His creation. Now we go back to the Bible for one last corollary.

Caiaphas, the high priest, prophesied that it was expedient that one man should die for the people rather than the whole nation perish.[83] He spoke of Jesus. Jesus, the son of God, who was crucified on Calvary. However, another also died that the nation should not perish. It was necessary that the son of perdition, Judas Iscariot, should also die. As stated earlier, he too, gave his life.

In the case of Judas, he took his own life.[84] He died before Christ, but his death had no saving power even for himself. Then, Christ was crucified for the sins of the world.

I am inclined to believe that Judas had no recourse. He was foreordained to this destruction and Caiaphas explained it in his prophecy. Someone had to betray Jesus, and the antithesis to Christ, the anti-Christ, had to die. It was necessary for balance. The first sacrifice, Judas destroying his life for his sin, was a service to Him who died after him, unfortunately, however, without redemption.

Another example of this truth is found in the narrative of the Exodus.

"And you shall take a bunch of hyssop, dip it in the blood that is in the basin, and strike the lintel and the two doorposts with the blood that is in the basin. And none of you shall go out of the door of his house until morning. For the LORD will pass through to strike the Egyptians; and when He sees the blood on the lintel and on the two doorposts, the LORD will pass over the door and not allow the destroyer to come into your houses to strike you. . .

And it shall be, when your children say to you, 'What do you mean by this service?' that you shall say, 'It is the

---

[83] John 11:49, 50
[84] Mat. 27:3-5

Passover sacrifice of the LORD, who passed over the houses of the children of Israel in Egypt when He struck the Egyptians and delivered our households.' So the people bowed their heads and worshiped. Then the children of Israel went away and did so; just as the LORD had commanded Moses and Aaron, so they did. And it came to pass at midnight that the LORD struck all the firstborn in the land of Egypt, from the firstborn of Pharaoh who sat on his throne to the firstborn of the captive who was in the dungeon, and all the firstborn of livestock. So Pharaoh rose in the night, he, all his servants, and all the Egyptians; and there was a great cry in Egypt, for there was not a house where there was not one dead. Then he called for Moses and Aaron by night, and said, 'Rise, go out from among my people, both you and the children of Israel. And go, serve the LORD as you have said.'" (Exo 12:22-23, 26-31)

The blood of the lamb saved the Israelites from the curse, but not the Egyptians. The firstborn of every household was under the curse of death. The lives of the Israelites were saved when the blood of the lamb was applied to their doors, but there was no such deliverance for the Egyptians.[85] Therefore, among both peoples there was death. In Egypt, it was the firstborn of each household. Among the Jews, it was the lamb. If Egyptologists are correct, pharaoh was not one of those drowned in the Red Sea. Rameses the Great ruled Egypt for 67 years—about fifty-seven(?) of these years after the Exodus. (Brier, 1999, p. Lesson 31) That timing certainly seems questionable.

---

[85] We do not know if there were any Egyptians who applied the blood to their doors as commanded by Moses.

Balance is required in all things: in judgment, in the formation of the universe, scientific theories, actions and reactions, and so forth. It is a principle of God. It is sometimes difficult for me to not concentrate on one side of a point I am making, especially when I am trying to emphasize the need for obedience to God. I sometimes spend too much time warning against disobedience and not enough emphasizing the blessings of obedience. Even in preaching and teaching, a balance is necessary.

Unchangeable Laws

Man enacts laws, which can be ignored, and as we said earlier, it is only illegal if you are caught. When we ignore God's laws, we are always caught. Of course, the same applies to scientific laws, but we must separate theoretical physics from physical laws. Physical laws have been proven, at least in specific circumstances.

The laws of relativity have been proven to be accurate for large objects; that is, atomic size and greater. Quantum physics has filled many gaps left by relativity, but neither relativity nor Quantum physics could fully unify the disparities provided by gravity. A relatively new area of physics (strings) is still theoretical, but it appears to unify the different branches of physics in some areas. The understanding of the laws of physics is constantly being refined. The laws of God are constantly being better understood, and scientists' research assists in that endeavor. Some of what you are reading may be outdated before you read it.

Einstein's relativity blew the socks off Newtonian laws of motion. Newton's laws had been proven correct to the level of physical knowledge available at that time, but there were questions still unanswered. Relativity answered many of those questions. Yet, closer study showed that relativity as initially proposed by Einstein did not answer certain questions that may not have existed before relativity was introduced. It only applied to objects in uniform motion: stationary or moving at a constant speed. This became

Einstein's special theory of relativity because it did not have universal application. It did not consider accelerating or decelerating motion, so Einstein developed the general theory of relativity.[86]

Problems surfaced as subatomic particles were discovered, and quantum physicists made discoveries that contradicted general relativity at the subatomic level. At the subatomic level, quantum mechanics was needed.

There was still no unification of the physics and attempts to include gravity into the equations resulted in infinity for answers, which indicated the answers were wrong. A fourth branch of physics began to develop in fits and starts: string theory. This branch of physics is still called theoretical regardless of some convincing steps forward.

Where laws of physics have been proven, they are absolute. If this event occurs, that result will follow. God has set these laws in place and does not have to supervise every action of every life form.

We ask questions like, "Why do bad things happen? Is God at fault? Why does He allow this or that to happen?" Since He is Love, should He not intervene? The answer is found in the law.

God has established His laws, and they are able to function without His interference. We have polluted the environment. This we have done through our own negligence and sometimes greed. I am not laying blame on mankind for global warming, but I do believe that we

---

[86] I should note that relativity is not a theory but a time-tested fact.

share in the responsibility if the environment is behaving abnormally.

We must certainly take responsibility for calamities like the Three-Mile Island and Chernobyl nuclear meltdowns. The plagues enumerated in the book of Revelation may simply be the result of wars and our misuse of God's gifts. Acid rain is attributed to industrial waste output and vehicle emissions, among others. It is detrimental to forests, a cause of fish deaths, etc. If we pollute the environment, the environment pollutes us. We will inhale the air we have fouled. It is the inevitable reaction to our actions.

If we ask why bad things happen, it is simply the result of bad things being done. Of course, we can argue that we, as individuals, have not done things to merit specific repercussions. I will not debate the merits of individual cases. While they have explanations, our focus here is on broader applications. We are experiencing the results to humanity due to abuses by humanity.

A Christian minister declared that Hurricane Katrina of 2005 was an act of God's judgments on New Orleans. I do believe that the plethora of disasters occurring around the world are reactions to our actions, the laws of God in motion. They are the manifestation of a tooth for a tooth reaction. However, I do not believe this hurricane was a judgment against New Orleans specifically. If it was a judgment against New Orleans, I must question why the French Quarter was barely touched. I was working with others in New Orleans to get homes and neighborhoods in shape for people to return home at the time for the first Mardi Gras celebration after the hurricane. I went into downtown New Orleans and found the French Quarter open for business, while thousands of devout people were forced out of their homes forever. One of the sights I saw in the spared heart of downtown New Orleans was that of two lesbians exchanging a passionate kiss[87].

I agree with Jerry Fallwell that the 9-11 disaster was a wake-up call. In the wake of this attack, America changed for the better. American flags were flying everywhere. Declarations of commitment to God were seen everywhere on billboards. People were reaffirming their faith in Christ, and they wanted the world to know that this is a Christian nation. We did wake up, for a while at least. For some, it was a permanent awakening. For others, it was less permanent.

Prayer provides some protection against repercussions from the law. Heartfelt repentance and loving communication with God are acts of goodness that will be repaid. The law is not overridden by prayer. The law is satisfied by heartfelt penitence. I will not attempt to rationalize every possible nuance or seeming exception to the balance I have suggested. When the laws are broken, there will be repercussions, but again, God can do anything? There are some things God will not do. I do not believe God will break His own laws. We see this demonstrated by Paul.

"For if I build again those things which I destroyed, I make myself a transgressor." (Gal. 2:18)

To me, even miracles are not the breaking of laws. Many things happen today that in Bible times would be

---

[87] For anyone, this should be reserved for a more private opportunity.

considered miracles: xrays, television, airplanes, motion sensing door openers, instant international communication, etc. They are all the results of technology. We have learned greater depths of the laws of God, and we have applied those laws to developing technologies.

I appreciated the support I recently discovered when learning that many years before my time on earth began, this same concept was proposed by St. Augustine who maintained that miracles are only apparent violations of the laws of God. (Shiff, 1901, pp. 321-322)

Do I minimize the power of Christ? God forbid! Science is not able to heal the blind through faith. Jesus, the incarnation of wisdom, God in the flesh, had the power of healing, life, and death. No other human has ever had the power of Christ. God did say, as we saw earlier, if the tower of Babel had been built, nothing would be impossible to the builders.[88] The lack of miracles since the early church is not due to a lack of Christ's willingness to perform miracles but a lack of faith on the part of the church.

The prophets could see the future. We can all see the future to some degree. We can see the potential that the mark of the beast "may" be a small transmitter placed under the skin to identify individuals.[89] This could be used to verify bank balances on a debit transaction and the identity of the person making the transaction. It could

---

[88] Gen. 11:6

[89] I am inclined to believe there will be a visible mark. I also expect perhaps voluntary electronic devices to be inserted under the skin. I have cautionary feelings about the latter, and I am strongly averse to the mark.

reduce identify theft and fraud, which would be an excuse to pass such a law. I have no firm stand on what constitutes the mark of the beast. At this point, it could be a tattoo, a microchip, or a combination. It also seems likely that it is visible.

The prophets, however, could see the future in detail. I have just outlined a possible mark of the beast and how it could be used for making purchases. I have given no details or stated that such will definitely happen in this way or that. The Book of Daniel lays out the future in such detail and accuracy that unbelievers (some refer to them as scholars) suggest a later date for its writing. (Larkin, 1929, p. 228) To substantiate this, they must also, and do, aver that Ezekiel was written years later than the author claims. The explanation lies in the fact that God, at any time, exists in the past, present, and future. He reveals to His prophets what he has already seen in the future.

The laws are not God. They are the rules that run the universe. If there is another universe (which I doubt), it may have a set of laws with many differences. There will be no difference in the laws of righteousness. Pride would still be sin. Surely there is a different set of laws that governs the spiritual dimension, a dimension that many scientists ignore or deny. Laws resulting from the personality and righteousness of God will be identical in every dimension.

God's laws judge us and bless us. If we do evil, we shall endure the repercussions of our evil. Penitence becomes part of the reactions when we turn from evil. We seek forgiveness from God, and this act has repercussions. As we have already seen, the repercussion of repentance is to avert the full effect of the evil we have done. It becomes a pillow, so to speak, which cushions our fall. It becomes part of the reaction.

Paul tells us the law is holy and just.[90] He clarified his view more fully to Timothy. "But we know that the law is good if one uses it lawfully." (1 Tim 1:8) The lawbreaker would not consider it good.

A criminal will blame the police when he or she is arrested. The law and any representative of the law are evil in the eyes of lawbreakers. To those who do not break the law, the law is a protection against those who do.

---

[90] Rom. 7:12

Here a Little

I thought to have titled this chapter, Word Chemistry. While not the same as chemistry, it does demonstrate some similarities. Chemistry is known for formulas for mixing different elements or chemicals. The number of ways these elements can be combined seems endless. The versatility of chemistry is analogous to the versatility of the Scriptures. Scriptural versatility is hinted at by Isaiah.

". . . precept must be upon precept, precept upon precept; line upon line, line upon line; here a little, and there a little. . ." (Is. 28:10, 13 KJV)

Properly dividing[91] and combining the Scriptures, we discover secrets of the snow.[92]

A deck of playing cards provides a simple example of chemistry. If you are at all familiar with cards, you probably know how to play 52-pickup. As the dealer, you simply fan the deck of cards into the air and have some poor unaware soul you have tricked into playing pick them up and put them back into the form of a deck.

No matter how many times you fan these cards into the air, they will always land in a new arrangement. Please excuse the unscientific use of the word always, but the likelihood that you will come up with the same arrangement in your lifetime is extremely unlikely. Regardless of how they are arranged, however, they are a

---

[91] 2 Tim. 2:15
[92] Job 38:22

deck of cards. Many games can be played with these cards by one or more people. Regardless of how many ways these cards are used, they are still the same deck of cards, and all these games are composed of these cards.

There are many more elements of truth in the Scriptures, and the depths of their riches are endless. As I am writing this chapter, it is Christmas Eve eve; so I will use the Christmas story as my first example.

The Christmas Story

The birth of Christ has been taught in so many ways and from so many angles that it seems doubtful there are many new ways to look at it; so, you may be very familiar with some or much of what follows.

The natural or literal knowledge of His birth is that the King of Kings was born in a stable and His bed was a manger, a feeding trough for animals. He was there with His parents, Joseph and Mary. Angels told shepherds that the Savior, the Messiah, was born and could be found in this stable. Had it not been such a grand announcement, I would expect that it would have been met with strong misgivings. After all, why would the King of the Jews be born in a stable? Much of the symbolism is obvious: Some is less obvious. Some may be offensive. The literal reality of what happened is one way to look at Christ's birth, but most if not everything literal has a spiritual understanding.

We are aware of the humility demonstrated by the Son of God coming to us in such a lowly manner. That there was no room in the inn is symbolic of there being no room in the hearts of men. Excuse me if some of the following symbolism is unpleasant, but we are talking about a savior that was born in the humblest circumstances to later die a cruel death.

The first spiritual lesson in the birth of Jesus is humility. The King of Kings, the Wisdom of the ages came to earth in a demonstration of pure humility – the same way He would die. From birth, he rejected the riches of this world, and He came to those that were lowly. He expects nothing less of us.

Jesus slept in a manger, a feeding trough for animals and became the food for humanity and demonstrated this at the last supper when He offered bread and wine to symbolize His body and blood. He told us to eat His body and drink His blood. Our body is both the stable and the manger. The stable is unclean and lowly. We partake of His body in that it is holy: We become holy, as He is holy. Before Christ, our food was our own will, our own desires.

We partake of His blood by the shedding of our blood. We do not necessarily do this by the physical shedding of blood, but by sacrificing our carnal ways and thoughts to take on His spiritual ways and thoughts. We give up our lives to take on His. [93] In addition, there are those today, more than any other time in history that are physically shedding their blood for Christ, dying for His name.

The shepherds were those that were told of the birth of Christ by the angels. The angels did not go to those steeped in possessions that could have provided better accommodations for the great King. There are a couple of thoughts about the shepherds.

---

[93] Lev. 17:11

First, they were an unskilled group of laborers. They had little to brag about, little for which to be haughty; so second, they also represent humility.

The angels announced the birth of Christ to those who would be humble enough to accept as their Messiah an infant born in a stable. God did not call us because of our great skills. He called us because we were humble enough to hear the message and give our hearts to Jesus. Yet, beyond the humility we displayed in accepting Jesus as our Lord and Savior, we have far to go. I speak for myself but assume that most others are in similar circumstances— greatly in need of more humility. The fact that these were shepherds indicates that they tended the flock. The angels spoke to a certain type of laborer. These shepherds would spread the word that the promised Messiah is born. It is the shepherd who has the wisdom and knowledge to lead others to Christ. Today, ministers of the Gospel are shepherds, but they do not work in isolation. Every Christian will, whether intentionally or not, testify of Christ. If we do not use words, we will use actions. Many people come to Christ through the love shown by Christians. Unfortunately, others have been discouraged from looking to Christ because the lives of some Christians demonstrated other than the love and righteousness of Christ.[94] There are weeds among the wheat, and all of us have at times acted more like weeds than wheat.

Wise men finally came to Jesus after a couple of years. Unlike the humble shepherd that readily accepts the Gospel, wise men (with or without humility) will seek the

---

[94] Matt. 13:25-43

truth. They will walk in the light they have until that light leads them to Christ.

There we have a literal and spiritual view of the birth of Jesus. Of course, there are other lessons. We will examine another dimension of Christ's birth shortly.

As Christians, we have become the stable and the manger. When we committed our lives to Christ, Christ was born in us. The shepherds that hear the proclamation that Jesus is born in a stable are the Christians surrounding us that see our commitment or the fruit of our Christian conversion. Wise men are those who have not yet committed themselves to Christ but do so after watching the life we lead before them or believe the words of the Gospel. They follow the light that leads to the conclusion that God has surely performed a work in us to be sought after.

Although we have given our lives to Christ, we are far from perfect. We are still very much like the original stable. In that stable is a manger where Christ was born. Christians and non-Christians will watch our lives. They will be influenced by our lives, for good or bad. They will (spiritually) eat of our flesh and blood. They will notice our righteousness or lack of it, and it will influence their lives. How we deal with our sufferings will encourage or discourage others. Exactly how we will influence the lives of others depends on how much we have partaken of the body and blood of Jesus. The more we have partaken, the more of His body and blood is within us for others to take through our witness and fellowship. Paul speaks of the riches of God as "Christ in you, the hope of glory." (Col. 1:27)

I promised another dimension to the birth of Christ. This may cause some discomfort, so proceed prayerfully. It deals with the linage of Jesus and what it means.

It was prophesied that Jesus would be born through the line of David.

"The LORD has sworn in truth to David; He will not turn from it: 'I will set upon your throne the fruit of your body.'" (Psa 132:11)

The first chapter of Matthew lists the linage of Jesus beginning with Abraham. Luke lists His linage beginning with God and continuing through Adam. However, Luke throws a curve in His chronology. From the start, Luke reveals a glitch in the linage. He says, "Now Jesus Himself began His ministry at about thirty years of age, being (as was supposed) the son of Joseph. . ." (Luk 3:23) Jesus was not the physical son of Joseph. He was the physical son of Mary and the Son of God. Of course, there is no obscure secret in this fact. The important point is that, physically, Jesus was born through the linage of Mary. The linages of Matthew and Luke between David and Jesus are completely different, except for a common beginning with David and ending with Jesus. Matthew shows the father of Jesus to be Joseph, son of Jacob. Luke shows the father of Jesus to be Joseph, son of Heli—more appropriately, son-in-law of Heli.

I will deviate from others who suggest that Mary's DNA was not in Jesus—that she was a genetically independent repository of an egg, but the life or the egg was not hers. I will illustrate by principle that Mary was the Mother of Jesus: that is, that the egg that nurtures the baby Christ was hers.

I understand the desire to draw the conclusion that the egg was not Mary's. It is driven by the desire to eliminate the imputation of original sin to Jesus. It is a concern I think God addressed in a different manner.

Granted that the mother is more than simply a passive repository of a baby: she contributes DNA, she nurtures the embryo, and she endures the agony of childbirth. At least as important as each of these, the mother is the protector.

We are introduced here to a principal that we shall not pursue extensively. Humility has been a major subject in this book and will be addressed further later; so, to me, comparisons to humility are not demeaning. Mary represents the humility linage of David—not the life source for Jesus. The life source is provided by the seed of the male. The seed of man is unregenerate; that is, it is still under the penalty of death. Mary provides DNA from David, but she does not provide life. Sin is not imputed through the egg, but through the seed of the male. The life of Jesus was provided by the Holy Spirit. Mary's DNA was the continuation of the line of David. Beyond this, Mary provides the physical house that shall nourish the Holy Seed that has miraculously fertilized her egg. While Mary was the mother of Jesus, she was subject to the penalty of sin.

Restated, Mary was surely a holy young woman, or she would not have been chosen as mother of the savior of the world, but she still needed the redemption that would be provided through her son. Jesus was pure in that he was the Son of God.

I never cease to be amazed at the length God will go to demonstrate His principles and the lessons He has for us. The birth of Jesus goes beyond being the vehicle to salvation: It becomes a lesson to us of how God works.

What is "illustrated" in the birth of Christ is how God works through us—how He provides salvation. Our flesh is the womb for the seed of the Holy Spirit to bring forth Christ in us. We are the clay through which He works. We are clay as was Mary. However holy our lives may have been before meeting Jesus, we were still dead in our sins. The death that is passed to each of us through inheritance from Adam is in the seed of the male. The life seed fertilizes the egg. The womb is the soil where the seed grows.

Therefore, pure seed was placed in Mary (good soil, if you will) in the same way that the Holy Spirit is placed in us. The Holy Spirit is not diminished, nor made unholy by entering our hearts. The Holy Spirit will bring forth Christ in each of us. Through us, the Holy Spirit ministers the cross to the world. Through the Holy Spirit, we become the body of Christ.

This segues nicely into the next subject.

Christ in you

It is only the sacrifice of Jesus that saves a soul from hell; yet we are saviors, too. It may be the example we lead that by His grace draws others to Christ. Having led them to Christ, He provides salvation for their souls. Our position as a savior is a distant second from the role of Jesus, but as part of His body, we are saviors.

His body is broken today into a world of individual believers, believers that suffer for His name's sake. Through the church, He is persecuted. Whatever is done to a follower of Christ is done to Christ. Through us, Christ is still on the cross. Every pain we feel because of Him, He feels. Yet, He still says, "Father, forgive them. They don't know what they are doing."

Our bodies, as individual believers, provide another cross. We have received His redemption and His Spirit. The Spirit within us suffers the pain of our continuing failures. By our actions, we push the crown of thorns tighter into His brow. He sees and feels the pain of our every act of hatred, vengeance, or disobedience. That Holy Spirit within us does not separate from us because of our sins: at least, not quickly. Instead, He forgives. He remains our advocate to the Father, reminding the Father that for this soul He shed His blood.

Allow me one more extension of the cross. By accepting Jesus into our lives, we have ascended the cross with Him. In one sense, we are the thief on the cross that asks to be remembered in paradise. The assurance is ours. It is promised by one who cannot lie. We will be with Him in paradise when our time on our cross is over.

We have followed the manger to the cross, delving further into the cross than I originally intended. But does this complete the analogies we are presented by the birth of Christ? No! The depth of truth in the Scriptures is inexhaustible.

As "A" conclusion to this subject, let me add a final word, which has already been alluded to.

Jesus died an agonizing death on the cross. The Father suffered as a result of this agony. That was illustrated when the sky darkened at Christ's death. The shadow from those clouds indicated the sorrow of the Father at His Son's death. So the Father and the Son suffered at His death, but it did not end there. A short time later, the Holy Spirit ascended the cross by indwelling in the church, the imperfect people whose sin the Holy Spirit endures to bring them to their fullness in Christ. One more, however! When you and I committed our lives to Christ, we volunteered to share the crucifixion of our sinful man that we might be raised up in the image of the Most Holy.

Do not bemoan your suffering. You may not have understood it, but you volunteered, and you shall be richly reward for Your sacrifice.

All Things Under His Feet

Are all things under His feet? Yes, and yet, no! Jesus put all things under His feet when He was victorious at the cross. You ask, "How was He victorious?" He was killed. His death was a victory in that He proved the overcoming power of humility and love. Instead of calling on the angels of the Father to rescue Him, he willingly endured the cross for the sake of mankind. If He had succumbed to the pain to save Himself, Satan and all that is his (fallen angels, humankind, kingdoms of the earth) would have won, but Satan was beaten at the cross. At this point, Satan bruised the heel of Christ, but the heel of Christ bruised his head. The evil of pride was defeated. Not only did Christ overcome the temptation to be delivered from the cross: He did not respond to His mistreatment with anger. Instead, from the cross, He prays for those who crucified

Him[95]. His victories on the cross are examples to us to this day in how to live. But! you point out, there is still evil, and it is getting worse. Satan still rules on the earth. He is not subjected to Christ. There is another level of understanding.

Jesus died, resurrected, and ascended into heaven. The man Jesus is the head of a body of believers. Every soul that dies in Christ is another case of Christ putting all things under His feet. We endure persecution, self-doubt, and temptations from the enemy; but in the end, having been faithful, we will ascend to God. You and I, by the power of the Holy Spirit within us, will crush the head of the serpent. We will put him and the lusts of our flesh under our feet, and our feet are the feet of Christ on earth today.

Yet, it is not fulfilled. Now, we wait for His appearing. At that time, Jesus will take dominion over all the earth and every living soul, ushering in the millennium—one thousand years of peace on earth. Satan will be bound in the abyss and completely subject to the authority of Christ. Then these prophesies of subjection of Satan and all else to Christ will be fulfilled.

Ah, but God is not finished. He will put an exclamation point on the victory. After the thousand years of peace, (Sabbath of these seven thousand years) Christ will loosen Satan for a final confrontation. Following this confrontation, Satan will be cast into the lake of fire. While enduring the death of the cross was the final and total assurance to the judgment of Satan, the lake of fire is the physical completion of judgment.

---

[95]   God help us!

Tabernacle and Temple

I doubt any student of the Scriptures has missed the point that the Tabernacle was a type of Christ. A few may have missed the lessons of the Temple as a type of Christ. We see the Tabernacle as a temporary sanctuary of God and the Temple as a permanent sanctuary of God. My mind swims as I contemplate the different lessons God has for us in these studies.

The Tabernacle was a type of Christ during His life on earth, but while on earth, Jesus was constructing the Temple.

". . . though He was a Son, yet He learned obedience by the things which He suffered. And having been perfected (consecrated), He became the author of eternal salvation to all who obey Him . . ." (Heb. 5:8, 9)

Having lived His life in submission to the will of the Father, He was perfect[96] and worthy to provide salvation to the world. Having finished His earthly life, He rose to heavenly realms where He sits by the Father until the Father makes the enemies of His Son a footstool for His Son. Thus, He was a movable tabernacle on earth, but is now a fixed temple.

However, He is not yet complete. His body still lives on earth as a Tabernacle with no permanent abode, i.e., you and me. When He casts death into the lake of fire, all His saints will be in their permanent abode.

---

[96] The rendering in the different translations is that Jesus was made perfect. I respect the knowledge of the translators, but the word here can also mean consecrated or complete. This was accomplished at the cross.

In Rev. 21, we see the Bride of Christ, who is described as a city, the New Jerusalem. This city has no temple; because, the Lord God and the Lamb are its temple. You may look at this city as the body of Christ, and God now has a permanent body worthy of His presence (through the blood of Christ). Now, we truly see that all things are under His feet.

Our wills, our vanities, our selves are subject to Him; and this we do willingly. As kings (overcomers) of the earth (our bodies), we will bring the glory and honor we have obtained from God into the city. According to Rev. 3:12, we will never leave the Temple that is in the city. We will truly be willing prisoners of God.

To summarize, the Tabernacle was a temporary house of worship in that that which is perfect was not yet manifest, but the temple is permanent. As Jesus walked the earth, He was in a corruptible body. It was a temporary abode for Him. The glorified body was a permanent body. The first body died, but the new body will never die. In His corruptible body, Jesus was the Tabernacle. In His glorified body, He is the temple.

When Jesus accepted the death of the cross, He put Satan under His feet. He was the conqueror. While Satan is still allowed to work in the earth, His fate was sealed at the cross. Jesus was at war with the spirits of this world. At the cross, He became the conqueror, and is now a prince of peace.

Yet, we see in Revelations that the prince of darkness, Satan, is yet to be cast out of heaven. Job 2:1 speaks of the sons of God (angels) coming to present themselves before God and Satan is mentioned as one being out of place as if he was cast out of heaven when he tried to usurp God's position. Yet, John 12:31 tells us that Satan is about to be cast out. Warfare is still being waged. The serpent told Eve that she would not die from eating the fruit, but spiritually, she died immediately. Later she died physically. What is completed in one sense is not necessarily complete in its final sense. In Rev. 19:11 we see Jesus on a white horse fighting against the enemy. He binds Satan for a thousand years before He lets him loose for a brief period. It still is not over. The prophesies continue.

After Satan is cast into the lake of fire, we see the bride of Christ, the New Jerusalem. In this city, no temple is seen. The battle is completely over. Now we see the final temple, the Lord God and the Lamb.[97]

Years ago, I had an understanding of salvation. It was unsatisfying. I saw it in a box, wrapped with colorful wrapping paper and topped with a ribbon. I was a young Christian, but, even then, I thought this was too simplistic. I got into a discussion with another Christian who quoted one Scripture verse, and because of that one verse, I saw the ribbon come loose and the paper peeled off my package. That evening I studied. I read the Scripture in question, and then paced the floor. Other thoughts came to mind, and I would chase those through Scriptures. For a couple of hours, I read a little and paced a little. Then answers began to come, but each answer generated at least one more question. They came faster and faster: answers and questions. I began to see a whirlpool as answers and questions kept coming faster and faster, deeper and deeper. I could not keep up. When I finished that evening, I knew

---

[97]   Rev. 21:22

a lot more than I did at the outset, but there were many new questions. That day I learned something about the depth of God's Word. When we think we understand God's Word, we have only begun.

We can combine Scriptures to uncover different truths and different levels of truth. We have seen this exemplified in this chapter, but care must be taken as to how we interpret Scriptures. The only real caution I give to students of the Scriptures is that they do not look for revelations that will cause problems. At the same time, do not deny truth for the sake of accommodating the Christian community.

Some are not able to go beyond what Peter called the sincere or pure milk of the Word.[98] Paul spoke of the milk of the word as necessary to grow until one is ready for meat.[99] Our understanding of the Scriptures must develop until we are able to digest solid foods. I confess that I do not consider what has been covered in this text as milk, and I confess to leaving many things unsaid. About many of those things, I have not received sufficient enlightenment.

We may combine Scriptures in many ways to learn many truths, but we must be prayerful to avoid misusing the Scriptures. A simple example of this occurred when a Christian woman asked me about divorce. "My husband is about to leave me," she said. "If he leaves me, I am free to marry again, right?" She was referring to 1 Cor. 7, where Paul states that if the unbelieving leaves, the believing spouse is no longer bound but may remarry. I was about

[98] 1 Peter 2:2

[99] 1 Cor. 3:2

to answer when I felt checked. Instead of agreeing, I said, "It depends." Depends on what, I did not know. She continued quickly, "Well, I think I've got him where he is about ready to leave." My response was immediate. "Your husband is not leaving you: You are chasing him off."

That is a rudimentary perversion of the Scriptures. Other problems are very honest: We may over interpret the Scriptures.

The best test of accuracy is the consistency of a meaning throughout the Bible. These things, I call principles: They prove themselves from Genesis to Revelations. The Laws of Physics, I believe are the laws of God in the physical world, and they have spiritual applications. Some comparisons, I have called analogies. They may not have the power of law but are merely useful comparisons.

As you have seen, I am not shy about interpreting the Scriptures. I do so with much prayer to avoid giving significance to the insignificant. I am also convinced that many do not interpret enough. God was very specific about the measurements of the ark of Noah. The numbers were important, not that the measure was in cubits. Some translations may convert cubits to a measure we understand intuitively but lose the knowledge God was trying to impart.

Regardless, I am human and make mistakes. If you see areas where you feel I have missed the mark, please pray that God will reveal His truth to whichever is missing the mark.

Why are some things Sin?

There are several ways to determine what is sin in the eyes of God and should therefore be sin in the eyes of Christians. The first determination of sin is the Ten Commandments.

Ten Commandments

The most obvious offences to God are actions that work counter to the Ten Commandments. As we have already seen, Jesus warned against breaking or teaching others to break the commandments.[100] Again, one may argue that Christ was speaking to the Jews, not the church. These verses contain a charge that, at the least, conformity to the righteousness of the Ten Commandments is necessary to enter the Kingdom of Heaven or Kingdom of God. This kingdom belongs to the church, both Christian and Jews. Thus, while we may be under grace, greater righteousness than that of the Hebrew scribes and Pharisees is required.

Yet, these commands could not be interpreted concretely. There were conditions applied to them that adjusted their effect depending on the intent and severity of the offence. While the commandments are usually thought of when discussing God's laws, the Ten Commandments

---

[100] Mat. 5:19, 20

is a compendium of God's laws that fall under the all-inclusive laws of God.

The Laws of God

As we stated earlier,[101] the laws of physics are also laws of God. If you can break a law of God, you can break a law of physics. The laws of physics are not broken.[102] Any action attempting to break a law of physics will be met with a corrective action. Likewise, any action attempting to break a law of God is met with a corrective action. This is the effect of balance, which we covered in the chapter on Balance.

If we do evil, we shall receive evil. If we do good, we shall receive good. As Job learned, "Those who plow iniquity and sow trouble reap the same." (Job 4:8)

It is difficult to define sin based on these causes and effects; however, because we can reap the suffering of someone else's actions to us. We may not be guilty of anything yet receive evil. The fact that Christ went to the cross is evidence of this fact. Our tenacity in doing good when it appears we are being unjustly rewarded evil for good will result in greater rewards in our next life.

The golden rule and ethics are difficult methods for assessing the value of our actions. A sinner may desire that everyone give to him all that he desires without any expectation of returning anything; yet, if you respond

---

[101] Page 124

[102] Advances in scientific discovery do sometime demonstrate a flaw in these laws as new insights are discovered.

in this way, it could be damaging to him. You could be feeding a problem that needs a treatment where they need to be deprived. Would any rationale human not versed in medical procedures consider it the best option to give drugs to someone who is addicted? In their circumstances, the good that can be done for them is to deny their desires, or perhaps measured doses will help decrease their reliance on drugs. So, how does one determine exactly what is the good thing to do? Maintain a close relationship with God and pray for enlightenment. That is my best suggestion currently.

Therefore do not let your good be spoken of as evil. (Rom 14:16)

Principles

God has established principles, which help reveal His will for us. Some principles show us how God works in some circumstances. In others, they reveal what pleases or displeases God. Those things that displease God must be considered sin. Our goal is to do His will. If we fail to do His will, we miss the mark, or we sin.

Principles are not necessarily declared openly but are revealed through the workings of God throughout Scripture. As principles of God, they have the force of law. In my book, The Elder Shall Serve the Younger, a principle is directly mentioned only twice in Scripture, but the truth behind that Scripture is expressed throughout God's Word. Genesis 25:23 declares concerning Jacob and Esau at birth that the elder shall serve the younger.

We see that principle demonstrated throughout the Scriptures, beginning in Genesis 1:5, "So the evening and the morning were the first day." Evening was mentioned first and then the day. Certainly light is greater than darkness; therefore, the evening or first part is the lesser part of the day.

Then God made two great lights: the greater light to rule the day, and the lesser light to rule the night. He made the stars also. (Gen 1:16)

Another principle of God was also established early in Genesis 2:24. "Therefore a man shall leave his father and mother and be joined to his wife, and they shall become one flesh." Granted, a husband and wife become one before God by agreeing in marriage. This, however, is not fulfilled physically until children are born to the marriage. Typically, this is through child birth, but it may be by adoption, formal or informal.

Before this, however, God had already instructed Adam and Eve to be fruitful and fill the earth.[103] It was God's intention, very clearly demonstrated that He expected this couple, male and female, to reproduce. Reproduction is not something that is possible when two people of the same gender comingle.

When Jesus came to a fig tree that bore no fruit, He cursed it.[104] Again, in the parable of the fig tree, Jesus spoke concerning fruit. "Then he said to the keeper of his vineyard, 'Look, for three years I have come seeking fruit on this fig tree and find none. Cut it down; why does it use up the ground?'" (Luke 13:7) He also says, "Every branch

---

[103] Gen. 1:28
[104] Mat. 21:19

in Me that does not bear fruit He takes away; and every branch that bears fruit He prunes, that it may bear more fruit." (John 15:2) One more example of expectation of fruitfulness is, "So you ought to have deposited my money with the bankers, and at my coming I would have received back my own with interest." (Mat. 25:27)

These verses demonstrate God's expectation that we bring forth fruit: physically and spiritually. He expects fruits, appropriate to the species: human, animal, or what grows from the ground.

But, God has not hidden His will in this regard in principles that must be discovered. He was very clear in His actions against homosexuality in Sodom and Gomorrah and in Paul's writings in the New Testament as well as throughout Leviticus.

"For this reason God gave them up to vile passions. For even their women exchanged the natural use for what is against nature. Likewise also the men, leaving the natural use of the woman, burned in their lust for one another, men with men committing what is shameful, and receiving in themselves the penalty of their error which was due." (Rom. 1:26, 27)

So, it is by principles and actions that the will of God is expressed toward homosexuality. It is obvious that God hates homosexuality. Let me be clear, however, that God hates homosexuality—not homosexuals.[105]

This is a very narrow application of the use of principles to determine sin. Also, realize that people are not condemned for proclivities, but for sin.

---

[105] God hates sin. I have here referenced one sin, but we all have our failures. Let God be your judge and redeemer.

What God Hates

"These six things the LORD hates, Yes, seven are an abomination to Him: A proud look, A lying tongue, Hands that shed innocent blood, A heart that devises wicked plans, Feet that are swift in running to evil, A false witness who speaks lies, And one who sows discord among brethren." (Prov. 6:16-19)

"But outside are dogs and sorcerers and sexually immoral and murderers and idolaters, and whoever loves and practices a lie." (Rev. 22:15)

Those things listed in these verses are obvious sins. God hates pride. He humbled Himself to present Himself in the body of Christ to suffer the humility of the cross. Consider that He who is far above all exists in dimensions so small that we cannot even detect, yet He is our savior. He declares, "I, even I, am the LORD, and besides Me there is no savior." (Is. 43:11) Greater humility than the humility of God does not exist.

Lying is mentioned in both of our reference verses. Murder is an obvious sin. We really do not need Scripture to tell us this. Those that have devised evil plans, such as robbing the life savings of employees by milking the value from their savings will stand in judgment before God. Also, governments that subject their peoples and control even how they think fit in this group.

Gossip in churches is certainly failing in pleasing God with tales about others, whether true or not. The old saying though not Scripture, "Believe nothing that you hear and only half of what you see," is worth heeding. How many times have you seen someone doing something questionable and drawn an erroneous conclusion? Years ago, I saw two Christian brothers talking secretively away from everyone else. I thought they looked like they were devising some dastardly plan for something. Thank God, I did not verbalize my thoughts to others. It turned out that one brother had a problem about which the other was counseling him.

Sexual immorality is rampant in America. It has become so common that the original taboos such as kissing on the first date are ancient history. Sexual intimacy has become common on the first date, perhaps the only date. James gave very few rules to the gentiles entering the church, but one of them was to avoid fornication.[106]

I will not spend significant more time on this subject, but I must mention again one more thing that God hates.

One translation appropriately renders Mal. 2:16, "'I hate divorce."

The following quotes excerpted from an article by <u>Audrey Barrick</u>, Christian Post Reporter dated April 4, 2008 Is both alarming and somewhat reassuring.

"After months of revived debate over divorce and its increasing acceptance among Americans, a new study affirmed born again Christians are just as likely as the average American couple to divorce.

The Barna Group found in its latest study that born-again Christians who are not evangelical were indistinguishable from the national average on the matter of divorce with 33 percent having married and divorced at least once. Among all born again Christians, which includes evangelicals, the divorce figure is 32 percent,

---

[106] Acts 15:29

which is statistically identical to the 33 percent figure among non-born-again adults, the research group noted."

"Still, the divorce rate among evangelical Christians – who are defined as meeting the born-again criteria plus other conditions – was lower (26 percent) than the national average. Meanwhile, those associated with a non-Christian faith were more likely to divorce (38 percent), the study showed."

This is a terrible testimony for Christianity. There are justifiable reasons for divorce, but are they being followed? Fortunately, I am not often called to make that judgment.

Is this the end of the sin list? No! There is another major area we need to address.

What is not of Faith

". . .whatever is not from faith is sin." (Rom. 14:23)

"For if our heart condemns us, God is greater than our heart, and knows all things." (1 John 3:20)

A good man and a fine preacher from my youth taught that whatever was sin for him was sin for everyone else. This is completely incompatible with the verse that instructs us to "work out your own salvation with fear and trembling." (Php. 2:12)

For several years, I smoked cigarettes. To me, smoking was a sin, and as a Christian, I had to give them up. I had faith that smoking was not right for me. Others, however, do not have this conviction, and I must respect that. It is a dirty habit. It stinks and is unhealthy, but it is not necessarily sin. The Bible does not mention smoking as one of the things God hates.

For many women, wearing makeup or slacks are sin. Makeup became sin because Jezebel painted her face.[107] If Jezebel's painting her face made makeup sinful, let's hope she didn't eat three meals a day or wash her hands before meals. She also looked out a window. Should we board up all our windows? We could argue that women use makeup because of pride. Maybe, it is merely the desire to look the best you can. Again, each person will have to answer that question for themselves.

As far as wearing slacks are concerned, there are slacks made for women that I would not wear on a dare. They are definitely not men's clothing.

Let me add here that I greatly respect these people in their zeal for holiness. I would rather the entire nation would follow their example than the reverse.

What is done without love

When we consider the laws of God, there is a law that trumps all others.

"'Teacher, which is the great commandment in the law?' Jesus said to him, 'you shall love the lord your god with all your heart, with all your soul, and with all your mind. This is the first and great commandment. And the second is like it: you shall love your neighbor as yourself. On these two commandments hang all the Law and the Prophets." (Matt. 22:36-40)

The lawyer was trying to catch Jesus, to trip Him up. His response to this answer, however, far from being upset

---

[107] 2 Kings 9:30

that he failed to catch Jesus in error, acknowledged that He answered well. It was undoubtedly an answer that he did not expect. Jesus took notice of the righteous answer from the lawyer by acknowledging that he was not far from the kingdom of God.[108]

Peter tells us that love covers a multitude of sins.[109] If we have failures, yet we serve Christ humbly and show love to others, our love becomes a force that turns aside the original response for sin.

Also, if we love, we will not intentionally do anything to harm others or offend God. Love not only covers sin: it prevents it. We fulfill the law of God through love. We may not be aware of the "thou shall nots," but the love of God in our hearts executes the law of God within us such that we do not break His laws. We walk uprightly before Him, not because there is a rule before us but because the Spirit of God is within us.

Caveat of Sin

There are two points to be discussed here. The first is that there are people who have come to see every form of immorality as acceptable. They will attempt to define sin as dependent on the social mores of the current society, or they will reinterpret the Scriptures to mean other than what is written. Such hypocritical behavior is not worthy of any Christian. They wish to liberalize God, but God has not changed and neither have His expectations. There

---

[108] Mark 12:29-34
[109] 1 Pet. 4:8

are also those who will cling to the faith argument that has some justification for those ignorant of sin. Those that cling to an argument simply to justify themselves are blinding their own eyes as they race toward a ditch.

The second point concerns the justification by faith mentioned above but when viewed honestly—not hypocritically.

"And that servant who knew his master's will, and did not prepare himself or do according to his will, shall be beaten with many stripes. But he who did not know, yet committed things deserving of stripes, shall be beaten with few. For everyone to whom much is given, from him much will be required; and to whom much has been committed, of him they will ask the more." (Luke 12:47, 48)

Suddenly, someone brings something to your attention. It is a sin of which you were not aware. God does not hold you to the standard that He holds someone who knew of a sin. Perhaps, James clarifies it best. "Therefore, to him who knows to do good and does not do it, to him it is sin." (James 4:17)

Strive for perfection but be content with yourself. You are, like all of us, a work in progress. As we grow in God, we become more aware of tiny faults, but they are still faults and must be dealt with. "We" all have at least a little bit of self. Oh, me!

Our goal is to see God face to face; but if we see God face to face, we will die. This is true, and this is the goal!

Spiritually, let us seek to see God face to face. Let us die to the flesh that we may live for the Spirit. These are but a few clarifications of what sin is. This is not exhaustive; but if we are able to live up to these standards, we do exceptionally well. We have "touched" on holiness in this chapter and discussed somewhat on what constitutes sin. We have said very little about HOW to overcome - how to live the life that pleases God. The resources for this subject seem endless. Let me point you to two resources that I rely on for instruction.

First, I suggest Hannah Whitall Smith's book "The Christian's Secret to a Happy Life." Second, I strongly recommend any book by Andrew Murray; for example, Humility. There is little use in my trying to repeat or improve on what God has spoken through their writings, however, an example in Mrs. Smith's book about a young lady, unable to do anything for herself exemplifies how we will attain holiness. "She did nothing but yield herself up utterly into his hands, and he did it all." That is how we will overcome.

We may go out to the battle, but it is God who gives the victory. In other words, we can do nothing within ourselves. We are powerless. When we overcome a fault, it is the working of the Spirit within us. We have merely yielded to him.

And do not present your members as instruments of unrighteousness to sin but present yourselves to God as being alive from the dead, and your members as instruments of righteousness to God. For sin shall not have dominion over you, for you are not under law but under grace. (Rom 6:13-14)

This said, permit me to make you aware of my recent book," Holiness, The Joyful Pursuit." It is much easier to digest than what we are covering here.

Many Aspects of Scripture

We have discussed multiple dimensions earlier but not specifically as an aspect of Jesus and their significance to our understanding of Scriptures. Again, science has concluded that there are at least ten dimensions and possibly eleven.[110] The extra dimensions beyond what we are all familiar with are not proven experimentally, but it has been mathematically demonstrated that they must exist. We can see multiple dimensions at work in the Scriptures, but we do not normally call them dimensions.

After the angel announced the birth of Samson, he ascended into a flame and disappeared.[111] He did not burn up. He simply disappeared into the flames. This was not something experienced in our dimension. The angel was extra dimensional. In our dimension, physical things burn up.

Jesus took Peter, James, and John into a high mountain, and He was transfigured.[112] His face was bright like the sun and His clothes were a brilliant white. Moses and Elijah appeared to Him. Both men had been dead for centuries, yet they appeared to Jesus; and somehow, the disciples recognized two people they had never seen before. The dimensions present here included not only physical dimensions but perhaps spiritual dimensions where they could see those who were dead. It was also intellectual or

---

[110] I suspect 12.

[111] Judges 13: 20-23

[112] Mat. 17:1-9

psychical in that they were able to recognize those they saw. This experience transcended dimensions known to most of us, certainly to me.

There are other examples of multiple dimensions. There is Jacob wrestling with an angel.[113] Paul knew someone who ascended into the third heaven.[114] Daniel was visited by angels who delivered messages to him.[115] Samuel rose from the dead in answer to Saul's summon.[116] An angel visited Zacharias to announce that he would be father of a son, John the Baptist, in his old age.[117] Notice that prophecies have knowledge about times that have not yet been to our knowledge. Is time multidimensional?

Permit me to digress for a moment. I had been meditating on this question of time. Since time is part of this creation, or at least the time we live in, God is greater than time. He is outside of time as we know it. In this, I agree with Saint Augustine. (Augustine, pp. Book 12, Chapter 6) Because of this, He is at once present in the past, present, and future. To Him, last year and next year are identical. He is present in both, concurrently. So, knowing the reaction to expect, I asked my wife if she thought we could pray for something in the past and affect history. She did not disappoint me. She thought it was ludicrous. Although I shared this opinion, I could not simply dismiss it. I continued to consider the possibility.

---

[113] Gen. 43:24-29

[114] 2 Cor. 12:2

[115] Dan. 8:16 9:21

[116] 1 Sam. 28:11-16

[117] Luke 1:11, 12

The conclusion I came to was if we are praying for known history; that is, if we are praying for things about which we already know the outcome, we are wasting our time. If we are praying about something we already know about and God was going to change history, why are we praying? It has already been changed. The fact that we are praying for something to change is indicative that it did not change, or we would not be praying.

That does not preclude praying for something we need. Praying for food that our family needs could result in a knock at the door with today's dinner. The person delivering it, however, may have spent most of the day preparing it, and they were bringing it as we prayed. Did God, knowing what our prayer would be, inspire someone to prepare this meal for delivery in fulfillment of the prayer we were yet to present before Him? There are many examples of such events.

To continue, Scriptures have always been alive with meaning. How many ways has the Christmas story been presented, yet, there are still new slants presented every December. One story does not diminish another. They are all different aspects of the same truth. Most of us have read and reread the same verses many times and suddenly noticed something that we had never noticed before, and we may be awestruck by the importance of what we had been overlooking. Sometimes these explode into important understanding of God's truths, but in my own experiences, they are often so simple that I feel like I must be the last one to have seen a truth. Yet when tested, others are often as surprised as me.

The many aspects of Scripture do not stop here. Look at the abomination of desolation spoken of by Christ. This prophecy was fulfilled by Antiochus Epiphanes in 168 B. C., yet Jesus told his disciples that when they see the abomination of desolation spoken of by Daniel, they should know that the end is near. Jesus was speaking of a future event that had already been fulfilled, but it was going to be fulfilled again. It did not disturb him in the least that it had been literally and dramatically completed almost 200 years earlier.

It was fulfilled again—after the death of Christ. This occurred in A. D. 70 when Titus invaded Jerusalem and burned the Temple. It was not burned before Titus entered the Temple, but it was burned against his orders. (Hadas, 1956, pp. 121-123) (Whiston, 1974, pp. 445-451)

Although this prophecy has been fulfilled twice, another occurrence is not precluded. Jesus told His disciples that when they see these things happen, the end of the dispensation was near.[118] This prophecy is to be fulfilled again at the time of the great tribulation.

We study the Scriptures looking for a single occurrence or fulfillment of Scripture. We also look for Scriptures to be fulfilled in a single manner. That this is an erroneous approach is glaringly obvious.

David wrote the Psalms from his own experiences. In the 22nd Psalm, David cries out to God, but his trials are prophetic of Christ. Jesus quoted from this Psalm when He spoke from the cross, "My God, My God, why have you forsaken me?" The sufferings of David were prophetic of Christ, and Jesus suggested that what happens to Him is

---

[118] Mat. 24:14-33

prophetic of what will happen to us. "If they persecuted me, they will also persecute you." (John 15:30)

He clearly stated that what is true of Him is also true of us.[119] An office belonging to Christ is given to all overcomers.[120] We are the body of Christ, and He is the head of the body. What exactly is the calling to be part of the body of Christ? How great is this calling?

Paul said, "eye has not seen, nor ear heard, nor have entered into the heart of man the things which god has prepared for those who love him." (1 Cor. 2:9) What magnificent things does Jesus speak of when saying, "If I have told you earthly things and you do not believe, how will you believe if I tell you heavenly things?" (John 3:12)

The return of Jesus offers us another opportunity to contemplate multiple aspects in this disputed event. Some say Jesus is coming before the tribulation. Others say he is coming after the tribulation. Another view is that He will return in the middle of the tribulations. Some say He will come for the church before the tribulation or in the middle of the tribulation, but He will return after the tribulation to set up His kingdom. It is also argued that the Scriptures do not support two second comings. It can even be argued that the Scriptures were never explicit about more than one coming; that is, he would appear and rule forever.

The Jews expected the Messiah to come and set up His kingdom on earth. They were not prepared for Him to be crucified. From the start, it appeared to be hidden from them. They were aware of only one advent. Even Nathanael, a righteous Jew, asked if anything good could

---

[119] Rev. 3:21
[120] Rev. 2:26-27

come from Galilee.[121] The Jews expected the Messiah to come from Bethlehem. Jesus was born in Bethlehem, but he lived most of His life in Galilee, and from there began His ministry. Now we expect Him to return to do what the Jews expected on His first appearance, but we are debating how many times He is yet to come.

We have already discussed that Jesus is still on the cross of our bodies, and this is another dimension[122] of His sacrifice. His Spirit is pierced by every sin we commit. The Holy Spirit within us cries out in intercessory prayer on our behalf for our souls. Also, as we are the body of Christ, Christ still suffers for the redemption of souls of men through the church—you and me. We, as the body of Christ, may also suffer for the sins of others. Some believe that our suffering may not always be for our own account. (Ruffin, 1991, pp. 58-60)

Why do bad things happen to good people? Bad things may happen to Christians far beyond any deserved penance. Could such suffering be for the sins of others?

Are we extensions of the savior? Who saves souls? We give the preacher credit for the salvation of souls, but who brings sinners into church? Is it not the church laity? If the laity does not evangelize by inviting people to church, those people may never hear the salvation message. The preacher may never be able to minister to them.

---

[121] John 1:46

[122] The subject of dimensions is not seriously addressed in this text. It is, however, of monumental importance. Scripture cannot always be taken simply at face value or having a singular understanding.

It is, of course, not the preacher who saves souls but the blood of Jesus Christ. Yet in some small way, we become saviors through witnessing of Him and our service to Him. By becoming like Him, we become living testimonies of Him. We intercede for the lost to Christ, and He draws them to the cross.

Many Christians are seeking transparency. When I first heard of this term, I did not understand what it meant. It means that through our lives, others see Christ—not us. By living an imitation of His life, we testify of Him. By our living an imitation of His life, He witnesses through us.

But before we forget, we left an earlier subject without completing it. We were discussing how many times Jesus has left to return. I cannot answer this question with complete confidence. Rev. 3:10 may be interpreted as saying Christ will return twice: once to rapture the church before the tribulation, once more to establish His kingdom on earth

"Because you have kept My command to persevere, I also will keep you from the hour of trial which shall come upon the whole world, to test those who dwell on the earth."

The word "keep" in this verse is also translated as guard. Guard has the implication of keeping you safe amid the tribulation. The fact that the church of Laodicea follows this promise to the church of Philadelphia may indicate that those belonging to the Laodicean church are not spiritual enough to be raptured and must therefore endure the tribulation. Another verse that strongly indicates a pre-tribulation rapture is "Watch therefore and pray always that you may be counted worthy to escape all these things that will come to pass, and to stand before the Son of Man." (Luke 21:36) This "could" simply indicate that they will safely overcome these tests.

From these Scripture verses, we could conclude that the church will not taste the great tribulation. Other verses suggest only that not all the church will experience the great tribulation. Mat. 24: 40, 41 tells us that of two working in the field, one will be taken, but the other will be left; or two will be grinding and one will be taken while the other is left. In these verses, both are working, but not both are taken.[123] The fact that any are "taken" is an indication that Christ is not setting foot on the earth at this time. Is He taking the church or, at least, part of it into the air with Him before the tribulation? Verses 36 through 38 speak of those prepared entering into the ark to escape the flood—another suggestion that the church will be taken before the tribulation, but the argument is weak. We may also see in this that we have already entered the ark, the body of Christ. The parable of the wise and foolish virgins in chapter 25 of Matthew suggests that the wise virgins are the servants of Christ who have kept the Spirit of God active in their lives and who will be raptured before the door is closed. This would not shut the door to salvation, as many will come to Christ during the tribulation. So, it implies that the faithful will be removed before the tribulation, but the rapture will be closed to those who are not spiritually prepared. Perhaps

---

[123] Is this a suggestion that they are working for the kingdom of God?

Elisha provides us some insight into qualifications for pre-tribulation rapture.

When Elijah was to be taken away, Elisha followed him tenaciously. Elijah finally stopped trying to send him away and asked Elisha what he would have done for him. Elisha asked for a double portion of Elijah's spirit. Elijah told him that if he saw him taken up, he would have what he ask.[124] I will interpret this story spiritually with a paraphrase of Elijah's response to Elisha.

Elisha, if you are close enough to God, if you are spiritually minded enough to see me taken into heaven, you will have what you have requested.

Similarly, if we are spiritually minded enough to see Jesus when He comes, we will go with Him. If we are still carnal minded, we may be one of those who come through great tribulation to get our white robes.

After the tribulation, Christ will appear in heaven, and every eye will see Him, and the trump of God will sound and all of God's people will be joined to Him.[125] The foregoing discussion is based on the premise that the rapture will precede the tribulation. There are arguments that support post-tribulation rapture. Regardless, He did promise overcomers that He will keep (protect) them in the trials coming on the earth. However the end time plays out, I do not believe He promises every halfhearted professor of Christianity that he or she will miss the tribulation.

Again, I seem to have digressed from discussing the many things Scriptures can reveal to the debate of when

---

[124] 2 Kg. 2:1-14
[125] Mat. 24:31

the rapture will occur. The important point in this chapter is the multiple dimensions or many aspects and revelations of Scripture and the workings of God. This is merely an introduction. The excitement comes when we allow the Spirit to open our eyes to the amazing blessings He has given us. We may not see these blessing, but they are ours. They may be in a dimension that we have not yet seen. There are many dimensions of truth in Scripture and all are true, but they are spiritually discerned.

Since I did bring up the tribulation and those going through it, I should also point out that this is a time of Jacob's troubles—not necessarily the church's.[126] While I have called the tribulation a time of Jacob's troubles, others consider Nazi oppression of World War II a time of Jacob's troubles.

There is no consensus to how many times Christ will return. His second coming could be in stages: a pre-tribulation rapture, and the return to earth to establish His millennial kingdom. If there is one return, it is one-dimensional. If not, it is multidimensional. We must also remember that the Jews saw only one coming and an immediate establishment of His kingdom on earth.

There are multiple dimensions physically. We live in four of them: time (if time is more than simply a measure) and three spatial dimensions, and scientists believe, through mathematics, that there are more. They do not claim to have found all the dimensions. We have seen also that there is at least one spiritual dimension. One example was the angel's announcement to Manoah concerning Samson's birth. It seems possible (likely) that

---

[126] Jer. 30:7

the dimension where Samuel was summoned from after his death was yet another spiritual dimension. As we cited earlier from Paul's writing's, there are, at least (I think only)[i], three heavens.

We have only spoken of one dimension of time, but multiple dimensions of time are also possible. Prophets somehow appear to tap other time periods. This may be how God reveals the future to them. One sees the future. He who sees the future exists outside of time, and that is God. Jesus, in His current glory said, "'I am the Alpha and the Omega, the Beginning and the End," says the Lord, "who is and who was and who is to come, the Almighty.'" (Rev. 1:8) He is, He was, and He is to come. His existence knows no boundaries in time. He exists outside of time; therefore, He sees the past, present, and future.

The way He stated His existence is that He exists in all times at the same time. He does not live in the present only. He also lives in the past and the future—concurrently. Time, as we know it, is part of the current universe and, even here, is not a constant. Let me explain.

Time is not a constant that is experienced by all people in all places at the same rate. Time passes at different rates for every human, but the difference is so small that we are not aware of it. It may be more correct to say that we each experience time in a different way, but it is so miniscule that it is imperceptible.

If you launch into space leaving your twin behind on earth as your spaceship travels at the speed of light, your twin is aging while you are not.[127] The faster something moves relative to something else, the slower time advances

---

[127] There are several assumptions made here for simplicity.

for that which is moving. If you return to your twin after the twin has lived thirty years, your twin will be thirty years older than you. Time for you may not have advanced one second.

Time is not only a dimension of this universe: it is a dimension of your existence. Walking across a room filled with seated people whom you are about to address, time for you is moving slower than for those seated. It's not just psychological, but it is exaggerated.

So, if time is a dimension of your existence and your activity in this universe, how much truer is it that time is a dimension of this universe—this creation. "In the beginning God created the heavens and the earth." (Gen. 1:1) Time as we know it did not exist before Genesis 1:1. This makes sense! God is outside of or greater than His creation.

Is there a dimension of time outside of our universe: this creation? It is likely that there is some dimension of time, but it may be different from the way we view time. Regardless of the existence of time outside of our universe, God is still outside of time. He is still the creator of any existence.

Our existence is the result of events that occurred before the creation of this universe. It seems that this universe is the direct result of those events, hence, original sin.

Another dimension of Scripture is found in this familiar verse of scripture.

"Therefore the Jews sought all the more to kill Him, because He not only broke the Sabbath, but also said that

God was His Father, making Himself **equal** with God." Joh 5:18

The Jews were going to kill Jesus for calling God his father, yet Jesus instructed us that when we pray to say, "Our Father". We are sons and daughters of God. Does that make us equal to God? Not in this dimension! We are and are destined to "become" the sons of God.

"Beloved, now we are children of God; and it has not yet been revealed what we shall be, but we know that when He is revealed, we shall be like Him, for we shall see Him as He is." 1Jn 3:2

In this dispensation and/or dimension we are not equal to God, to be sure! Even understanding that we will be like Him only hints at what we shall be. I think it is incomprehensible in our current estate to fully understand what we shall be, but it will be beyond anything we can imagine.

Original Sin

"You were in Eden, the garden of God..." (Ez. 28:13)

The Eden spoken of here goes beyond the garden of Eden. It is the heavenly Eden. Let's bring in more of this prophecy.

"Son of man, take up a lamentation for the king of Tyre, and say to him, "Thus says the Lord GOD: 'You were the seal of perfection, Full of wisdom and perfect in beauty. You were in Eden, the garden of God; Every precious stone was your covering: The sardius, topaz, and diamond, Beryl, onyx, and jasper, Sapphire, turquoise, and emerald with gold. The workmanship of your timbrels and pipes Was prepared for you on the day you were created. You were the anointed cherub who covers; I established you; You were on the holy mountain of God; You walked back and forth in the midst of fiery stones. You were perfect in your ways from the day you were created, till iniquity was found in you. By the abundance of your trading You became filled with violence within, and you sinned; Therefore I cast you as a profane thing out of the mountain of God; and I destroyed you, O covering cherub, from the midst of the fiery stones. Your heart was lifted up because of your beauty; You corrupted your wisdom for the sake of your splendor; I cast you to the ground, I laid you before kings, that they might gaze at you.'"(Eze 28:12-17)

This prophecy is about Satan. It names the current king of Tyre, but it goes far beyond that earthly king. This is the tree of knowledge of good and evil that was in Eden. As a tree, He is referred to in another prophecy by Ezekiel.

"I made it beautiful with a multitude of branches, So that all the trees of Eden envied it, that were in the garden of God." (Ez. 31:9)

In this garden, there was another tree that appeared less desirable. This tree was Christ.

"For He shall grow up before Him as a tender plant, and as a root out of dry ground. He has no form or comeliness; and when we see Him, There is no beauty that we should desire Him." (Isa 53:2)

Explained simply, Christ is the image of humility. Humility has no beauty to the carnal mind.[128] The carnal nature desires power, honor, and position. Lucifer promoted himself. His iniquity was known, and he was cast out. From the iniquity of Satan, we see a new program come into existence.

Many angels appeared to have been taken in by Satan. "His tail drew a third of the stars of heaven and threw them to the earth." (Rev. 12:40)

It appears that we (you and I) were affected by this introduction of sin. This universe seems to have been put together for the sole purpose of bringing judgment (mercy and retribution) to God's creation. There were angels who fell and angels who were not affected by Satan. Another group, not angels, seems to be caught in the middle.

---

[128] Fulfilling this depiction of Christ spiritually does not imply that humility was the only intent of this prophecy. We are repulsed at the idea that Christ was not handsome, but this may also have been fulfilled physically. For spiritual understanding, it is appropriate.

"For You have made him a little lower than the angels, And You have crowned him with glory and honor." (Psa. 8.5) Of course, this prophecy was specifically about Jesus, but what form was a little lower than the angels. He was made in the likeness of sinful man. Jesus "made Himself of no reputation, taking the form of a bondservant, and coming in the likeness of men." (Php. 2:70)

So, in one form or another, it appears that we existed before the physical universe was created. It is evident that He knew us before this physical creation. Those of us who will be saved had our names written in the Lamb's book of life before the universe was created. Thank God for His tenacity!

"The beast that you saw was, and is not, and will ascend out of the bottomless pit and go to perdition. And those who dwell on the earth will marvel, whose names are not written in the Book of Life from the foundation of the world, when they see the beast that was, and is not, and yet is." (Rev. 17:8)

This verse speaks of those whose name has not been in the Book of Life from the foundation of the world. From the conception of creation the names of overcomers were known. As He declares in IS. 46:10, God knows the ending from the beginning. That we were preexistent becomes even more apparent from Eph. 1:4. ". . . He chose us in Him before the foundation of the world. . ." Even before there was time as we know it, we were known by Him, and we certainly lived in a dimension about which we have no recollection now. That the dimension was physical is somewhat doubtful, but not impossible.

A point to make here is that while God knows the end from the beginning does not confirm nor deny predestination on a general level. There were, of course, some absolutely predestined.

Again, make your calling and election sure.

More Aspects

Before we move to the attributes of Christ, let us go out on one more limb. I heard a young minister tell a loyal congregation that he took every verse of Scripture literally. What was troubling about this statement was that it limited how God could communicate with him through Scripture. It is more likely that every verse of Scripture has a spiritual meaning than a natural meaning. We limit what God can show us. We have preconceived ideas about different subjects and shedding ourselves of these ideas is very difficult. Of course, we should allow for a literal reading of Scripture as well.

The outside-the-box puzzle has been used so much in recent years that it is common knowledge to most of us. In case you have not encountered it, here it is.

Make a square consisting of three rows of three dots. There will be three dots lined up horizontally and three dots lined up vertically for a total of nine dots. Take a pencil and without lifting the pencil from the paper draw four straight lines that connect all the dots. You may wish to stop reading until you verify the solution. You may see the correct solution on page 218.

The solution has lines that are not limited by the box created by the dots, but when many people try to solve it, they create that additional limitation rendering any solution impossible.

If you travel far enough across the sea, you will fall off the edge of the earth! That was the common view before

Columbus proved to the world that the earth was round. I assume you are aware that a flat-earth society exists that still believes the earth is flat. You may wish to join their discussions at theflatearthsociety.org. Talk about hard to convince! Did people ever question why the water did not fall off the edge of the world?

Galileo proved the earth was not the center of the universe, but the church threatened to deliver him to the inquisition if he did not recant that view. The inquisition would have meant certain death, so Galileo admitted he was wrong. He spent the rest of his life under house arrest. Copernicus preceded Galileo to suggest that the earth was not the center of the universe, but he was not threatened with the inquisition.

Of course, Galileo was not wrong, and he knew it. People were so caught up in the notion that the earth was the center of the universe that they would kill anyone who declared otherwise. It was not open to discussion. There was to be no hearing of the proofs. For no reason beyond human egocentricity, everything had to revolve around the earth.

Just because something is outside the realm of what we normally think possible or impossible does not make it untrue. When I first heard of time and space compression, I was convinced that someone spent too much time at the punch bowl. Now, not to accept it as fact would put me in an ever-decreasing number of doubters. Avoid gullibility but allow yourself to think outside the box.

About fifty years ago, I discovered (by the grace of God) that there are four levels of understanding Scriptures, and a literal understanding is only the first way to understand them. Recently, I was pleased to learn that this was well known to Hebrew scholars centuries ago. However, our explanations of the levels do not completely coincide. The first level is the literal understanding of the Scripture. The second level is to understand how this Scripture applies to each of us, personally. The third level is allegorical. Finally, there is the mystic level—the heavenly revelation that Jesus spoke of while talking to Nicodemus in John 3:12.

While we are here, let us again connect briefly to the subject of dimensions. There are three physical dimensions that we are normally aware of: height, depth, and breadth. If these can correlate to the first three methods of interpreting Scriptures, could time not relate to the mystic level? How can we measure time? What is its volume? Can we touch it? Will it wear out? Does it have a color? Surely, time is much more difficult to rationalize than the other dimensions. I am sorely tempted to deny the existence of this thing called time; that it is nothing more than a measure we have created to delineate between events. I am tempted but I am not convinced. If time exists as a reality, we should be able to travel in it as in science fictions. We certainly see it in spiritual realms, but is time a physical reality or is it merely a measure? Excuse my philosophical ramblings, please?

For one final example, let us look at a Scripture we all know and clearly understand. Those who are inspired by God speak things they do not themselves fully comprehend. Did David realize that his psalms were prophetic of the Messiah? Did Peter understand the full implications of Acts 2:38? Did Caiaphas realize that he spoke by inspiration of the Holy Spirit when he was justifying the crucifixion of Jesus?[129] John certainly understood what he was saying in the first chapter of his Gospel, but as wonderful as it was, he may not have realized the extent of the truth he was teaching. He begins,

"In the beginning was the Word, and the Word was with God, and the Word was God. He was in the beginning with God. All things were made through Him, and without Him nothing was made that was made. In Him was life, and the life was the light of men. And the light shines in the darkness, and the darkness did not comprehend it." (Joh 1:1-5)

Continuing,

"And the Word became flesh and dwelt among us, and we beheld His glory, the glory as of the only begotten of the Father, full of grace and truth." (John 1:14)

We all fully comprehend that John was relating the entry into this world by the Messiah: He who, in His spiritual being, created the world. Jesus, as the Word or Logos or Wisdom, created all things. The purpose of this creation was to teach us of the Father. All creation testifies of God. He is revealed to us through His physical creation. Perhaps the extent of this begins to run together for you. Are we now talking about the man Jesus or about the universe? The answer is yes, and more.

There is an important difference, in that the universe did not die for our sins[130]; but the universe and the laws of the universe are a physical testimony of God. For

---

[129] John 18:14

[130] The earth and the works therein are eventually to be burned up. 2nd Peter 3:10.

example, some very intelligent researchers have been able to get a glimpse at the intelligence of God, and based on one measure alone, determined that God is, at a minimum,1098 more intelligent than humans. (Ross, 2001) That is a bunch of zeros after the number 10, but this is the minimum. By studying the laws of the universe, we can get some insight in how God deals with us. That was covered earlier.[131]

The Word continues to be made flesh in the body of Christ. As extensions (unfit as we are) and servants of our King, we are living testimonies of God. This has already been stated but not relative to understanding these verses.

Let us recall Satan being cast out of heaven and take it a bit further. We saw that he was cast out before the foundation of the world. He was also cast out when Jesus was crucified. Finally, he was cast out in Revelations. Was he or was he not cast out of heaven each time? If he was cast out of heaven, is there a clue to us concerning the number of heavens? Paul said he knew a man caught up to the third heaven.[132] Satan was cast out of heaven three times. Are we beholding three dimensions of heaven? Is it then necessary for Satan to be cast out of each heaven?

All of this, this entire chapter, is merely a glimpse into dimensions. Indeed, our intellectual capacity is too limited to delve deeply into God's mysteries, but we must not stop trying. He is willing to reveal great knowledge to us if we persevere. The Spirit that He has given us searches even the deep things of God.[133] We have a beginning of

---

[131] Page 121

[132] 2 Cor. 12:2

[133] 1 Cor. 2:10

understanding God's wisdom, but we have not begun to delve into it here. Pardon the timeworn cliché; but when it comes to understanding the awesomeness of God, we have only scratched the surface. Ah, to join those who have at least scratched the surface of God's revelations!!

More About Satan

He has been called the prince of darkness, but not in the Bible. Referred as such or not, he is indeed the Prince of Darkness. He was in the Garden of God, the heavenly garden, long before Eden[134]. He was the anointed cherub that covered or protected. What did he protect? What can we find in darkness that needs protection? How could he have failed God with such awesome responsibility. What if anything of value can be found in darkness?

I will give you the treasures of darkness And hidden riches of secret places, That you may know that I, the LORD, Who call you by your name, Am the God of Israel.

Isa 45:3

He made darkness His secret place; His canopy around Him was dark waters And thick clouds of the skies.

Psa 18:11

He reveals deep and secret things; He knows what is in the darkness, And light dwells with Him.

Dan 2:22

"The secret things belong to the LORD our God, but those things which are revealed belong to us and to our children forever, that we may do all the words of this law.

Deu 29:29

The secret of the LORD is with those who fear Him, And He will show them His covenant.

---

[134] Pleasure

Psa 25:14

Notice a very important attribute of Satan. Three places in Ezekiel he was referred to as a creation, not as someone in any way born, but created. He was promoted to a very high position, but he was not borne of God.

You were in Eden, the garden of God; Every precious stone was your covering: The sardius, topaz, and diamond, Beryl, onyx, and jasper, Sapphire, turquoise, and emerald with gold. The workmanship of your timbrels and pipes Was prepared for you on the day you were created.

Eze 28:13

Lucifer was in the Garden of God. This was the heavenly Eden. He was the protector of the deepest mysteries of God. Notice that he was covered with precious stones: nine of the twelve found in the breastplate of the priests of Israel. I am not prepared at this time to explain the significance of each stone satisfactorily, but in every reference that I am aware of, two or three stones are missing for Lucifer. The significance of those stones eludes me at this point. I could speculate that one of those missing stones represented humility.

It is a, perhaps merely personal belief that humility must precede love. We know love is represented as a very desirable trait but love without humility may merely be lust. Humility is the purifying element for love. Indeed, Pride was the original sin that led Eve to eat of forbidden fruit.

Attributes of Jesus

We have spent time on some of the more arcane traits of Jesus, and now we will attempt to summarize a few major characteristics. John said that there would not be enough books in the world to contain all the acts of Jesus, but that covered only the years of His ministry. Christ is from everlasting to everlasting. Remove sin from the equation, then everything about everything is about Christ. Whether you study the Scriptures, nature, or the various fields of science, their truths are all about Christ. So, all of Christ's attributes will not fit in these pages. Every day, I learn a little more about Jesus, and I am in awe. That some of these attributes work together should not be surprising. In the end, they all work together.

Jesus sent his disciples out in pairs. I am confident that they were paired for compatibility; that is, who would work best and most effectively together. Who, when working together, would best present the Gospel? It is as though some attributes are married. I could have used the word united but married seemingly implies a closer bond.

Love and Humility

Love is the greatest commandment. This is the attribute above all attributes. It is the one attribute that identifies God.[135] Love, however, works through humility.

---

[135] 1 John 4:8

There are numerous examples of God's love working through humility in the Bible. "This is the attribute above all attributes. It is the one attribute that identifies God. Love, however, works through humility. There are numerous examples of God's love working through humility in the Bible. The greatest example is that He gave His only begotten Son, that whoever believes in Him should not perish but have everlasting life. (John 3:16) God so loves the world that He took on the form of His lowly creation and suffered the death of the cross that we might live with Him forever.

For forty years traipsing through the wilderness from Egypt, Israel tested God's love. On several occasions, He would have killed the Israelites, but others stood in the gap for their lives.

Phinehas stopped a plague that sin brought upon Israel.[136] When he destroyed those who sinned, God relented. He humbled Himself to allow Israel to live. While the sinners had been destroyed, the capacity for sin remained, yet God spared them. The current temporary estrangement of Israel from God is evidence that the capacity for sin remained.

Moses prayed for the people on several occasions, but on one occasion God would have destroyed Israel and make a nation of Moses.[137] This is an example of Moses' love for Israel and his humility in that Israel was more important to him than becoming a great nation to replace these millions. His love and humility countered the sin of Israel and saved their lives.

---

[136] Num. 25:7
[137] Ex. 32:10

Faith and Righteousness

We do not need a plethora of verification of the unity between these attributes. There are, however, several very direct references, but we will repeat only one.

"Yet indeed I also count all things loss for the excellence of the knowledge of Christ Jesus my Lord, for whom I have suffered the loss of all things, and count them as rubbish, that I may gain Christ and be found in Him, not having my own righteousness, which is from the law, but that which is through faith in Christ, the righteousness which is from God by faith. . ." (Php. 3:8-9)

Refer also to Gal. 5:5 and all of Romans 4 and Hebrews 11 and James 2:18.

Wisdom and Knowledge

After Solomon had dedicated the Temple, God appeared to him in a dream and asked him what he desired of Him. His prayer and God's response were, "Now give me wisdom and knowledge, that I may go out and come in before this people; for who can judge this great people of Yours?" Then God said to Solomon: "Because this was in your heart, and you have not asked riches or wealth or honor or the life of your enemies, nor have you asked long life—but have asked wisdom and knowledge for yourself, that you may judge My people over whom I have made you king—wisdom and knowledge are granted to you; and I will give you riches and wealth and honor, such as none of the kings have had who were before you, nor shall any after you have the like." (2Ch 1:10-12)

God gave Solomon much more than he requested. The wealth of Solomon is of mythical proportions even to this day. Yet, wealth was merely an add-on.

If the extra blessings of God to Solomon were so great that it is still spoken of, how great was the wisdom and knowledge that God gave him? One example of the greatness of his wisdom and knowledge is reflected in that the queen of Sheba (Yemen) travelled many miles to hear him speak.

There are many Scripture references where wisdom and knowledge are combined. A few are listed here. (Eccl. 1:18 Prov. 2:10 8:12 9:10 14:6 Rom. 11:33 Col. 2:3)

Knowledge can be acquired through study. Wisdom, however, is a gift of God that supplements knowledge. While knowledge is obtained through much study, humility is acquired through submission to His spirit.

Tolerance

Preparing for summer-long mission trips, a key subject is flexibility. At training with one organization, it is pointed out that one will encounter significant cultural differences and those encountering those differences will need to handle them with a Christian attitude. You also live for that time with people you may never have met before. Each person has his or her way of doing things, and sometimes those differences can be very aggravating. For summer-long trips, a good deal of time is used to become acquainted with the differences; but you cannot discover all the differences during this period. Therefore, you will encounter them in-country.

There are things that one should try to determine before getting to the country; for example, you do not want to learn on the first day in country that one of your team members smoke. I met a team member one year who, when I referred to him as Gregory, let me know in no uncertain terms and without any thought for a Christian response, that he was not Gregory. He was to be called Greg, so that was one thing I could get out of the way before we got to our assignment. Such an attitude should have been a warning of the amount of tolerance that would be required. I did appreciate that he was humble enough to accept correction without rancor.

While being acquainted with personality and cultural differences between team members is important, the cultural differences of the country would also be a challenge. My first trips were to Russia, and my assignment was an excellent entrance to experiencing different cultures. One could not always find a grocery store where you could meander through the store and hand pick each item you wanted. It was necessary to go to the counter and communicate to the person behind the counter the needed items and quantities. I would not care for this if the person behind the counter spoke English. Since they did not know a single word of English, it was even more trying. It was also trying of their patience to receive a request by pointing. This, of course, is just the beginning.

After six summers in Russia, I thought I would have encountered about everything, and I really did not have to concern myself with being flexible. Was I wrong! I learned that there is always something new to learn, more to tolerate.

Consider for yourself, your friends, and family. Do you still find things about them that you must try to endure patiently? Tolerance is an ongoing development, but unless we explicitly address tolerance, we will not become more tolerant.

Fortunately, for Christians, our savior is ultimately tolerant. He understands our faults and weaknesses. It amazes me that He continues to endure my failures. I am very thankful for that tolerance, but I hate that it is necessary for Him to be tolerant. As Paul said, "For what I am doing, I do not understand. For what I will to do, that I do not practice; but what I hate, that I do.

Rom 7:15

Selflessness

Jesus demonstrated selflessness when He went to the cross. Praying in the garden of Gethsemane, He was willing to surrender His will to the will of the Father.

"Father, if it is Your will, take this cup away from Me; nevertheless, not My will, but Yours, be done." (Luk 22:42)

Again, "So He said to them, 'When you pray, say: Our Father in heaven, Hallowed be Your name. Your kingdom come. Your will be done On earth as it is in heaven.'" (Luke 11:2)

His very purpose was the will of the Father.

"Then I said, 'Behold, I have come— in the volume of the book it is written of me— to do your will, o God." (Heb 10:7)

The Scriptures are clear. We are to put His will before ours. If we put His will before ours, we will obtain our hearts desire.

Holiness

At this point, we will touch only briefly on Holiness. Again, I refer you to my book, Holiness, the Joyful Pursuit.

"It is written, 'Be holy, for I am holy.'" (1Pe 1:16)

This verse states emphatically that holiness is an attribute of God. Another verse explains its importance.

"Pursue peace with all people, and holiness, without which no one will see the Lord. . ." (Heb 12:14)

We could spend much time and many words explaining what constitutes holiness, but we will not. The Scriptures tell us to "work out your own salvation with fear and trembling." (Php 2:12)

Notice that the verse states to work out your salvation with fear and trembling. Another verse instructs us to make our calling and election sure. (2 Pet. 1:10) Some will try to tell you what sin is. Others will tell you what is not sin. With an honest heart, "search the Scriptures, for in them you think you have eternal life; and these are they which testify of Me." (Joh 5:39)

Some will condemn you for playing a musical instrument. Others will encourage you for condoning homosexuality[138]. Find the balanced path and rely on the Scriptures. We do not have to walk a tightrope, but we must be separate from the world. Remember that Jesus is not trying to trick you. That was not the purpose of His suffering the cross. If your zeal for holiness causes you great distress, lighten up. Stress is destructive, and neither you nor I will be perfect in this life, but do not mistake this as an approvable of debauchery.

Unity

Unity is difficult to understand fully. The concept is simple enough, but if we understood it completely, I think we would seek it more earnestly and the results would preempt ever letting it go. As we saw in the chapter on unity, it holds the keys to great power with God. Understanding unity, I think, would help greatly in understanding the godhead. A few things about it are obvious.

Unity requires agreement. Total agreement is not possible in this life. Each of us differs from others in some viewpoints.

Unity requires love. When you love others, you enjoy sharing their company, occasionally. If we love others, we will sometimes overlook their mistakes. At other times, we show love by pointing out mistakes.

---

[138] I have made several references to homosexuality in this book, and they have not been supportive. This is not an accident: however, I have worked with people in the ministry with this preference. Their lives were otherwise impeccable and their ministries effective.

Unity requires ALL the attributes of Christ. "For where two or three are gathered together in My name, I am there in the midst of them." (Mat 18:20) We have already seen that to be in His name requires being in His nature. To pray in His name is to pray in His nature and will. When we are gathered in His nature and seek what He would seek, we will be in unity; and our prayers will be answered. All He asks is "seek first the kingdom of God and His righteousness, and all these things **shall** be added to you." (Mat 6:33)

We begin to comprehend that the attributes of Christ are too numerous to list. Here, we have listed a few of the most important ones. If we can master these, we will do well.

The Final Glory

This chapter centers on the nature of Christ in us. The study of New Jerusalem as it is presented in Revelation presents us with more attributes that Christ expects in. It tells us what will be in the heavenly kingdom. Whether or not you agree with the following, I hope I may at least have presented something that will benefit your own studies.

New Jerusalem, The Holy City

The Holy City, the New Jerusalem, the bride of Christ: Here is the reward we have longed for. In Revelation 4:1 we heard a voice from an open door in heaven instructing us to "Come up here," and once there we found ourselves in a temple-like setting. Now, the messenger says, "Come, I will show you the bride, the Lamb's wife." (Rev. 21:9)

Move forward, thoughtfully. We are told to "come up here." That is to enter into the Spirit that we might understand what we are seeing. Leave carnal understanding behind.

The description of the Holy City is breathtaking—awe-inspiring. It is described as precious gems and gold. It is described in terms that attempt to express its grandeur. This is the reward for Christians who have given their lives to Christ, yet, for all the grandeur, there are several things about the city that I find contradictory in the literal, and some things are unsettling. However, it may be congruent with Scriptural principles that the city is to be viewed spiritually and not literally. We will examine this when we address the government number, twelve.[139]

Now I saw a new heaven and a new earth, for the first heaven and the first earth had passed away. Also, there was no more sea. (Rev. 21:1)

We have been looking forward to a new heaven and a new earth. We came to Christ seeking conversion to His righteousness, and we long to be clothed upon with our heavenly house[140]. Our hope is that our mortality, our physical being, will be replaced with a spiritual house—in this case, the Holy City.

Jesus said, "In my Father's house are many mansions (John 14:2)." The Hebrew/Greek dictionary identifies residence or abode as a suitable replacement for mansion. How well does this verse correlate to the Holy City! A city is a place with many abodes. The kingdom of God is the body of Christ that consists of all the children of God. ". . . behold, the kingdom of God is within you." (Luke 17:21) The kingdom of God IS the Holy City. Paul wrote, "For the kingdom of God is not meat and drink; but righteousness, and peace, and joy in the Holy Ghost." (Rom. 14:17)

As we saw earlier, it has sometimes been taught that the kingdom of heaven is a heavenly kingdom high in the sky while the kingdom of God was the spiritual kingdom. We also saw that this difference simply is not true. Yet, there is a coming kingdom that we behold dimly, as Paul

---

[139] Page 342
[140] 2 Cor. 5:2-4

taught[141], but these kingdoms of heaven and God are one and the same. However, there may be more than one dimension of this kingdom. That is, while referred to in singular, there may be a physical and spiritual reality of the kingdom.

"For in this we groan, earnestly desiring to be clothed with our habitation which is from heaven." (2Cor. 5:2)

Compare this Scripture to the following.

"Then I, John, saw the holy city, New Jerusalem, coming down out of heaven from God, prepared as a bride adorned for her husband." (Rev 21:2)

The Holy City is the new body, the glorified body that we shall receive at the coming of Christ and which will be occupied by His people after the millennium.

"Behold, I tell you a mystery: We shall not all sleep, but we shall all be changed—in a moment, in the twinkling of an eye, at the last trumpet. For the trumpet will sound, and the dead will be raised incorruptible, and we shall be changed. For this corruptible must put on incorruption, and this mortal must put on immortality." (1Co 15:51-53)

The new heaven is the new mind that we seek from Christ. The new earth is the body that we will inhabit in eternity. I expect that it will be like the body Christ had when he appeared to His disciples after His resurrection. These are not things we already have. The revelator clarifies this by adding that there was no more sea. Sea sometimes typifies tribulations and worldliness. Remember that Peter was able to walk on water to Jesus until he

---

[141] 1Cor. 13:12

looked around at the wind and waves of the sea.[142] He was successful in walking above the troubles of earth until he became mindful of them. Noah's ark, also, was carried above the flood of tribulation that was poured out upon the earth. For those in the ark, it was a baptism cleansing them of sin. For those outside the ark, it was destruction of sin through their deaths.

Remember that in the fourth chapter of Revelation there was a sea of glass before the throne. There we could see a perfect image of ourselves. Here, there is no more sea. We no longer have our own image, for we have been transformed into His image. We have attained that level of transparency where His nature and our nature are identical. Previously, we looked into the sea before the throne to see our image, but at this time, we have become so united with Christ that we will simply reflect Him. There is no more tribulation, neither is there any imperfection. Our baptism into the nature or name of Jesus is perfect. That nature dwells within us as we dwell in the Temple; the Lord God and the Lamb.[143]

The fact that we must still endure tribulations indicates, if nothing else does, that we have not reached this place of the new heaven and new earth. But certainly the fact that we still possess our original body demonstrates that we still live in the old earth. There is nothing heavenly about these bodies that progressively deteriorate, but we look forward to a holy city whose builder and maker is God. We do not fully comprehend what the new heaven

---

142 Mat. 14:28
143 Rev. 21:22

and new earth will be: We can merely see a shadow of its reality.

In this vision, the first heaven and earth have passed away. Here, we no longer desire the things we once desired. We experienced this to some extent following conversion. Many things that enticed us to worldliness no longer had the same effect on us. It was not a complete transition, but it typified the fullness of conversion to come. If you have not attained that pinnacle of perfection that you covet so earnestly, if you cannot understand why holiness eludes you so effectively, be encouraged. Jesus promised, "Blessed are those who hunger and thirst for righteousness, For they shall be filled." (Mat 5:6)

We SHALL be filled with the holiness we seek. Even the body may have experienced a regeneration following conversion, yet this earth will be replaced with a glorified earth.

"Then I, John, saw the holy city, New Jerusalem, coming down out of heaven from God, prepared as a bride adorned for her husband." (Rev 21:2)

The symbolism here is stark. The city of the great King descends from God. It is brought down from its heavenly reality to something we can understand, something to which we can relate. Consider that what we are seeing here with our natural reasoning is something that is unprecedented in human history—a city descending from heaven for us to inhabit. Only an unbeliever would say it could not happen. God can do anything, but does He? I may truly be blown away by witnessing such a literal occurrence someday, but I think not. The city consists of the many mansions we mentioned before—the resurrected souls of God's blessed, the redeemed. In my perhaps myopic vision, it does not consist of buildings made of clay or even of gold. These things men can make. The city of God only God can make. Notice the similarity between what is happening here and what Paul spoke of in first Thessalonians and first Corinthians.

"For the Lord Himself will descend from heaven with a shout, with the voice of an archangel, and with the trumpet of God. And the dead in Christ will rise first. Then we who are alive and remain shall be caught up together with them in the clouds to meet the Lord in the air. And thus we shall always be with the Lord." (1Th 4:16-17)

"Behold, I tell you a mystery: We shall not all sleep, but we shall all be changed—in a moment, in the twinkling of an eye, at the last trumpet. For the trumpet will sound, and the dead will be raised incorruptible, and we shall be changed. For this corruptible must put on incorruption, and this mortal must put on immortality." (1Cor 15:51-53)

Jesus appears from heaven and calls for His people who are then caught up to be with Him, and we are changed. Our mortality puts on immortality. Our old heaven has surely passed away for that which is perfect has come. Lusts of the flesh no longer entice us. We have a new body, the New Jerusalem—immortality.

The symbolism continues: It is as a bride adorned for her husband. It is resplendent with white and gold and jewels—those things that denote purity and wealth. Is the bride of Christ a natural city of gold and jewels? Consider for a moment yourself as being wed to a city. Not likely! The bride of Christ is the body of believers that sacrificed unto death, and the jewels and gold and white are the attributes of the holiness of the bride, the spiritual glory with which the saints are endowed, and the authority they have been given. In addition, I said that they sacrificed unto death. The sacrifices are the lusts of the flesh that they (we, hopefully) have overcome. We deny ourselves these worldly pleasures until death or until they are no longer desired. However, we may indeed sacrifice literally unto physical death.

Many Christians throughout the world refuse to deny Christ and are subsequently imprisoned or killed for their persistence in testifying for Christ. In this case, the sacrifice is very literal. We should give much thanks to God if we are spared such suffering, and we should pray fervently for those who are persecuted so greatly. We should pray God's grace and strength that they are able to endure their sufferings.

The next verse begins to explain the nature of the city.

"And I heard a loud voice from heaven saying, "Behold, the tabernacle of God is with men, and He will dwell with them, and they shall be His people. God Himself will be with them and be their God." (Rev. 21:3)

The tabernacle or habitation of God is with men. God's house is each individual Christian. God shall dwell with us, in us. He will not leave us: We shall never be devoid of His presence again. Those times that we have walked through valleys of despair, unable to sense the presence of God, are past. We have become His permanent abode. We will be His people, subject to His will, as we have desired in this life to be. He will be our ever-present God, leading and directing our lives in eternal righteousness.

In verse two John tells us that the city is prepared as a bride adorned for her husband. The implications of this statement are humbling, because we know from Genesis 2:24 that the man and the woman, the husband and the bride will be united. We become one with Christ and are called by His name. That does not imply that we will lose our identity. Remember that name is synonymous with nature, so the name we are given is the marriage name of our nature to Christ's nature as we saw in our study of Rev. 2:17.[144] We will retain our unique relationship with Christ as well as the uniqueness of who we are.

This is a slight digression, but I cannot help but to point out the first part of Rev. 2:17. We will receive of His hidden manna. This manna is the Word of God—the living, breathing, earth-shaking truth of the Living God. I believe He is giving us this manna in measured portions now—before His coming. Jesus gave His disciples a taste of this manna, and many left Him. Of this manna He said, "The words that I speak to you are spirit, and they are life." (John 6:54-63) The life-giving Word of God continues:

"And God will wipe away every tear from their eyes; there shall be no more death, nor sorrow, nor crying. There shall be no more pain, for the former things have passed away." (Rev. 21: 4)

With this verse we either diverge from current natural laws, or we enter a higher understanding of these laws. We looked at this subject earlier, and here we will extend our discussion of the laws to emotions. Every religion on

---

[144] Page 129

earth recognizes two forces: good and evil. They wrestle with one another. They are two energies: one takes us into a valley of despair and one takes us to a mountain of joy. We experience two sides to emotions. We exist because of such variation.

Variety is not just the spice of life; variety is the essence of life. You have noticed a sweet smell upon entering a room with scented candles, but after a while, except for an occasional whiff, you may no longer notice the smell. It has become constant, and your senses have adjusted to it. You can hear because of sensory organs that respond to vibration (variation). You have vision because of a constant fluttering within the eyes to detect motion. Without the constant variations, we would cease to smell, hear, or see. (Morris, 1993, pp. 86,87,95) We require opposites. The heart fluctuates between contraction and rest. Without this variation, life would be nonexistent. Without some sorrow, we will not recognize joy. Elation is an unusual emotion that is caused by unusual events. Sadness is, or should be, an unusual emotion that is the result of specific causes.

Now, suddenly, there shall be no more sorrow or pain. We will experience constant and eternal happiness. Natural laws, as we know them, appear to cease to exist relative to emotions, or we begin to live in a level of those laws of which we were not familiar before.[145] The Scriptures indicate that the former things are gone. This could be taken very literally, or it could mean merely that we are no longer subject to those laws, or as we just stated, we live at a level of physical laws of which we were not previously aware.

---

[145] Miracles – Page 206

In this New Jerusalem, we shall never sin; therefore, there is no reaction to sin. There is, we recall, a hell, and we shall touch briefly on this subject shortly. Suffering is the result of sin and we will no longer sin. Even now, many people suffer more than seems appropriate. I will only say, trust God that He has a purpose, and those who suffer disproportionately will be rewarded.

It also appears that the world we live in is temporary, and by world, I am referring to the entire universe. Stars have exploded into super novae. Some, science suggests, have imploded by growing dense enough to form black holes that the force of gravity is able to keep even light from escaping. Our sun is estimated to have a remaining lifetime of about five billion years after which changes in the sun will result in earth's destruction. (Bill Arnett, nineplanets.org/sol.html) Five billion years may sound like a long time, but it is not eternity. Our sun, along with every other star in the universe, is burning up its fuel. Although the universe is expanding, and that expansion is accelerating, it will die. It will become unable to support life. Will gravity eventually take over and draw all the matter in the universe to an infinitesimally small dot resulting in another big bang? If this happens, every living thing in the universe will be destroyed. Regardless of how it is accomplished, life in this universe will end. Whether God can or cannot prevent the death of the universe is not in question. He can do anything. The questions are what He will do, and does it matter. The first part of that question is answered in Hebrews 1:11, "They will all wear out like a garment." How will a new creation of the physical world affect "heaven?"

"Then He who sat on the throne said, 'Behold, I make all things new.' And He said to me, 'Write, for these words are true and faithful.' And He said to me, 'It is done! I am the Alpha and the Omega, the Beginning and the End. I will give of the fountain of the water of life freely to him who thirsts. He who overcomes shall inherit all things, and I will be his God and he shall be My son.'" (Rev 21:5-7)

He that sat upon the throne, He that rules declares that He makes all things new. Of course, Alpha and Omega is Christ, and He rules. He will rule with the Father. In addition, spiritually, He will sit upon the throne of our minds, and the waters of life that we will drink are those heavenly truths from the depths of the living Word of God.

Christ said, "It is done." The war between good and evil is over, and evil has been judged, good has been blessed.

"But the cowardly, unbelieving, abominable, murderers, sexually immoral, sorcerers, idolaters, and all liars shall have their part in the lake which burns with fire and brimstone, which is the second death." (Rev 21:8)

So much for not having opposite forces! We have seen in preceding verses that the sons of God are blessed and shall know no pain or sorrow. Now we see those that shall know no peace. The opposites still exist but are more focused. Sons of God shall know only good; unbelievers will know only misery. Until this time His sun warmed both good and evil, and the rain watered both good and evil. Now His Son warms the good, and sin burns the evil. The word "sorcerers" in this verse is another word for pharmacist or poisoner. Of course, pharmacists have not been singled out for the lake of fire, but if we interpret pharmacist in this verse in its negative connotation then it may refer to drug dealers and developers of illicit drugs. It then contains much significance for the present age.

"Then one of the seven angels who had the seven bowls filled with the seven last plagues came to me and talked with me, saying, 'Come, I will show you the bride, the Lamb's wife.' And he carried me away in the Spirit to a great and high mountain, and showed me the great city, the holy Jerusalem, descending out of heaven from God. . ." (Rev 21:9-10)

Again, John is told to come, and again, John must go up. Earlier, he was told to come up hither. This time the angel takes him up. It is done; man's work is over. Now he is taken higher without any of his own effort to a great and lofty mountain. John is taken into a high mountain, carried away into the Spirit. The implication here is that to see and understand the city of God, God must take one high into the Spirit. Therefore, what we are seeing here is an outline. This is only a beginning.

Notice that John ascended before the city could descend, hence, a second possible reason for John going higher. It is a principle of God that man must make steps toward God, and God will then move toward man. Acts 2:38 commands men to perform two acts, after which they shall receive the gift of the Spirit from God. Namaan had to wash himself in Jordan seven times before God granted him his desire. Moses had to go up into the holy mountain before God met with him and gave him the commandments. Likewise, John had to obey the angel before he was elevated to a spiritual level where he could see the city of God descend. The principle is that of man ascending spiritually before God will descend to meet with him. Also remember the verse that says those who seek righteousness shall be filled. (Mat. 5:6)

We have done everything possible to ascend into the presence of God, but here we, as John, are carried into a mountain. Now we are ascending, but there is no effort on our part. Remember Rev. 3:20?

"Behold, I stand at the door and knock. If anyone hears My voice and opens the door, I will come in to him and dine with him, and he with Me."

God is not pushy.[146] He lets us know He is with us, but we must allow Him entry. Likewise, His angel told John to come and He would show him the Lamb's wife. John had to permit it. He had to relinquish control and put himself in God's hands. Likewise, we will overcome when we put our complete trust in God.

Would it seem strained if we point out that John was carried away in the Spirit—not flesh, and being in the Spirit, what John saw was spiritual not physical. Dreams that we read of in the Old Testament used symbolism to communicate their meaning. Joseph's dream of the sheaves bowing before his sheaf,[147] and Pharaoh's dream of the ears of corn[148] are two examples. Nebuchadnezzar's dream of

---

[146] Draw me away! We will run after you. (Son 1:4) We may ask God to be pushy with us—to push us in the ways we should go. We may read this verse as "Drag me." Whatever it takes, draw me to your will. Be pushy. I invite your authority to rule over me.

[147] Gen. 37:6-11

[148] Genesis 41

the great image[149] foretelling of kingdoms of the earth was another. Methinks this phenomenon is repeated here.

If the city was a vision to be interpreted, what are the meanings of the various elements? What are the meanings of the measurements?

Continuing with the next verse it reads, "having the glory of God. Her light was like a most precious stone, like a jasper stone, clear as crystal." (Rev 21:11)

The significance to this verse is apparent. This city, naturally or figuratively, has the glory of God—the glory of a precious gem. The glory of God has the purity of crystal. It is a glory like that experienced by Moses[150] after having been in the mountain with God. Moses was merely a reflection of the glory he had witnessed in the mountain, yet his face was so dazzling bright that the Israelites could not look at him. With this city, it is no longer a reflection. In addition, Moses saw only God's backside (humility), and this description is merely the backside of the reality of this city.

"Also she had a great and high wall with twelve gates, and twelve angels at the gates, and names written on them, which are the names of the twelve tribes of the children of Israel: three gates on the east, three gates on the north, three gates on the south, and three gates on the west." (Rev 21:12-13)

Verse 12 is more obscure than the preceding verses. It had a great wall (excuse me, she had a great wall), which was necessary to have gates. "She" is the necessary pronoun as we are talking about the bride of Christ. Be aware,

---

[149]   Daniel 2
[150]   Exodus 34:29-35

however, that "she" is added: the word is not in the original manuscript. It is not necessarily wrong, however, to refer to a bride as she. Continuing, there were twelve gates, and each gate contained the name of one of the tribes of Israel. As we have seen, name is synonymous to nature in the Scriptures, so to possess the name of a tribe of Israel is to possess the nature of that tribe. The position of the gates, three to a side, reminds us of the positions of the tribes of Israel around the Tabernacle[151] when they camped in the Wilderness. We will study the gates further when we study verse twenty-one. Now, we shall look at the foundations.

"Now the wall of the city had twelve foundations, and on them were the names of the twelve apostles of the Lamb." (Rev 21:14)

The wall is constructed on twelve foundations, the apostles. These walls are the walls of salvation, a salvation based on the teachings of the twelve apostles. They are great and high, offering great security against any opposition and any temptation. They are for protection— to shield us from the enemy. Paul spoke of the whole armor[152] of God, but there is no direct correlation between these walls and that armor. This wall and foundations would be a combination of the teachings, ministries, and living testimonies of the apostles. The words of God that they have left us in the writings of the New Testament have strongly fortified us by that armor.

Do we need armor in this city? Do we need protection? It becomes our eternal inheritance. Imagine, we will never again fail our God. There is no breaking down these walls

---

[151] Numbers 2
[152] Eph. 6:12-17

of the Holy City. They are strong and impenetrable. The Holy City is a place of spiritual development in Christ where recidivism, backsliding, is impossible.

"And he who talked with me had a gold reed to measure the city, its gates, and its wall. The city is laid out as a square; its length is as great as its breadth. And he measured the city with the reed: twelve thousand furlongs. Its length, breadth, and height are equal." (Rev 21:15-16)

How do we measure up with this reed? The reed is golden, which symbolizes purity obtained through fire. When we have gone through the fires of tribulations, how good a testimony for Christ have we been? We have all failed, and in this life, we will continue to slip; but Lord Jesus, help us to admit our mistakes and continue to improve.

This measure of purity, or holiness, is perfect for this city. This city, after all, is the ultimate goal of every Christian. This is our reward, and however much we may have fallen short in holiness before, at this point, through the grace of Jesus Christ, our measure will be perfect by this reed.

The angel was to measure the city, the gates, and the wall. The order of the measurements is interesting. Usually, we would proceed to the walls, through the gates, and into the city. This would typify our approach to God as we might view it in the Tabernacle, but here, the measure is reversed. The city is our final goal and the angel is looking at the city from the inside out. We see ourselves now **in** the city of our final glory, measuring our final spiritual stature in Christ. We are no longer measuring the outside to see where we must tone up and trim down to enter.

The city has a strange shape. It is either pyramidal or a cube. In one sense, it must be pyramidal, because later it will say that the Lamb is the light of the city. Excuse me? I mean no affront to anyone but permit me this one attempt at a humorous comment to accentuate my point of the city's spiritual aspect. If the city is literal, it must be pyramidal because the Lamb is the light, so He must be at the peak of the city like the angel on Christmas trees. It is inconceivable to me that Christ will forever act naturally as a light bulb to the Holy City.

Its visual design is not, however, pyramidal: Its symbolism is cubical. The Holy City is the correlative to the Most Holy Place in the Tabernacle and temple. The measurements of the Most Holy was 10 cubits by 10 cubits by 10 cubits—a cube. The Most Holy in any Biblical temple or tabernacle is a cube. The fact that the length, breadth, and height here are equal is intended to capture this correlation. (Moore, I Must Decrease, 1999)

The length, breadth, and height of the city are twelve thousand furlongs.[153] This measure was most perplexing until some simple math came to mind. If there is anywhere I am stretching to find a spiritual interpretation for the city, it is here. Twelve is the number of government, so the city is perfect in government. The fact that this perfection is multiplied by a thousand implies an eternal

---

[153] It is interesting that the length, height, and width are each 1377 miles or about 2300 kilometers. Imagine any building 1377 miles tall. It makes any skyscraper in the world microscopic by comparison. Other calculations would find the city to be a cube of 500 miles, wide, long, and tall.

government. A thousand years is like a day[154] to the eternal God. The psalmist was using this comparison to denote the eternal existence of God. The use of a thousand as a multiplier to government (twelve) may tell us that the government established in this city will last forever. Jesus used multiplication to denote infinity when He said, I do not say to you, up to seven times, but up to seventy times seven." (Mat. 18:22) This He said to Peter who had asked if he should forgive a brother's offenses seven times. What obsessive-compulsive personality is going to count the number of offenses, so they forgive up to 490 times? It is simply a way to specify infinity in this instance.

That God does use multiples of a thousand for literal purposes should not be ignored. I firmly believe that we are living in a period measured in thousands of years and this period will shortly end as we enter the seventh millennium of Biblical history. That, of course, is the thousand-year earthly reign of Christ.

Oops! We almost forgot the unit of measure, furlongs. Perhaps I should have slipped on. There are instances when the unit of measure is, I think, unimportant. Noah's ark was measured in cubits. The NIV translators changed it to feet, so instead of being one hundred cubits long, the ark is one hundred and fifty feet long. It is the number, not the unit of measure that is important here as it was for Noah's ark.

Furlong means race. Two other places in the New Testament use this same word but translate it as race—not furlongs. We are in a race to come under the authority or government of Christ. The word race or furlong is derived

---

[154] Ps. 90:4

from another word that means covenant or establish. When we attain this place in Christ, we have certainly run the race and won. Having attained this position, we are established forever. The source for furlong also means continuous. The use of this word reemphasizes the permanence of the government of God and the New Jerusalem.

"Then he measured its wall: one hundred and forty-four cubits, according to the measure of a man, that is, of an angel." (Rev 21:17)

The wall has a dimension of 12 cubits times 12 cubits. The purity and perfection of this wall is symbolized by the measure of the angel—the golden reed. Why use 144 instead of twelve? It just confuses things! After all, a wall 12 cubits high would be approximately eighteen feet. That is a pretty good wall. I strongly suspect that the meaning of the number 144 is significantly more than I am aware of currently; nevertheless, I offer the following primer on this number.

Sometimes, when you or I say something, we want to make very certain it is heard, so we repeat it; we emphasize it. God emphasized His message to Pharaoh by giving him the same dream twice.[155] By exponentiation the number emphasizes it more strongly yet. It is as though God was reaching to the very depth of His Spirit to declare the perfection and absolute authority of this government in terms we can understand. If this is the message God is delivering to us, we see from the twelve thousand furlongs and the 144 cubits the perfection and eternity of this government.

---

[155] Gen. 41:32

"For unto us a Child is born, Unto us a Son is given; And the government will be upon His shoulder. And His name will be called Wonderful, Counselor, Mighty God, Everlasting Father, Prince of Peace." (Isa 9:6)

The government is upon the shoulders of Christ or at the headship. Our goal is to be in the headship with Christ, governing with Him. What we are looking at when we see the Holy City is the headship of Christ, the throne of Christ, and the glory of it is that we shall rule and reign with Christ. We must show some ruling authority in this life to have ruling authority in the next. This ruling authority is not necessarily ruling other people, it is not running the church. It is ruling over our own being: keeping our thoughts pure, serving instead of ruling. The fact that we are Christians demonstrates that we have exercised some ruling authority; otherwise, we would simply deny Christ and live according to the lusts of the flesh. If you are like me, I suspect you have areas of your life that are still not completely under control. Lord Jesus, grant that we may submit to your ruling authority. Then that authority will make us rulers over ourselves.

"The construction of its wall was of jasper; and the city was pure gold, like clear glass." (Rev 21:18)

The wall is made of jasper, which we saw in verse 11 is clear as crystal. What a difference this presents! Now, we hide what is within us. We do not want the world to know our faults, our failures, or when we might utter an untruth. It is difficult for the light of God to emanate from us when we are deceiving ourselves and others. We are the light of the world, and many people professing Christianity darken a room with their testimonies. Racists and reprobates must build walls of putrid flesh in attempts to hide the sin within. God help us to not fall into this category. Redeem us from our failures.

The completed Christian has no need to hide what is within. He or she is so pure that there is no remorse in others knowing what is within. The ruling government of God is transparent—readily revealing the holiness within. My pastor related this wisdom that another had related to him. It applies to you and me in our current lives. He was told that if you felt a need to confess your sins, you should go to the woods, find a rabbit, confess your sins to the rabbit, then shoot the rabbit. If you are Catholic, don't shoot the priest.

What is being revealed by this transparent wall is the purity of the city within, which is so holy that it becomes sparkling and gloriously clear.

"The foundations of the wall of the city were adorned with all kinds of precious stones: the first foundation was jasper, the second sapphire, the third chalcedony, the fourth emerald, the fifth sardonyx, the sixth sardius, the seventh chrysolite, the eighth beryl, the ninth topaz, the tenth chrysoprase, the eleventh jacinth, and the twelfth amethyst." (Rev 21:19-20)

We already know from verse 14 that the foundations have the name of the twelve apostles. The simplest understanding of the foundation is that the city is founded on the teachings of the twelve apostles.

The twelve tribes, the twelve stones, and the twelve gates represent the government of God. Until God grants us greater insight, this much is apparent: The twelve foundations are the principles upon which the city is built.

Those foundations are the teachings of the twelve apostles. The eternal city is based on these principles. When our spiritual foundation is built on these principles, the gates of the city of God will be open to us, forever.

Ephod of the Priests??????????

Sardius	chalcedony; sardius; chrysolyte;; chrysoprasus;
Topaz	topaz
Carbuncle	
Emerald	emerald
Sapphire	sapphire
Diamond	
Ligure	jacinth
Agate	
Amethyst	amethyst
beryl	beryl
onyx	sardonyx
jasper	jasper

Twelve Gates

The gates of the city represent virtues, characteristics of Christ that must be at work in us. Keep in mind that we will not be perfect in this life. The very flesh we live in hides from us the beauty of holiness that we shall know in this city. When we enter the city, the dark glass[156] is out of the way and we can see clearly.

The twelve gates were twelve pearls: each individual gate was of one pearl. And the street of the city was pure gold, like transparent glass. (Rev 21:21)

"Open to me the gates of righteousness; I will go through them, And I will praise the LORD. This is the gate of the LORD, Through which the righteous shall enter." (Ps. 118:19,20)

These gates may each be a single pearl of spiritual wisdom, twelve pearls in all, that provide entrance into the city. A pearl is a truth, represented here as virtues—virtues that we should have active in our lives. There is only one door to salvation, and that is Jesus. The word "this" in verse 20 can also be translated "these," so there is no disagreement in tense between the two verses.

It is quite possible that you will discover a different virtue for a gate or a different purpose for the gates. That may or may not negate what is being presented here. The Wisdom of God is such that He could present us with many lessons from the gates. If you have not received such enlightenment, I hope these descriptions will stir the revelations of God in your mind to the lessons He has for us, whether the lessons on these pages or others.

There are twelve pearls and each one has the name of a tribe of Israel. To discover what these pearls are, it seems necessary to learn something of the nature of the tribes. When Jacob blessed his children on his deathbed, he revealed something of their natures. In some cases, the nature is clearly revealed in their names. As we have already

---

[156] 1 Cor. 13:12

discussed, that a name is important in the Scriptures is demonstrated in those to whom God gave new names to identify their new office.

Abraham was first named Abram, high father; but when God spoke to Abram about the birth of his son Isaac, He changed his name to Abraham—Father of a Multitude. Likewise, Sarah's name was changed from Sarai (domineering) to Sarah (queen). Abraham was fathering a new nation and Sarah was the queen of that nation. I can't speak on the significance of Sarai's domineering.

Be that as it is, however, the meanings of names are not always known, or its spiritual significance is not intuitive. In the case of the sons of Jacob, we know the meanings of their names; but like Reuben, his lust cost him his blessing as the heir. This loss changed the significance of Reuben in Scripture. The blessing normally due to the firstborn was not bestowed on Reuben.

Reuben

"Reuben, you are my firstborn, My might and the beginning of my strength, The excellency of dignity and the excellency of power. Unstable as water, you shall not excel, Because you went up to your father's bed; Then you defiled *it*— He went up to my couch." (Gen 49:3-4)

By rights of birth, Reuben was Jacob's primary heir. Look at the grandiose words used to describe Reuben: firstborn, might, beginning of strength, and excellence of power. Jacob lauded the position that Reuben held, yet for all these acknowledgments of Reuben's exalted position, Reuben lost the blessing that should have been his.

Jacob continued to describe Reuben as unstable as water: "Turbulent" is translated unstable in the KJV. Jacob then blessed(?) him saying, "You will no longer excel." Instead of obtaining a blessing of exaltation that was his by right of birth, he found himself humbled, all but disowned, and we see, perhaps, the most important characteristic that we must grow into, humility. Hence, the principle of the first gate, the first pearl of wisdom appears to be humility.

It is not uncommon that those who come into positions of power (exaltation) abuse the power. They are neither aware of the responsibility that comes with their power nor of the tool to retain it, humility. Humility and exaltation appear to be opposites, but they are not: They should coexist within us. We should first learn humility, and then we shall grow into power. Consider Joseph who remained faithful to God in all the tribulations he endured and was subsequently raised from the position of a lowly shepherd to rule Egypt, second only to Pharaoh.

Reuben means "see a son." This name could have been given to Reuben identifying him as the firstborn and therefore heir to the double portion blessing due the firstborn.

Many may not consider humility to be a great prize, but it is the first things we should learn as Christians, as I have "finally" realized. It is a virtue we should chase. When our hearts are touched by the call of Christ, we must be humble enough to accept that call, submit, and commit our lives to Christ. It was stated earlier that love works by humility. We feel the love of Christ when He reaches out for us. We then humble ourselves to let that love flood our being, so humility is the first gate. As pride was the

<u>original</u> sin[157] in the Garden of Eden, humility is the first gate to the city of God.

Humility is a purifier. If you have love without humility, your love may be perverted to lust. It is still a love, but it is impure. Humility is a prerequisite for pure love.

The next blessing was to the next two sons in line, Simeon and Levi.

Simeon and Levi

"Simeon and Levi *are* brothers; Instruments of cruelty *are in* their dwelling place. Let not my soul enter their council; Let not my honor be united to their assembly; For in their anger they slew a man, And in their self-will, they hamstrung an ox. Cursed *be* their anger, for *it is* fierce; And their wrath, for it is cruel! I will divide them in Jacob And scatter them in Israel." (Gen 49:5-7)

You will notice that for Reuben we used the words of the blessing to discover the principle to be learned from him, and it was counter to the blessing of his birthright. For Simeon and Levi, we look to their names. Using only the name of Reuben could have led us to different conclusions. Simeon's blessing is tied very tightly to Levi's, as one. Simeon means hearing and is derived from a word meaning obedience,

"You go near and hear all that the LORD our God may say, and tell us all that the LORD our God says to you, and we will hear and do it.' Deu 5:27

---

[157] Original sin 281

(for not the hearers of the law are just in the sight of God, but the doers of the law will be justified)

Rom 2:13

It does not appear to be accidental that these two words, hearing and obey, are tied so closely together. I have cited only two verses where hearing and obedience are paired. The importance of obedience cannot be overemphasized. King Saul thought that sacrifice would erase his error when he failed to comply with directions from God, but Samuel corrected him.

"… Behold, to obey is better than sacrifice, And to heed than the fat of rams."

1Sa 15:22

For his sin of disobedience, Samuel pronounced judgment on Saul.

So Samuel said to him, "The LORD has torn the kingdom of Israel from you today, and has given it to a neighbor of yours, who is better than you.

1Sa 15:28

For one sin of disobedience, Saul lost his kingdom. It would later be passed to Saul's exact opposite. Instead of a head taller than others of Israel, David was a child. Instead of seeking his own kingdom, David sought God's will. How many times after Samuel anointed David king of Israel could David have killed Saul who was trying to kill him? To David, however, Saul was the anointed of God, whether he had lost the blessing of God or not. David honored the anointed of God so consistently that when an Amalekite confessed to killing a dying Saul, David had the Amalekite killed for daring to lay a hand on God's anointed.[158]

David so diligently sought God that even after having Uriah killed and taking his wife Bathsheba as his own, that he had the following testimony.

"because David did what was right in the eyes of the LORD, and had not turned aside from anything that He commanded him all the days of his life, except in the matter of Uriah the Hittite." (1 Kg. 15:5)

There are doubtless lessons to learn from David's error in his treatment of Uriah, but I am not cognizant of them currently; however, there are adequate areas of study to continue.

Simeon, from hearing and heeding, presents us with the principle, **obedience**. The meaning of Levi is hinted at in the blessing to Simeon and Levi. Levi means joined, intertwined, or unity. Jacob cautioned against being united to their anger. He even cursed them that they should be scattered in Israel. It is easy to see the results of Levi's blessings, so we will return to that, shortly.

"The inheritance of the children of Simeon was included in the share of the children of Judah, for the share of the children of Judah was too much for them. Therefore the children of Simeon had their inheritance <u>within</u> the inheritance of that people." (Jos 19:9)

Simeon's inheritance was certainly not dispersed. The closest we can come to considering Simeon scattered in Israel is that instead of receiving their own allotment, they received part of Judah's inheritance.

---

[158] 2 Sam. 1:1-15

Levi, unlike Simeon, was clearly scattered in Israel. Also, unlike Simeon, the dispersion of Levi adds clarity to the meaning of Levi—unity. While Levi was dispersed among all the tribes of Israel, as the priesthood, they were the glue that held the twelve tribes together as a single nation. Unity is a very important principle. Unity, if not more powerful than faith, is a powerful catalyst to faith. That explanation was presented earlier. Our lesson from Levi is **unity**.

The principle portrayed by the fourth son of Israel is completely transparent. Yet, for all that transparency, there exists an amazingly elusive caveat.

Judah

"Judah, you *are he* whom your brothers shall praise; Your hand *shall be* on the neck of your enemies; Your father's children shall bow down before you. Judah *is* a lion's whelp; From the prey, my son, you have gone up. He bows down, he lies down as a lion; And as a lion, who shall rouse him? The scepter shall not depart from Judah, Nor a lawgiver from between his feet, Until Shiloh comes; And to Him *shall be* the obedience of the people. Binding his donkey to the vine, And his donkey's colt to the choice vine, He washed his garments in wine, And his clothes in the blood of grapes. His eyes *are* darker than wine, And his teeth whiter than milk."

(Gen 49:8-12)

The first three sons were bypassed: the fourth son is the one to be praised, the one with a great blessing. The scepter shall not depart from Judah. Judah shall reign continually among the tribes of Israel. Even the name Judah means praise. Thus, the fourth principle is praise.

Praise is a principle that is easily demonstrated as a gate to the city. When you are going through a dry place, feeling isolated from God—forsaken, praise God without reservation and without restraint. I have never seen praise fail to provide access to the Spirit, but it may at times take a while depending on your spiritual condition. There is much more to the blessing of Judah, but this is enough for finding the principle. The elusive element concerning Judah, the caveat, praise shall be addressed with the blessing to Joseph.

Zebulun

"Zebulun shall dwell by the haven of the sea; He *shall become* a haven for ships, And his border shall adjoin Sidon."

(Gen 49:13)

Zebulun is more esoteric, but there seems to be sufficient information for understanding of the principle represented through him. The name is from a word meaning habitation or "dwell with." One meaning for water in the Scriptures is the Word of God, and Zidon means catching fish from a root word meaning catching animals. Jesus told his disciples that He would make them fishers of men, and they would fish with the truth of the Word. We also find solace, or a haven, in the Word and in the good words of friends. We find strength in words of encouragement.

"not forsaking the assembling of ourselves together, as is the manner of some, but exhorting one another, and so much the more as you see the Day approaching." (Heb. 10:25)

All these taken together sums up to fellowship. We need the **fellowship** of other Christians, and the greater our troubles, the more we need each other. We provide a haven and solace for each other. This fellowship is where we share the Gospel, the Word of God. Where the Gospel is delivered is where new children are born into the kingdom of God.

Issachar

"Issachar is a strong donkey, Lying down between two burdens; He saw that rest *was* good, And that the land *was* pleasant; He bowed his shoulder to bear *a burden,* And became a band of slaves." (Gen 49:14-15)

Whew! This is a blessing? Issachar is going to work. The Christian labors between two loads: the Old Testament law, and the New Testament grace. It is sometimes difficult to balance the two. Where does the benefit of works end, and how gracious is grace? We may have difficulty keeping the workload in balance, but seeing the prize we labor voluntarily, cheerfully for Christ. We are driven by the Spirit. Paul referred to himself as a prisoner to Christ for the Gentiles.[159] He was a prisoner of

---

[159] Eph. 3:1

Christ, laboring on behalf of the gentiles. And even though salvation is by faith, the reward is based on works.[160]

"Come to Me, all you who labor and are heavy laden, and I will give you rest. Take My yoke upon you and learn from Me, for I am gentle and lowly in heart, and you will find rest for your souls. For My yoke is easy and My burden is light."

Mat 11:28-30

We are called to labor in the field of the world for the name of Jesus and the salvation of souls. We are called to service to lift His name and the message of the cross.

That does not mean that we are all called to minister in the Word as pastors or teachers. We may minister by baking bread or mowing the lawn of the church or for an ill neighbor. Sometimes, an outreach ministry presents an opportunity to provide service to our communities, to the sick, or to those in prison. We serve God by also serving others, and **service** is an important principle of God.

Issachar is blessed through Service.

Dan

"Dan shall judge his people As one of the tribes of Israel. Dan shall be a serpent by the way, A viper by the path, That bites the horse's heels So that its rider shall fall backward. I have waited for your salvation, O LORD! (Gen 49:16-18)

Dan means judgment, and while we often look at judgment as a negative attribute, it has two sides:

---

[160] Rev. 2:23

punishment and reward. In other words, Dan provides justice. We see both sides of judgment in these verses. First, judgment is as a serpent that brings punishment. Second, mercy or compassion is implied in waiting for God's salvation. For Dan to judge his people requires judgment or wisdom, and wisdom is a stronger term for this gate.

Dan is providing justice through judgment—the meaning of his name. These verses speak of both penal judgment and mercy or deliverance. Examples of this principle is found in several coincidences(?).

Dan is the fifth son of Jacob, and the number five is the number of judgments. The judgment number is usually illustrated with the negative side of this principle, but not always. When Joseph was sharing a meal with his brothers, he provided five times the portion for Benjamin than he provided to his other brothers.[161] Later, he provided Benjamin with five sets of clothes while providing his other brothers only one.[162] When the Philistines made a guilt offering to God after capturing the Ark of God, they sent golden replicas of tumors and rats—five of each.[163] In Revelation[164] locusts with stings of scorpions were to torment mankind for five months.

What is required to execute judgment? Solomon demonstrated this when he ordered the child who two women were arguing over to be cut in half and divided between the women. The real mother readily gave up parental rights to her child, while the woman falsely

---

[161] Gen. 43:34

[162] Gen. 45:22

[163] 1 Sam. 6:4

[164] Rev. 9:5, 10

claiming to be the mother was willing to see the child divided.[165] The next verse, verse 28, names the principle associated with good judgment, wisdom.

This is not a wisdom that comes from man but from God. I know people who have trouble forming a meaningful sentence, yet God reveals things to them that are not accessible by very educated men and women. They are manifesting the wise **Judgment** of the Most High.

Many consider five as a number for blessing, and it is. That is half the story. Judgment has two sides: one a blessing, another a penalty. Judgment is properly dispensed through wisdom.

Gad

"Gad, a troop shall overcome him: but he shall overcome at the last." (Gen 49:19)

Gad shows perseverance by not giving in to those who overcome him. He fights back to victory over his oppressors. Gad demonstrates perseverance or tenacity. Likewise, as Christians, when we fail Christ in some way by giving in to the flesh, we refuse to give up. We fight back until we have victory over our flesh, our tempers, and such. Gad symbolizes determination or willpower. All of this reminds me of what Jesus said: "By your patience possess your souls." (Luk 21:19)

Thus, the lesson from Gad is *patience*.

While we may realize our need for this virtue, many Christians, including myself, are loath to pray for patience

---

[165] I Kg. 3:16- 27

because of Romans 5:3, which states, "tribulation worketh patience." (KJV) The NKJV is no less distressing with "tribulation produces perseverance." The fact remains, however, that any sincere Christian who seeks to see God manifested in his or her life *will* experience trials.

We read of Job, and we realize that for the most part, our sufferings are miniscule by comparison. People make the mistake of praying for a Job experience. Whew! That's chancy!

I seek God in my life. I seek to see His nature subdue my nature, but I do not desire a Job experience. I do pray to see God manifesting His righteousness and His Spirit in me, but I do not ask for a Job experience. After once praying a certain prayer, I experienced the worst six months of my life. Only once since then have I prayed that prayer; nevertheless, whatever it takes for me to be everything I can be, let it be Lord. Yes, Lord Jesus: Let it be!

The truth is, however, that every Christian has one or more Job experiences. A Job experience is any experience that tries your faith to the nth degree. Many Christians have experienced the loss of a child or watched helplessly as a loved one suffers an agonizing illness. This may be their Job experience.

Asher

"Bread from Asher shall be rich, And he shall yield royal dainties." (Gen 49:20)

Asher is a word meaning happy. God expects His people to be happy; in fact, He insists on it.

"Because you did not serve the LORD your God with joy and gladness of heart, for the abundance of everything, therefore you shall serve your enemies, whom the LORD will send against you, in hunger, in thirst, in nakedness, and in need of everything; and He will put a yoke of iron on your neck until He has destroyed you."

Deu 28:47-48

This verse, among the blessings and cursing's in Deuteronomy, warns of a curse if we do not serve the Lord with joyfulness. How many times has this gotten us into trouble? Having forgotten to rejoice in the blessings that God has given us, we invite trouble by bemoaning all the terrible things that have happened to us.

At times, we do have a right to be sad but never with God. We may lose loved ones, but God is even nearer to us when we are enduring such pain. Spiritually, we may feel very close to God, even while we endure despair from our loss. Having suffered a loss or hardship, we should –by the grace of God- bounce back. Unfortunately, we sometimes cling to our sadness longer than necessary. Sometimes, it is difficult to see why we should rejoice. If we have lost our jobs, it is often hard to see any way out of the financial strait where that loss has placed us. What makes such a problem more distressing is that our families rely on the income from that job to provide food and shelter. We should still try to trust God that things will work out.

There are, however, those of us who never see the good in our lives or the health in our bodies. We will whine constantly, and no one wants to be around us. Defeatism does not make a very good witness of our experience with Christ.

Therefore, **joy** is a principle for entering the city. There will not be any tears there.

Naphtali

"Naphtali is a deer let loose; He uses beautiful words." (Gen 49:21)

The fact that Naphtali gives good words implies that he encourages. A hind let loose has numerous implications. A hind is a female deer. We may extrapolate from the fact that this hind gives good or encouraging words that Naphtali nurtures in a motherly manner, encouraging goodness and gentleness in her children. Gentleness is implied through the female gender symbolizing humility. The principle that emerges from Naphtali is encouragement. As Christians, we should encourage others to be all they can be. Too often, children have become all too aware of their limitations. We have had unrealistic limitations placed on us. We have been told all the things we cannot do and too seldom encouraged to try the impossible.

My father told me, based on past scholastic performance, that I would fail high school Algebra. I should take the simpler math course. He based his opinion on the solid evidence of the past. For a brief period in high school, I was an honor student, even getting A's in Algebra. What I do not know, unfortunately, is how well or how poorly I would have done if I had been encouraged in my choice of classes. As it was, I probably needed the challenge.

There is evidence that people will often become what they have been told they are. If we are told we are no good, we may begin to believe it and behave accordingly.

A student in one of my classes told me on a couple of occasions that she was dumb and knew she was dumb. I rebuked her for admitting such and told her she was not dumb. Later, she told me that she wished she had studied in my class. I was astonished that she passed my class without studying. Others, with a background in the subject would struggle to get a C; yet she, without any background in the subject, passed without studying. I made her aware of my amazement. The next semester she got a B in a class I taught that was known for ending 4.0 GPA's.

Attitude is important, and we should encourage others, as well as ourselves, to have a positive attitude. "Can't" must be excluded from our vocabulary. We can do anything. We may be slower in some things than others, but we can do anything.[166]

I am amazed at what I see handicapped people accomplish. How can a blind person get a college degree and that with honors? How can those with learning problems graduate from college? How can those with Down's syndrome effectively hold down a job and even earn accolades from supervisors and fellow workers?

A young man I met in Yemen was blinded in an accident, yet he was consistently optimistic. He kept people around him laughing from a constant barrage of jokes. He wrote poetry. He spoke perfect English and was close to graduating from college. He was very optimistic about life. He acknowledged that his loss of sight resulted in greater

---

[166] I struggle with acrophobia. Reluctantly I climb ladders.

awareness through his other senses. Being around him was enjoyable. His optimism was encouraging.

Negative, defeatist attitudes can be converted to positive attitudes where we realize that we can do anything. Of course, it is dipping into that inner power that enables us to accomplish goals. Paul said it best and succinctly in Philippians 5:13, "I can do everything through him who gives me strength."

Saints encouraged and were encouraged by others in the church.[167] Even meeting other Christians is encouraging.[168] So the principle set forth by Napthali is **encouragement**.

Something that presents itself in this principle is that encouragement obviates criticism. If we are criticizing our fellow Christians, or nonChristians for that matter, we are not encouraging them.

Joseph

"Joseph is a fruitful bough, A fruitful bough by a well; His branches run over the wall. The archers have bitterly grieved him, Shot at him and hated him. But his bow remained in strength, And the arms of his hands were made strong By the hands of the Mighty God of Jacob (From there is the Shepherd, the Stone of Israel), By the God of your father who will help you, And by the Almighty who will bless you With blessings of heaven above, Blessings of the deep that lies beneath, Blessings of

---

[167] Acts 15:32, 16:40, 18:27, etal.
[168] Acts 28:14

the breasts and of the womb. The blessings of your father Have excelled the blessings of my ancestors, Up to the utmost bound of the everlasting hills. They shall be on the head of Joseph, And on the crown of the head of him who was separate from his brothers." (Gen 49:22-26)

Joseph typifies the attitude that Naphtali encourages. Joseph is my Biblical mentor. I try to keep the life of Joseph in mind when I face discouragements. Joseph had dreams that showed him in situations where he ruled. These dreams separated him from his brethren, and even upset his father, Jacob. Joseph was, however, through his entire life the ruler that he saw in his dreams.

His brothers sold him into slavery, yet he ruled in the house of his slavery.[169] He was cast into prison after rejecting the advances of Potiphar's wife, but even in prison, Joseph ruled: He was put in charge of the prison. Then, after victoriously enduring these hardships, he was promoted to rule Egypt, second only to the Pharaoh. In the end, he ruled over his family as he had seen in his childhood dreams.

Joseph had **faith** in God and lived with a positive attitude, a ruler's attitude. He ruled over the conditions where he found himself. Joseph did not rule over his brothers immediately. This did not come till years later, but it did come. Likewise, Abraham, was told that he would be the father of many nations, but he and Sarah were beyond hope of having children. Even after the miracle of Sarah bearing a child at ninety-nine years of age, she had only one child—hardly a nation. Today, many nations call Abraham father: some naturally, some spiritually.

---

[169] Gen. 39-41

"Without faith it is impossible to please God." (Heb. 11:6)

That one verse illustrates the importance of faith. Indeed, the entire eleventh chapter of Hebrews is a testimony to the importance of faith. The writer of Hebrews named several ancients who pleased God with their faith. If it is not possible to please God without faith, we must develop a characteristic of faith. This faith will enable us to become the kind of Christian we desire to be.

We may wonder why we have not advanced as we think we should. We still have faults that we have struggled with for years, but we do not seem to be able to overcome. Jesus encouraged us.

"Blessed are those who hunger and thirst for righteousness, For they shall be filled." (Mat 5:6)

He has promised us that if we hunger and thirst to do well, we shall do well. If you have not seen the performance of this promise thus far in your life, trust God that you will surely be filled with His righteousness. We trust the promise until we see the performance. The **faith** that Joseph portrays shall bear fruit in **our** lives.

When we discussed the blessing of Judah, we mentioned a caveat.[170] Notice that Judah was him whom his brothers would praise, and the scepter would not depart from between his feet. Yet, it was Joseph who Israel saw wearing a crown. The rewards of faith are not immediately known. Joseph was sold into slavery and thrown into prison before he received his crown, and the blessings of his fathers were upon him. Additionally, it was not Judah who received the double portion due the firstborn. That

---

[170] Page 351

blessing, reserved for the firstborn, was bestowed upon Joseph. The words, "From there" in the phrase "From there is the Shepherd, the Stone of Israel," in the blessing of Joseph may be interpreted as referring to God: but after removing punctuation it can also be applied to Joseph. (Moore, The Elder Shall Serve The Younger, 2007)

Not being a translator, I cannot state that one understanding is absolute or simply likely. It seems odd, however, that Israel after already prophesying about Christ, found it necessary to reaffirm the birth of Christ in his blessing to Joseph. Joseph received the blessing of the firstborn. He was present in two portions in Israel, Ephraim and Manasseh. Ephraim would later lead ten of the twelve tribes, leaving Judah only two.

Why did Israel bless the youngest, Ephraim, above the eldest? Of Jacob, his mother Rebekah was told that the elder would serve the younger. Was Jacob remembering this as he was blessing his children? Are we seeing a separation in Israel that teaches a physical and spiritual linage?

Benjamin

"Benjamin is a ravenous wolf; In the morning he shall devour the prey, And at night he shall divide the spoil." (Gen 49:27)

How amazing it is to have begun with Reuben, symbolizing humility, and to end with Benjamin. Benjamin means son of the right hand, and the right hand symbolizes power—in this instance **spiritual power** in service and ministry. After Jesus had been crucified and buried, He resurrected in power.[171] In a somewhat similar manner, we began our study of the children of Israel with humility and complete it with the power symbolized by Benjamin. Jesus further affirmed the principle of the right hand of power.

". . . hereafter you will see the Son of Man sitting at the right hand of the Power, and coming on the clouds of heaven." (Mat 26:64)

The children of God have power. I am reminded of a story, the veracity of which I cannot attest. A Christian had just been robbed when he remembered the Scripture that told how five of God's people shall put a hundred to flight.[172] He chased the robber in the name of Jesus and ordered the thief to return his possessions. The thief dropped his wallet and kept running.

---

[171] Matt. 28:18
[172] Lev. 26:8

While I do not suggest this action, it does demonstrate that God's people do have power. There have been times when I –God forgive me- questioned how much God moved in my life, only to be amazed at the number of prayers that were answered.

According to an article by Debra Williams, D.D.,[173] the power of prayer has been scientifically substantiated, and that power is not diminished by distance. Every Christian has this power.

A qualifying attribute of this power is revealed in the blessing of Benjamin. In the morning or in the day season he will devour the prey. When we are living in the sunshine of God's blessings, we will store up the strength afforded by those blessings. This is like the seven years of plenty when Joseph stored the abundance of grain. In the night season, or in the season of darkness, when we walk by faith, without the warmth of God's Spirit, we must survive on the ration of those blessings. At this time, we will live by faith instead of feelings. It is sometimes referred to as the Word season because our faith is derived from the Word of God that we have internalized. It is worth noting that as the drought continued, the people of Egypt became more dependent on the ruler of Egypt. Likewise, the more problems Jesus brings us through, the more reliant we become on the anointing of Christ.

This power is overcoming power, the fruit of which is righteousness. We recognize that all power belongs to and proceeds from God. Even our righteousness is from

---

[173] Scientific Research of Prayer: Can the Power of Prayer Be Proven?
http://www.plim.org/PrayerDeb.htm

God. ". . . and be found in Him, not having my own righteousness, which is from the law, but that which is through faith in Christ, the righteousness which is from God by faith" (Php 3:9)

The first gate symbolized humility and the last gate represents power. The appropriateness of this order is found in 1st Corinthians 15:43, "It is sown in dishonor, it is raised in glory. It is sown in weakness, it is raised in power." The seed of God's grace is sown in our weakness and develops into an overcoming servant of the Most High.

Benjamin, as we saw earlier, means son of the right hand. Reuben means "see a son" as if to point to the heir. Neither Benjamin nor Reuben inherited the double portion, and Benjamin had no claim. That honor fell to Joseph when he received two portions in Israel through the tribes of Ephraim and Manasseh.

Rachel was the favored wife of Jacob. When Israel (a name given to the ten tribes led by Ephraim) was carried into captivity, children of Rachel would have no seed remaining; except that Benjamin remained with the tribe of Judah. Interestingly, the apostle to the gentiles, Paul was of the tribe of Benjamin.

Many of the prophecies to Israel were to the ten tribes led by Ephraim. Some of these prophecies refer to the reunification of Israel and Judah. While the physical lineage of Ephraim is to be called out by God as He knows every one, the church may be a spiritual lineage of Ephraim. If this is so, then prophecies to Israel as the dispersed of the ten tribes may refer to the church as well as physical Israel (Ephraim).

We summarize our findings in the following table.[174]

Sons of Israel	Pearl
Reuben	Humility
Simeon	Obedience
Levi	Unity
Judah	Praise
Zebulun	Fellowship
Issachar	Service
Dan	Judgment - Wisdom
Gad	Patience
Asher	Joy
Naphtali	Encouragement
Joseph	Faith
Benjamin	Overcoming Power

These gates of pearl to the Holy City are open. You may notice the omission of love for any gate, yet if you observe the combination of pearls, you will see that each one is an exercise in love. As the apostles were the disciples of Jesus, so also, these twelve principles are discipled through love. Without love, these principles are without meaning. Again, faithful Paul explains this point.

---

[174] You may come to other conclusions concerning the gates. I am comfortable with the conclusions here, but they can certainly be refined. God and His revelation are too magnificent to be boxed in by my small level of intellect, which hopefully, has been somewhat enhanced by His Spirit. Regardless, He cannot be fully understood or explained by any person, and the gates can contain much more than presented here.

"Therefore, as God's chosen people, holy and dearly loved, clothe yourselves with compassion, kindness, humility, gentleness and patience. Bear with each other and forgive whatever grievances you may have against one another. Forgive as the Lord forgave you.

"But above all these things put on love, which is the bond of perfection.

Col 3:14

Love is the virtue that binds every other virtue in perfect unity. Love gives meaning to everything we do, and it binds together the virtues that protect us from attacks from outside the walls of our city.

These spiritual characteristics work outwardly. We execute them in our service to others. The source of their strength is the love that dwells within us. Love works outwardly from the heart to empower these natures in service to others. For that service we may receive glory and honor, but as John said, that glory and honor go inward to the Temple within, the Lord God and the Lamb.[175]

The second part of our source Scripture, Rev. 21:21, spoke of the street of the city: pure gold, as clear as glass. This simply speaks of holiness, the purity of the bride. This holiness comes from trials in the fire burning out the dross. The bride's holiness is so perfectly pure that it is transparent. With that, we complete this study of the city and its gates.

---

[175] Rev. 21:22, 24

Faces of God's Laws

We have discussed the Laws of God and some of its aspects. We have seen in our study of the Holy City how the laws seem to work differently for the unbeliever and the believer.[176] We see that the physical creation is decaying: It is wearing out. Likewise, all physical life forms have a finite existence. It is the effect of the Law of Moses and goes far beyond the scope of this text. What we can see are those things Paul taught us.

"Now we know that whatever the law says, it says to those who are under the law, that every mouth may be stopped, and all the world may become guilty before God." (Rom 3:19)

The laws are applied to that which is physical, carnal if you will, and brings evidence of unbelief. It is our accuser.

"… the law brings about wrath; for where there is no law there is no transgression. "(Rom 4:15)

Sin entered the world before the Law of Moses. There was but one law in Eden. Do not eat of the tree of knowledge of good and evil. Death was pronounced on Adam and Eve in the Garden of Eden. They died spiritually immediately, but physically, they lived many years longer.

"Or do you not know, brethren (for I speak to those who know the law), that the law has dominion over a man as long as he lives?" (Rom 7:1)

While we are in this flesh, the law of that which is natural, has dominion over us. We were born and, immediately, we began moving toward death. That view

---

[176]   Page 326

may appear pessimistic, but not when we realize that death merely introduces us to the other face of the law. We have been subject to the law from its other face since the day we committed our lives to Christ. Nevertheless, this flesh must complete its course.

The other face of the law is that which moves from chaos to order, and it operates in the spiritual realm. Paul explains this as, "if Christ is in you, the body is dead because of sin, but the Spirit is life because of righteousness." (Rom 8:10)

Our body is dead because we have forsaken our lives in the flesh to follow Christ in the Spirit. Our spirit continues to thrive and grow stronger.

"But if the Spirit of Him who raised Jesus from the dead dwells in you, He who raised Christ from the dead will also give life to your mortal bodies through His Spirit who dwells in you. Therefore, brethren, we are debtors—not to the flesh, to live according to the flesh. For if you live according to the flesh you will die; but if by the Spirit you put to death the deeds of the body, you will live." (Rom 8:11-13)

"For he who sows to his flesh will of the flesh reap corruption, but he who sows to the Spirit will of the Spirit reap everlasting life. (Gal 6:8)

There are two differences in the faces of the laws. That is focus and results. Our focus is on faith in Christ or that which is spiritual. The result is life and that most abundant. The focus of law in the natural realm is those things that sustain the physical. That which is physical is foreordained to subsequent decay.

"As smoke is driven away, So drive them away; As wax melts before the fire, So let the wicked perish at the presence of God. But let the righteous be glad; Let them rejoice before God; Yes, let them rejoice exceedingly." (Psa 68:2-3)

At the presence of God, the wicked perish. Those walking after the flesh are destroyed by the laws of God. However, those that walk after the Spirit discover life in those same laws. God judges based on those laws, and the blood of Christ and our commitment to Him positions us favorably before Him. Following Christ in the law of Love prepares us for the "Final Chapter" in this walk of life.

Temples Revisited

This material IS challenging! In this section, we will view examples of lessons not widely considered. There are lessons in the Temples not normally covered, and have you viewed the Exodus as a lesson of salvation beyond the lamb's blood on the doorposts? The windows of the Scriptures constantly reveal insights we may never have considered.

In my book, The Elder Shall Serve the Younger, we see that this simple statement about the birth of Esau and Jacob was more than a prophecy stating the relationship between the two brothers. It is the stating of a principle—a principle that resurfaces throughout the Bible. After I published that book, I gained new insights and discovered that it is a principle important enough that it was presented in the first chapter of Genesis, not once, but six times. Each time God states this same principle but not obviously. Six times in the first chapter of Genesis, it is written, "the evening and the morning were the . . . day" Evening came before morning, but after the final judgment there shall be no more night.[177] Likewise, we continue to see relevancy in the Scriptures to our daily lives.

---

[177] Rev. 22:5

The Temples

Our earlier study of the Temple was very superficial.[178] There are many more gems of wisdom, more I am sure than any living being has mastered. Here, we shall broaden our understanding of Temples but still merely as an overview.

Charts of the Temple showing the three compartments are common, but not all Temples have three compartments. We should first enumerate the number of temples and their types. There are two types.

The first type has a single chamber instead of the three we usually associate with temples. These, for lack of a better term, I will call non-redemptive temples. The reason for this name is that they simply do not provide redemption. Sin is not permitted, and immediate exile is the penalty for sin. The second type is the temple we see most in the Scriptures. This "redemptive" temple consists of three chambers. Each chamber demonstrates spiritual growth in the redemptive process. So, let us first enumerate the temple types and their iterations.

Redemptive Temples

There is reason to believe that this list is not complete. Further study may reveal additional iterations of the temple. Others may be able at this time to identify additional temples. God seems to want to make sure we

---

[178] Valuable resources for the study of the Tabernacle or Temple (Price, 2005) (Pink, 1974) (Hicks)

understand redemption; although, many Christians seem to do very well with little or no understanding of temples.

In my opinion, the key verse in Scripture to explain salvation is a picture of the spiritual growth that the temple illustrates. That verse is Acts 2:38. Why I say this will become clear as we proceed. Following is a list of redemptive temples.

Tabernacle

Solomon's Temple

Herod's Temple

Tribulation Temple

Ezekiel's Temple

Jesus

Church

Christian

Non-Redemptive Temples

Garden of Eden

New Jerusalem

Pre-creation (heavenly) Eden

First, we will briefly discuss the non-redemptive temples.

Eden, a picture of the heavenly temple

Notice that there are no compartments: no courtyard, no holy place, and no Most Holy. There is only Eden. The entire temple was most holy. Like the New Jerusalem, there is a Tree of Life. A river was also there. It was to water the garden; therefore, it was a river of life. There is one thing here that is missing in the New Jerusalem, the Tree of knowledge of good and evil.

The Glory of God, the indwelling presence was also in the garden. This is the Lord God who walked in the Garden. Adam and Eve had to hide themselves from Him when they realized that they were naked. In other Temples, the Glory of God left the Temple because of the presence of sin, but in the Garden of Eden, God expelled Adam and Eve. There was also no forty days, weeks, or years of purification. God did, however, establish a method of redemption before expelling Adam and Eve. God gave them skins to cover their nakedness, foreshadowing the blood of Jesus that is the covering for our sins.[179]

New Jerusalem

In the New Jerusalem also, there was only one compartment: the Most Holy Place. Why is this different? The reason is obvious. Neither of these Temples are

---

[179] Thanks Jean.

redemptive temples. The different compartments in redemptive temples represent levels of spiritual development. There was only one level of development allowed in the Garden of Eden--perfection. Not measuring up to that level, Adam and Eve were evicted. It becomes evident what sort of people will be allowed in the New Jerusalem, not that we have yet attained that status.

"And the nations of those who are saved shall walk in its light, and the kings of the earth bring their glory and honor into it. Its gates shall not be shut at all by day (there shall be no night there). And they shall bring the glory and the honor of the nations into it. But there shall by no means enter it anything that defiles, or causes an abomination or a lie, but only those who are written in the Lamb's Book of Life." (Rev 21:24-27)

While these verses speak generally of those that are saved, they also enumerate characteristics that will not enter. It shall be a perfect environment with those who are perfectly holy. Anyone less than perfect would defile the Temple, and that is not allowed. Of course, we are not perfect now, but we shall be perfect when we are clothed with our new body.

'And as we have borne the image of the man of dust, we shall also bear the image of the heavenly Man. Now this I say, brethren, that **flesh and blood** cannot inherit the kingdom of God; nor does corruption inherit incorruption. Behold, I tell you a mystery: We shall not all sleep, but we shall all be changed—in a moment, in the twinkling of an eye, at the last trumpet. For the trumpet will sound, and the dead will be raised incorruptible, and we shall be changed. For this corruptible must put on incorruption, and this mortal must put on immortality. So when this corruptible has put on incorruption, and this mortal has put on immortality, then shall be brought to pass the saying that is written: "Death is swallowed up in victory." "O death, where is your sting? O hades, where is your victory?"' (1Co 15:49-55)

At the last trumpet, we shall all change from an imperfect being to one of perfection. Remember also, what is said of us after we have entered this final non-redemptive temple.

He who overcomes, I will make him a pillar in the temple of My God, and he shall go out no more. I will write on him the name of My God and the name of the city of My God, the New Jerusalem, which comes down out of heaven from My God. And I will write on him My new name. (Rev 3:12)

We shall not again leave this temple. This is God's promise to us that we shall never fall from grace. We shall never again offend Him. And what does it mean that He will write on us His new name?

Under every covenant since we were evicted from Eden, the very best we can hope to achieve is to be a witness of His name. Again, name in Scripture identifies a nature or characteristic. One of the main characteristics of Christ on earth was suffering. Here are a few verses to identify what Christ expected of us.

". . . commanded that they should not speak in the name of Jesus, and let them go. So they departed from the presence of the council, rejoicing that they were counted worthy to suffer shame for His name." (Act 5:40-41)

For I will show him how many things he must suffer for My name's sake." (Act 9:16)

These words, God spoke to Ananias when he balked at ministering to Paul after his conversion.

But Jesus said to them, "You do not know what you ask. Are you able to drink the cup that I drink, and be baptized with the baptism that I am baptized with?" They said to Him, "We are able." So Jesus said to them, "You will indeed drink the cup that I drink, and with the baptism I am baptized with you will be baptized." (Mar 10:38-39) Most the apostles suffered martyrdom.[180]

Do not fear any of those things which you are about to suffer. Indeed, the devil is about to throw some of you into prison, that you may be tested, and you will have tribulation ten days. Be faithful until death, and I will give you the crown of life. (Rev 2:10)

These few verses illustrate that we are expected to suffer for His name. Are there blessings while we are suffering? Did not Peter and John rejoice that they were found worthy to suffer for His name? There must be something about suffering for the name of Jesus that overwhelms the suffering, but there is suffering. Jesus suffered rejection by the people He came to save. He was even rejected by His family. If your family members are not faithful followers of Christ, you too may be rejected by those of your own household. Yet, with whatever suffering we must endure, we find it true that "Whom having not seen, ye love; in whom, though now ye see him not, yet

---

[180] It is my personal belief that John did not experience death. Of course, there is neither historical nor scriptural evidence of this of which I am aware.

believing, ye rejoice with joy unspeakable and full of glory." (1Pe 1:8 KJV)

In this new temple, there is no more (baptismal) sea: a sea which washes away sin. We have no more sin and have no more need to be baptized in His name of suffering. We have forever, the river of water of life or the depth of understanding of God. I imagine the pursuit of this understanding will take eternity to fathom. It is worth repeating that we have received the promise, "To him who overcomes I will give <u>some</u> of the hidden manna to eat. And I will give him a white stone, and on the stone a new name written which no one knows except him who receives it." (Rev 2:17) This name is not known (understood, if you will) by anyone else. The reason it is not understood is that this name is the nature that results from our perfected nature united to His ever-perfect nature. The name to which our name is joined is His new name which no longer suffers. Instead, His new nature is one of ruling authority.

Where It All Began

You were in Eden, the garden of God; Every precious stone was your covering: The sardius, topaz, and diamond, Beryl, onyx, and jasper, Sapphire, turquoise, and emerald with gold. The workmanship of your timbrels and pipes was prepared for you on the day you were created. (Eze 28:13)

The garden of Eden where Adam and Eve began life was an earthly garden. Although it was an earthly Temple, it had only one compartment—the whole garden. It was not a redemptive Temple as Adam and Eve had not yet fallen and needed no redemption and Lucifer will have no redemption. The garden where Adam was employed was not the garden referred to by Ezekiel. Ezekiel spoke of the heavenly Eden—the heavenly Temple that preceded creation.

No one in the earthly garden was covered with topaz and diamonds. Ezekiel had more to say about this person, referred to as the King of Tyre.

"You were the anointed cherub who covers; I established you; You were on the holy mountain of God; You walked back and forth in the midst of fiery stones. You were perfect in your ways from the day you were created, Till iniquity was found in you. By the abundance of your trading You became filled with violence within, And you sinned; Therefore I cast you as a profane thing Out of the mountain of God; And I destroyed you, O covering cherub, From the midst of the fiery stones. <u>Your heart was lifted up because of your beauty; You corrupted your wisdom for the sake of your splendor</u>; I cast you to the ground, I laid you before kings, that they might gaze at you. You defiled your sanctuaries by the multitude of your iniquities, By the iniquity of your trading; Therefore I brought fire from your midst; It devoured you, And I turned you to ashes upon the earth In the sight of all who saw you. All who knew you among the peoples are astonished at you; You have become a horror, And shall be no more forever." (Eze 28:14-19)

This garden was the "Mountain of God," the heavenly garden. Satan was cast out of this garden. Notice again, that God does not forsake non-redemptive Temples: He casts out the polluters. Being cast out of these temples for defiling it was accomplished immediately, so more than one compartment was not necessary.

So, we see three non-redemptive temples. Each of these has one compartment, and no sin is permitted. Judgment is immediate. The sinner is cast out; therefore, Satan was cast immediately out of the heavenly temple.

There is an anomaly here in that Satan has access to the heavenly Eden, even now. This same anomaly was present in the earthly Eden in that the serpent was present. In the case of the serpent, there is no mention of his being cast out of the garden.[181] Satan's office was the ministry of Law. Of course, he would be very powerful in a position such as this. The reason he is still permitted to appear before God is that he might accuse the saints, as he did with Job. He uses the Laws of God to destroy our victory with Christ. He uses God's Laws to accuse us. He reminds us of our failures. Yes, we have earned the accusations, but Jesus looks at us as through the cross and forgives. This was Satan's sole purpose of appearing before God in Job. He wanted to cause Job to curse God, but he was constrained by the limits of God's permission.

Redemptive Temples

Solomon's Temple

This Temple was built for a dispensational earthly resting place for the glory of God. His dwelling was no

---

[181] It appears Satan was cast out more than once. Would this amount to being cast out of each one of the three heavens Paul alluded to? 2Cor. 12:2

longer a tent that needed to be assembled and disassembled to move with Israel in their journeys. It was constructed on the same order as the Tabernacle. It had three sections: outer court, holy place, and most holy.

Tabernacle

Take note of these facts about the Tabernacle. Israel was freed from their bondage to Pharaoh by the blood of the lamb and crossed the Red Sea. Before there is a Temple or Tabernacle, there is a purification or a preparation. This purification was accomplished at the baptism in the Red Sea. Remember from the Flood, that there were forty days of proving oneself through the constant forty-day rain. For the Tabernacle, there was forty days of fasting on the part of Moses before the Tabernacle was blessed.[182] After Moses forty-day fast, he pitched the tent and called it the Tabernacle of Meeting, and each time Moses entered the Tabernacle the anointing of God stood at the door of the Tabernacle.[183] Not until all the work of the Tabernacle was complete did the glory of God go into the Tabernacle. When the work was completed, the glory of the Lord filled the Tabernacle.[184]

---

[182] Exodus 24:18

[183] Ex. 34:7-9

[184] Ex. 40:33-35

Jesus

Jesus is a Temple. Indeed, all other (temporary) temples are representative of Jesus and His dealings with His people until the end of the Millennium. Solomon's prayer of dedication for the first temple was an excellent picture of God's people in their relationship to God. When the people sinned such that they were carried away into other countries, Solomon prayed that they would repent and pray toward this temple. Jesus is the Temple through which we have access to the Father.

Jesus was anointed with the Shekinah glory after He was baptized. John bore witness of it when he testified about the Holy Spirit descending on Jesus in the form of a dove. The Shekinah glory of God will not stay in the presence of sin. Jesus, as a Temple of the Holy Spirit, witnessed to this when He prayed, "My God, my God. Why have You forsaken me." At that point, He took all the sins of the world on Himself. Once this was done, He could end His suffering as He did when He said, "It is finished."

A seeming deviation from the rule of forty days before the anointing of a temple is that Jesus was anointed immediately after baptism. Then he was driven by the Spirit into the wilderness to be tempted. Consistency returns when His fasting preceded the start of His ministry; that is, Jesus' ministry began after 40 days of fasting. One possible explanation for the deviation is that Jesus was pure from birth.

That Jesus was a temple is confirmed by His own words.

'So the Jews answered and said to Him, "What sign do You show to us, since You do these things?" Jesus answered and said to them, "Destroy this temple, and in three days I will raise it up." Then the Jews said, "It has taken forty-six years to build this temple, and will You raise it up in three days?" But He was speaking of the temple of His body.' (Joh 2:18-21)

Also, every temple is sanctified by the shedding of blood. Herod accomplished this after the birth of Jesus when he ordered the killing of the innocents in an attempt to kill the Messiah who the wise men told him was born. These innocents, sheep, as it were, died in His place. As mentioned earlier, Moses also was spared from death while Pharaoh had the innocents killed.

Church

The church received the Shekinah glory, the indwelling Spirit of God, on Pentecost. This was after **forty** days of ministering from Jesus after His resurrection, revealing to them the significance of all that had happened to Him and why. As there was for every Temple, there was a period measured as a multiple of forty before it was blessed. The Holy Spirit, likewise, entered the church after those forty days of teaching. It was, of course, the blood of Jesus that purifies the church as a temple. After it is purified, it is anointed by the Spirit.

A redemptive temple can be forsaken by the anointing, as occurred for Solomon's Temple. This did not occur until the sinfulness of the Jewish people reached a certain point. We do not know exactly when the anointing left Solomon's

Temple, but after leaving, it never returned. The church is a building of millions of people, so the sins of Christians have not been sufficient to have the anointing removed; therefore, the anointing has remained on this temple for almost 2,000 years. This anointing <u>may</u> leave the church at the rapture. One could easily argue that the anointing is not what it has been in the past. Indeed, during the middle ages, it seemed that there were no truly anointed people. As in the days of Elijah, God has reserved for Himself a faithful people.[185] Truly, I don't believe the anointing will leave the church before the end of the millennium.

This brings up a point of immense importance to Jews and the church. Only when the anointing leaves the church can the Temple in Israel receive the Shekinah glory. Historically, only one temple is anointed at any time. It seems, if the pre-tribulation temple is to be anointed, the church (those with the anointing) must be removed first. This is tantamount to removing the Shekinah glory from whoever remains of the church. This is an indication to me that the church may be raptured before the tribulation. The church remaining will be in the same position as the Jews—facing the tribulation. Recall Matthew 24: 40-42. Two would be working: one would be taken, the other left. Two would be grinding: one would be taken, the other left. Pair this with 2 Thessalonians 2:7 that states, "that Day will not come unless the falling away comes first, and the man of sin is revealed, the son of perdition. These two events will likely take place at or about the same time, after the antichrist assumes his position in the Temple. This does present a problem with no one knowing

---

[185] 1 Kg. 19:18

when Christ will come; therefore, the antichrist revealing himself as antichrist may precede, but very close to, his taking his position in the Temple. The main point is that the Holy Spirit will not leave the sanctified church without His anointing. Those lacking oil in their lamps will be left behind. As Jesus said, "the master of that servant will come on a day when he is not looking for him and at an hour that he is not aware of and will cut him in two and appoint him his portion with the hypocrites. There shall be weeping and gnashing of teeth." (Mat 24:51,52)

One may discern the existence of two concurrent temples here: the temple of the Jews, and the temple of the church. Is this possible? Jesus referred to Himself as a temple. I have identified the church as a temple. Jesus lived concurrent with Herod's temple, and the church thrived during the last forty years of that temple's existence. There has, however, been only one anointed temple in existence at any time. After the destruction of Solomon's Temple, there was no anointed temple until Christ.

If however, the next temple is not blessed with the Shekinah glory of God, the church could remain until the end of the tribulation. There have been long periods when there was no anointed temple, so the church could remain throughout the tribulation. In the next section, we will discuss a slight discrepancy to this point.

Other Temples

Another temple we have not discussed is you, the individual devotee to Christ. Although we are a many membered body and therefore, one temple, we are each a temple. Currently, we are an earthly tabernacle progressing from one level of spiritual development to the next.

"Do you not know that you are the temple of God and that the Spirit of God dwells in you?" (1Co 3:16)

It is interesting that we are both temples individually and as part of the body of Christ. The Shekinah glory (Holy Spirit anointing) can be removed from each temple, individually. It can also be removed from the remaining church at the coming of Christ. Those who are taken will retain their anointing.

Noah's Ark

The earth was declared unclean by God; therefore, it must be purified. God sent a Flood to wash away the impurity. Noah found grace as a minister of God. He preached for 120 (40*3) years that God was going to destroy the earth.

When the ark was finished, God told Noah that it would begin raining in "forty" days; so he gathered the animals to enter the ark. The world to whom he preached would not accept his message. A rain of "forty"[186] days ensued. Adding the days enumerated in the telling of the ark, Noah and his family were in the ark for 400 or 401 days. I am inclined to infer that they were in the ark for 400 whole days. The reason for this inference that it fits with the multiple of forty. At the time of this writing, I have no further reason for that inference. The Ark here is a temple of God. Notice that the ark contains three levels,

---

[186] Preparation?

like the outer court, holy place, and most holy of the Tabernacle.

All redemptive temples are temporary. They demonstrate our path to a perfection and redemption that will be everlasting. One could also question the ark as a temple, but from the fact that it provides a picture of the salvation achieved through faith in Christ, it is a temple. It is also composed of three compartments as other redemptive temples. These compartments are stacked on top of each other, but this only adds to the concept of spiritual elevation as we progress from one level to another. Notice that the window is placed in the top of the ark, so the view into heaven is only for the highest floor. It also provides a view of things above.

The fact also, that "the Lord shut them in" (Gen. 7:16), demonstrates that our salvation is dependent on God. All the work of building the ark was useless if the ark had not been sealed. Sealing them in from the destruction of the floods was a work of God. If Noah had not been obedient in building the ark, they would have had no ark in which to be saved. If it had not been for the sealing power of God, they would have died despite all their work. Without Christ, all our works are nothing, but by our obedience to Christ we obtain His saving grace.

Conclusion

There are two types of temples: non-redemptive and redemptive. The non-redemptive temples have one compartment. No sin is allowed in this temple. God does not remove His anointing from this temple. Those who commit sin are cast out of this temple. One does not have to grow into a maturity level within this temple. One only enters this temple if he is perfect.

The second type of temple is the redemptive temple which has three levels.[187] Each level depicts a level of readiness for the non-redemptive temple. Those who attain the third level of this temple are ready to enter the non-redemptive temple. Paul tells us that he knew the level he had attained, when he said, "I have fought the good fight, I have finished the race, I have kept the faith. Finally, there is laid up for me the crown of righteousness, which the Lord, the righteous Judge, will give to me on that Day, and not to me only but also to all who have loved His appearing." (2Ti 4:7-8)

Again, he tells us of his readiness in two places in Galatians.

I have been crucified with Christ; it is no longer I who live, but Christ lives in me; and the life which I now live in the flesh I live by faith in the Son of God, who loved me and gave Himself for me. (Gal 2:20)

From now on let no one trouble me, for I bear in my body the marks of the Lord Jesus. (Gal 6:17)

Those of us who are aware of our failures and lack of readiness to enter the non-redemptive Temple will be readied in a moment, at either death or rapture. I am inclined to believe that even the holiest saints lived the

---

[187] The Tabernacle and the Temple contain extensive lessons for us concerning salvation. For a more thorough presentation on the redemption message of the Temples, I suggest my book, "I Must Decrease."

entirety of their lives with unintentional sin, but even these will be gone when He has changed us at His coming.[188]

One will ask, "What must I do to be ready?" To the best of your ability, be obedient to the Spirit. Walk humbly before Him. In the final analysis, He is the judge.

I may have stirred more questions than provided answers. If I could be more conclusive, I would. I continue to seek enlightenment and I pray that God will give you understanding in all things.

---

[188]   1 Cor. 15:51,52

The Exodus

Lessons from Exodus are closely related to lessons from the redemptive temples. The first lesson we find in the Exodus is salvation through the blood of the lamb. OK. It isn't the first lesson, but it is the first obvious lesson. The first lesson is found in Moses as written in the following verses.

"And the LORD said to me: 'What they have spoken is good. I will raise up for them a Prophet like you from among their brethren, and will put My words in His mouth, and He shall speak to them all that I command Him." (Deu 18:17-18)

I cannot comprehend the wisdom of God. As I am reviewing this material, I am struck by another iteration of these truths. When we think of a "Prophet like you," I am reminded of the parallel between Moses and Jesus in their early lives. Pharaoh ordered all the male children killed at birth. While other children were killed because of this order, Moses survived. This account in Exodus 1 and 2 does not specifically say any children were killed. Many were saved by the midwives. The account implies that children were still killed after the midwives saved them. Moses was not put into the basket and the water until it was no longer safe to hide him, so evidently, the young males were killed when they were discovered. This corresponds to the children in Bethlehem being killed while attempting to kill Jesus. So those children killed in Egypt may be considered the blood sacrifice for Moses.

After Moses was placed in the water, Pharaoh's daughter pulled him from the water and raised him as her own, so this was his baptism.[189] The name Moses means "drawn from water." Water is a type of trial or suffering, and part of the nature of Christ in His redemptive purpose was (is)[190] suffering. After he fled Egypt, Moses dwelt in Midian for forty years until an angel of God appeared to him and ordained him to deliver the children of Israel out of Egypt.[191] So the death of the Hebrew children, Moses being placed in water, and being ordained denotes the plan of salvation that Peter preached in Acts 2:38. It is evidenced from these Scriptures that Moses prophecies that God would raise up one like him speaks of Jesus.

Now Moses faces Pharaoh and commands that he allow the children of Israel to go into the desert to worship, and after great plagues (great tribulations), Pharaoh has ordered them to go. The blood has been shed and Israel has been saved from the judgment that killed the firstborn of every family in Egypt who did not have the blood applied to their doorposts.

They could not stay in Egypt, however. Egypt has been their prison for four hundred years, but the deliverance of God requires that they leave. As Christians, we cannot remain in the same place we lived before we were saved. We had to follow where Christ would lead us. Israel marched

---

[189] There are no coincidences in Scripture. This leaves me to meditate on what if anything the fact that Moses was saved by a ruling Egyptian signifies.

[190] Until the second coming of Christ, He will endure the suffering of His people. Through His body in the form of the church, He suffers when we suffer.

[191] Acts 7:30-34

to the Red Sea, but after a while the bondage of Egypt (Pharaoh) chased after them. Pharaoh decided to return them to bondage. Israel was saved from the judgment of death, but the bondage that held them for four hundred years tried to reclaim them.

Israel crossed the Red Sea, but they were not entirely free from their bondage. The enemy still had the ability to draw them back into the total submission with which they served Egypt for these many years. After Israel's "baptism," the Egyptian army was destroyed. Egypt no longer held them in bondage. In like manner, baptism[192] destroys the power of Satan to rule over us.

This does not mean they (or we) are perfect. They are headed for the promised land, and they have many battles before reaching their goal. It was possible that they could have entered the promised land soon after leaving Egypt. Shortly after they started their journey, Moses fasted forty days, and God wrote the Ten Commandments on tables of stone. This represents the hearts of the Israelites and young converts. More on that shortly!

In the meantime, Moses fasted, and God wrote the commandments for him. Before they were even carved in the stone, Israel was tempted to return to Egypt, their bondage. After destroying the commandment stones in response to their sin, Moses had to return to the mountain to get fresh copies of the commandments.

Now, having the commandments, they assembled the Tabernacle and dedicated it. The presence of God accepted this tent of meeting as their place of worship. God would meet with Moses at the Tent of Meeting, the earliest form

---

[192] Study of God's Word

of the Temple. The Spirit of God had been with Israel since the Red Sea, but now they had God dwelling in their midst. He took up residence in the Tabernacle. This is the difference between having the presence of God in your life and the baptism of His Spirit abiding in your soul.[193]

Complete victory is in sight. It is just a short journey now to their ultimate destination, the Promised Land. They journeyed to the border of the Promised Land and sent a delegation of spies to count the cost. After spying out the land, they decided that they could not conquer the enemies before them. In our case, those enemies are the failures that we carried out of Egypt. In Egypt, we had food to eat. We were in bondage, but we could survive. This land, Canaan, was truly blessed. It was a fruitful land, but we are not strong enough to overcome those who would keep us from inhabiting this place of plenty.

Therefore, God declared that the faithless who would not rely on Him to fight and conquer the enemy, would not enter the Promised Land. Forty years would be required to destroy the faithless from Israel. You and I also, must endure a life of trials until our faith is great enough to overcome the enemies. This period represents the testing period signified by years of quantity forty. We see this number repeatedly in the Bible representing a period of trial or testing. It is a period of troubles or suffering that will mature us. Of course, perhaps, our lives, not being lessons for subsequent generations may not have deliberate periods such as the forty years Israel endured.

So we continue our journey under the leadership of Moses. After forty years, we are ready to enter Canaan

---

[193] Acts 18:24-19:6

and conquer the land, but they must have new leadership. Moses was disobedient at Meribah (provocation) and was forbidden to enter Canaan. Remember that his name means "of water." Moses ministry was the ministry of baptism. We were baptized in the Red Sea and that baptism continued through forty years of testing in the wilderness. The blessing has been that we have been sustained by heavenly food from God, and we have enjoyed the continuing presence of God in our lives, the baptism of His Spirit. While we have had the presence of the Spirit in our lives, we have still harbored doubt that had to be destroyed. Our leadership has been through suffering. This leadership is not qualified to take us into the land of great fruitfulness with God. We must now take confidence in the leadership of the Spirit.

Moses ordained Joshua to replace him as leader. He has brought us to Canaan, but Joshua will lead us into Canaan. We have been getting closer to our goal through the schoolmaster. We have learned our lessons well and are ready for the final battles. Yes, battles. The Promised Land is inhabited by giants. We must destroy them.

Joshua (Yeshua) Is Hebrew for Jesus. The Holy Spirit has used trials and blessings to help us wend our way to this point. We are not guided by trials but by the anointing of the Holy Spirit. Notice that Joshua is referred to as Joshua or Joshua, son of Nun. The lineage of Nun is not revealed in the Bible, and this seems appropriate. Joshua is the son of Nun or the son of "Perpetuity". I don't think it is a stretch to say that Joshua is a "type" of Jesus, the Son of the Eternal God. Now that Jesus (Joshua) is fully established as our leader, we are ready to take control of our destiny and conquer the giants in our lives.

It is also interesting that the entrance to the promised land is through Jordan, which means descender. Naaman was commanded by Elisha to wash in Jordan seven times to receive healing for his leprosy.[194] He initially refused. He was willing to wash himself in the rivers of Damascus but not Jordan. By his assessment, the rivers of Damascus were better than the Jordan. Being urged by his servants, he washed himself in the Jordan and received his healing; that is, he descended through humility to obey the instructions of the prophet. Likewise, we are to obey the prophet of humility to cross into the promised land through a baptism in humility.

Relating this to the Temple, we have progressed from the courtyard, between freedom by the blood of the lamb and baptism. We have progressed to the Holy Place where we lived in the desert. The priest in the Holy Place is alone, as Israel was isolated on its forty-year journey through the wilderness. Coming to Jordan, we are ready to enter the Most Holy where we will dwell in the presence of God. We will still be separated from the world, but we will reside in the eternal presence of the Most High God. We are ready to overcome our greatest enemies: pride, greed, judgment, lust, intolerance, etc.

Notice that after Israel was saved from death by blood, they were under the ministry of water baptism (depicted by the leadership of Moses) for forty years, during which time they grew in faith in God as the knowledge of their bondage lessened through the death of the generation that

---

[194] 2 Kings 5:9-14

came out of Egypt. When they took on their new leader, Joshua, they entered the power of the Spirit to overcome their greatest enemies—those who would keep them from their promised heritage. Thus, we see the ministries of blood, fire, and water: the overview of the extended understanding of Acts 2:38.

Allow me to clear up what could be confusing about the leadership of Moses and Joshua. You and I are led of the Spirit of God throughout our Christian experience. The Moses leadership is that of the Spirit. The difference between Moses and Joshua is our level of spiritual maturity. As children, we are directed by parental love and direction, which sometimes requires punishment. As we mature, we receive less punishment and more rational direction. It is difficult to make a rational argument with a child. When they want something, they want it. No amount of reason will change their demands. As we mature, punishment lessens. Instead of spanked or given a time-out, the keys to the car are withheld. There, many times, becomes a place where we are mature enough to survive in the adult world. That is when we face the giants. Hopefully, all the good and bad we have experienced getting us to this point will enable us to be successful in whatever we undertake. The Moses ministry of the Holy Spirit has brought us to the Joshua or Jesus ministry of the Holy Spirit.

Before moving any further, let us return to a subject I promised more clarification about; that is, the tables of stone with the Ten Commandments. As you are probably aware, these stones represent our hearts. The laws of commandment were written on stone because that was the medium of the day but also to demonstrate that our hearts have been stony. They were written as rules and were not to be interpreted. We were in no spiritual condition to interpret them. We would only pervert them. Remember what the Judaic priesthood did to the fifth commandment. We repeat it here.

He answered and said to them, "Why do you also transgress the commandment of God because of your tradition? For God commanded, saying, 'Honor your father and your mother'; and, 'he who curses father or mother, let him be put to death.' But you say, 'Whoever says to his father or mother, Whatever profit you might have received from me is a gift to God"—then he need not honor his father or mother.' Thus you have made the commandment of God of no effect by your tradition. Hypocrites! Well did Isaiah prophesy about you, saying: 'THESE PEOPLE DRAW NEAR TO ME WITH THEIR MOUTH, AND HONOR ME WITH THEIR LIPS, BUT THEIR HEART IS FAR FROM ME. (Mat 15:3-8)

The interpretation of the priests was a perversion of the law. They dared to pervert the Laws of God. To us and to Israel following the tribulation God says, "Then I will give them one heart, and I will put a new spirit within them, and take the stony heart out of their flesh, and give them a heart of flesh, that they may walk in My statutes and keep My judgments and do them; and they shall be My people, and I will be their God." (Eze 11:19-20)

The Word of God is alive, so we are not done. We have seen the steps of redemption in several areas, but we may have missed the redemption emphasis. Noah's flood was one that seems incomplete. The flood also does not minister these steps of regeneration completely, or I have not properly discerned them. The redemption message began when God covered the nakedness of Adam and Eve with skins. This was the shedding of blood that was required and worked with the baptismal flood, but where is the fire?

But the day of the Lord will come as a thief in the night, in which the heavens will pass away with a great noise, and the elements will melt with fervent heat; both the earth and the works that are in it will be burned up. (2Pe 3:10)

One could argue that the burnt offering offered by Noah after the flood would complete the blood, fire, and water sequence. The covering of animal skins provided by God was a blood offering that applied to everyone on earth at the time. The flood affected every living being. The fire spoken of by Peter will be a universal fire. However, lest we forget, that there was a fire at Pentecost; the baptism of the Holy Spirit.

There was blood shed in Eden. There were baptismal waters at the flood, and there was fire at Pentecost.

Did Jesus have to die?

Muslims have a problem with the idea of Jesus dying. They simply won't accept that He died. They argue that Judas died in place of Jesus and accuse Christians of hiding this from the world. Annually, they celebrate a holiday called Eid. On this holiday, they kill a goat and have a feast with family and friends. It is a celebration of the sparing of the son of Abraham by offering a ram in his place. They celebrate it with a lack of understanding. The first error is that they think the son was Ishmael, not Isaac, but that is not necessarily the important message in this sacrifice. In the Garden of Eden, man yielded to sin. The penalty for sin was death. They miss the important point that the sacrifice offered spoke to us of Jesus, He who died in our place.

And the LORD God commanded the man, saying, "Of every tree of the garden you may freely eat; but of the tree of the knowledge of good and evil you shall not eat, for in the day that you eat of it you shall surely die." (Gen 2:16-17)

God, to test Abraham's faith, commanded him to sacrifice his only son. The ram was a replacement for his son.[195]

Muslims also argue that God is too magnificent to live in a human body, much less allow men to abuse Him. This is what they and probably most of Christendom miss.

---

[195] Gen. 22:12,13

As a death was required to satisfy the penalty of death, the replacement had to be perfectly free from sin. To save mankind from this death penalty, to atone for all the sins of the entire world required an offering that was perfect. That offering also had to be of such immense value that it exceeded every sin ever committed. The only one who could meet such requirements is God. Therefore, God took on the form of a body and allowed men to kill Him, in that form, that He might be the salvation of the world.

Jesus was made a curse by allowing his enemies to hang him on a tree. The Christ was killed for the salvation of the world. He was the sacrifice portrayed by the ram.

The origin of all sin in the world was from the pride of Lucifer. God is holier than any of his creation, and He hates pride.[196]

"The fear of the LORD is to hate evil; Pride and arrogance and the evil way And the perverse mouth I hate." (Pro 8:13)

Again, "But He gives more grace. Therefore, He says: 'God resists the proud, but gives grace to the humble.'" (Jas 4:6)

This sacrifice for the sins of the world requires the ultimate humility, a level of holiness of which only God is capable. God is holier than any human or angel. He humbled himself to come to earth in human form and to allow sinful man to curse Him, beat Him, spit in His face, and finally to crucify Him. Because of His sacrifice, you and I are now heirs of the Most High God. This sacrifice is great enough to atone for all sin ever committed. For the salvation of mankind, God was manifest in the flesh in the

---

[196] Job: 40:11, 12, Pro.6:17, Pro.21:4

person of Jesus Christ and provided this ultimate sacrifice. It is reasonable that ignoring this sacrifice is worthy of retribution.[197]

If not such a tragic suffering on the part of Jesus, it would be humorous that the very thing that defeated Lucifer was his sense of self-worth. He was so proud that he exalted himself. Jesus was so humble that He accepted such humiliation for the salvation of the world.

---

[197] Heb. 2:3

You cannot see My face

But He said, "You cannot see My face; for no man shall see Me, and live." And the LORD said, "Here is a place by Me, and you shall stand on the rock. So it shall be, while My glory passes by, that I will put you in the cleft of the rock, and will cover you with My hand while I pass by. Then I will take away My hand, and you shall see My back; but My face shall not be seen." (Exo 33:20-23)

I am awed at the depth of God's Word. So much "seems" to contradict proven scientific facts. The Word even seems to contradict itself. Neither is true. The Word was written to be understandable and, in a way, to present spiritual insight. An example of this is a day of creation, which we covered earlier. It was written to present exactly what transpires; for example, the revelation by the angel to Manoah about the birth of Samson. (Judges 13:1-22)

These two references form the crux of a much deeper understanding of God's working with men, but we shall not delve beyond the surface. The experience of Manoah and his wife demonstrates a contradiction (?) to the reference from Exodus. Our previous confrontations with apparent contradictions have prepared us to expect a resolution to this problem, and God has not disappointed us.

We are already aware of different depths of understanding, and that is what we are facing here. The cause for confusion in Manoah's statement after watching the angel ascend into the flames was, "We shall surely die, because we have seen God!" (v 22) Yet, they did not die. Considering all that happened to their son, they may have wished they had. Samson caused the Philistines so much trouble that they sought to kill him, and this was a source of great sorrow to his parents.

Regardless of subsequent events, Manoah and his wife did not die. Did God change his mind? He was emphatic to Moses. Did Manoah misspeak? The answer to both questions is no. God did not change His mind and Manoah did not misspeak. Also, this is not the first time God appeared to men. He appeared to Abraham on several occasions. (Gen 17:15, 18:1) On each of these occasions, God was referred to as an angel or as a man, or even as three men (another revelation of the Godhead).

Without expanding this subject beyond its key point, we see that God has been seen by men. Our reference verse said no man would see Him and live. We derive two points from these verses.

God may appear in different ways.

Man may die in more than one way.

Man may die physically. This is what we take away from our reference verse. This is what Manoah feared. The key to why one will die and why none of these individuals died after seeing God is found in that part of our verses that stated, "you shall see My back; but My face shall not be seen." It is, then, that we cannot see God face to face and live.

Therefore, God has revealed Himself as He has through the Scriptures. We cannot see the fullness of the Scriptures and live, for this is how God is revealed to us. It makes sense that everything about God is revealed to us in parables and apparent contradictions. Each veil of mystery that is pulled back reveals a little more of God and His plan for man. The veil is pulled back as we can receive it. As the veil is pulled back, we may find it necessary to realign our thinking. Our ability to understand has broadened and perhaps also our concepts must broaden.

Do not mistake that for saying that we must accept things we thought were sin are ok. Sin is sin. A deeper understanding of Scripture will give us clearer understanding of sin as well as a deeper understanding of grace and holiness.

As we draw nearer to God, more of our carnal nature dies. The more we see of God, the less we pay attention to temptations: the less we are affected negatively by what goes on around us.

Regardless, as we draw nearer to Christ the veil surrounding God's mysteries will be drawn back a little more. Revelations will occur, and the elect of Christ will become stronger and holier.

This is purposely a very short chapter. I hoped to again demonstrate the depth of the Word. Imagine! Revelations so magnificent that our minds and bodies could not survive them. It makes the radiance on the face of Moses after being in the presence of God understandable. Since we do not experience the need to cover our face, so others can look at us tells us one or two things. One is that we are not close enough to God that our faces would reflect the blinding light resulting from merely(?) seeing the back side of God in His revelations. The second is that we are not holy enough to radiate the reflection of His holiness.

The Final Chapter

No, this is not the final chapter of this book. It is the final chapter of our dispensation. It is the final chapter of premillennial history. We are looking for the return of our savior. What spiritual truths could hint at the timing of the return of Christ or, if separate, the end of this dispensation and the ushering in of the millennium? Everyone knows the end is near. We look expectantly for the return of Christ and the end of the age. Are they the same? That question, I will not attempt to answer. What I explicitly want to address here is when (I believe) this dispensation <u>must</u> end, and the Millennial kingdom begin. Mad? Obviously! So, let us continue.

There are several givens that are not otherwise treated in this chapter. We will quickly address a couple of those givens here, and it may be unapologetically repetitious.

Dispensations

There are three primary dispensations in human history.[198] The first is what I call the dispensation of blood. It began in the Garden of Eden when God covered the guilt of Adam and Eve with the skin of an animal. The second dispensation was that of water, ≈1650 years later,

---

[198] There are other dispensations. The dispensations I refer to here are the three dispensations that relate to God's plan of salvation.

when God saved eight souls from the flood that destroyed sin in the known world. The third dispensation started is that of fire and began on the first Pentecost when the Holy Spirit was given. These dispensations cover human history to this point, a total I believe to be almost 6000 years. After the current dispensation is a one-thousand-year dispensation of peace, the Sabbath, the Millennial reign of Christ.

You may have noticed the similarity between these dispensations and Acts 2:38 that answered the question, "What must we do to be saved?" That is no accident. Everything in the Bible happening prior to the crucifixion of Christ was bringing us to this point: salvation! Then Peter said to them, "Repent, and let every one of you be baptized in the name of Jesus Christ for the remission of sins; and you shall receive the gift of the Holy Spirit. (Act 2:38)

Since I opened the door, permit me a brief side-trip. There are three parts to Acts 2:38: repentance, baptism, and receiving the Holy Spirit. Salvation was demonstrated in the dispensations of Biblical history. Adam and Eve were saved from death by the blood of the animal whose skin covered their nakedness. Later, mankind was saved from the power of sin that came from outside influences by the destruction of that power through the baptism of Noah's flood. External temptations were destroyed. That baptism destroyed the power of outside temptations when we wish to overcome. The fulness of baptism is only achieved, however, through study of God's Word, the baptism of water by the Word. Again, as Paul said, "Husbands, love your wives, just as Christ also loved the church and gave

Himself for her, that He might sanctify and cleanse her with the washing of water by the word." Eph 5:25-26 It is by searching God's Word that we gain power over the enemy. Receiving the Holy Spirit gives us the power of the indwelling Spirit of God to overcome, (whether we use it, or not). The Holy Spirit is the last, but not least element in the fulfilling of our salvation. The parable of the sower illustrates this with the seed that falls into good ground and brings forth fruit thirty, sixty, and hundred-fold. The thirty are those who have repented and bring forth thirty-fold increase. The blood offering of Jesus Christ saves us from damnation. Those baptized, especially, in the Word are those who bring forth sixty-fold. Finally, those who go on to receive the gift of the Holy Spirit, are those who bring forth a hundred-fold increase. This enables us to overcome the internal influences of sin. I wish I could say that overcoming was instantaneous, but I can't. Also, because we are in a specific fold, thirty, sixty or hundred, does not imply that we are living up to our full potential at that level. It is, at least, a potential. Let me also admit that the understanding of these levels and their relationships are not fully revealed to me.

Forty

Many books have been written on the significances of numbers. Our primary interest here is the number forty. This number has been called the number of probation, and it is. It is also the number of preparation. Finally, forty is a number for ministry. These are seen in Israel's travelling in the wilderness for forty years as probation for their negative report when told to spy out the Promised Land in preparation for capturing it.

In the life of Moses, he spent forty years in preparation before going into the wilderness. During this period, he was being taught in all the wisdom of Egypt. Then he was another forty years in maturing through trials in the wilderness before he was called to his ministry at the burning bush. His ministry was the forty years he spent leading Israel from Egypt to the Jordan where they would enter the Promised Land.

Each of the first three kings of Israel ruled the country for forty years. We find the duration of Saul's reign in the New Testament (Acts 13:21).

Even the life of Jesus demonstrates the number forty. It has recently been concluded that Jesus was born in 4 B.C. The "latest possible" year for the crucifixion and hence, Pentecost was 36 AD. That would mean Christ was forty years old when He was crucified. He also fasted forty days before beginning His ministry. Remember, forty is a number for ministry.

The Prophetic

The subject we address in the remainder of this chapter has brought an immense amount of scorn on the Scriptures, such that I am hesitant to address it. Nevertheless, I feel I must share what I believe to be a realistic and Scriptural summary of coming events and their approximant timeline. The return of the Lord will occur within seven years or concurrently with the end of this dispensation; so, when is that? In my opinion, it is close enough that all of us should be seeking His face more diligently than ever. I will become more specific, shortly.[199]

We can know neither the day nor the hour that Christ will return. There is also disagreement over when the church will be raptured relative to the end of this dispensation and the tribulation. These are, however, two different questions.[200] We see signs of the end. Accepting that we can know neither the day nor the hour of the end, how close can we estimate the end of the dispensation?[201] The end of the current dispensation marks the establishment of Christ's millennial kingdom on earth. The beginning assertion for determining this timing may seem weak, but I think it will take on credibility as we proceed. That assertion is that each thousand years of religious history represents one day in God's timetable of dealing with man.

But, beloved, do not forget this one thing, that with the Lord one day is as a thousand years, and a thousand years as one day. (2Pe 3:8)

As of this writing in 2012, the year on the Jewish calendar is 5772. Therefore, according to the dating by

---

[199] As an aid to move forward in readiness for the return of Christ, may I humbly suggest my book, "Holiness, the Joyful pursuit".

[200] I have hinted earlier that the rapture must occur before the tribulation, but there are also strong Scriptural indications to the opposite.

[201] If anyone can be so certain as to the hour of Christ's return, two things are required. They must be able to specify the time zone for the hour specified, and they must provide Scriptural support. I doubt either of these will be made known to us. He did tell us that no man knows the date nor time. Matt. 24:36, 25:13, Mark 13:32

the Jewish calendar, in 228 years, religious history will reach 6000 years or six days based on this verse from 2nd Peter. For purposes of this study, the date we will start our reckoning from is 36 A.D, a "likely" latest year of Christ's crucifixion and the event of Pentecost and a likely Jubilee year.

The accuracy of the Jewish calendar is also questionable. It is not Scripture, so it is subject to error. Archeologists have proven the accuracy of Biblical events by adjusting the calendar-year reckoning by about 150 years or more. (Rohl, 2003, pp. 211-216) That minimal adjustment would set the year of this writing at about 5922, much closer to the 6000-year mark.

It is widely believed that we are living in the end time. Some very knowledgeable persons have made predictions concerning end-time approximations by what I consider only somewhat off target. Some of these predictions have been based on reasonable considerations, hence, the world would end in the year 2000 or again in 2012. 2012 has come and gone, and the world has not ended. It is alive, if not well. Also, Christ has not returned by the predicted date.

Since this is the dispensation of the church (fire of the Holy Spirit), this dispensation began with the anointing of the Holy Spirit. Pentecost occurred between 30 and 36 A.D. and was the start of the church age. Therefore, to fit the assertion of six thousand-year days and reckoning of the first Pentecost as 36 A. D., the return of Jesus must be by Pentecost of 2036 with one additional caveat. It can, indeed must, in my view precede that date. This date is the most distant in time for Christ's return. Matt. 24:22

and Mark 13:20 says those days shall be shortened. The question arises: "Why must it end at this time? Why not longer?" Is God that specific about timing? We will revisit this shortly.

A pastor once openly denounced my assertion that God's creation of man was incomplete, but after I further explained my statement, he agreed. Each thousand years of human history represents one day on God's calendar. This calendar week is the six days that God is forming man into His image and likeness. This is a more perfect creation than the original Adam. After six days, we must observe the Sabbath, the thousand-year millennial reign of Christ. This paragraph explodes into a much broader area of questions that are not part of our main subject matter here, and my answers to many of those questions would be purely hypothetical, so we proceed with care.

And I saw thrones, and they sat on them, and judgment was committed to them. Then I saw the souls of those who had been beheaded for their witness to Jesus and for the word of God, who had not worshiped the beast or his image, and had not received his mark on their foreheads or on their hands. And they lived and reigned with Christ for a thousand years. (Rev 20:4)

Again, the thousand years referred to by this reference is the seventh or Sabbath day. The Law of God has not been suspended because we are in the dispensation of grace. He still expects us to live holy lives and abide by the Ten Commandments, including the Law of the "Sabbath."

"Remember the Sabbath day, to keep it holy. Six days you shall labor and do all your work, but the seventh day is the Sabbath of the LORD your God. In it you shall do no work: you, nor your son, nor your daughter, nor your male servant, nor your female servant, nor your cattle, nor your stranger who is within your gates. For in six days the LORD made the heavens and the earth, the sea, and all that is in them, and rested the seventh day. Therefore, the LORD blessed the Sabbath day and hallowed it."

(Exo 20:8-11)

If God gave us rules to follow, remember that it was first God himself that rested on the Sabbath.

And on the seventh day God ended His work which He had done, and He rested on the seventh day from all His work which He had done. Then God blessed the seventh day and sanctified it, because in it He rested from all His work, which God had created and made. (Gen 2:2-3)

Based on these facts, we are living at the very end of the sixth day of religious history. Following this day, we will celebrate the Sabbath—one thousand years of peace. Peter was not speaking idly when he wrote, "But, beloved, do not forget this one thing, that with the Lord one day is as a thousand years, and a thousand years as one day." (2Pe 3:8) The end of this dispensation will mark the end of God's workweek of forming mankind into children worthy of His eternal Kingdom.

It seems reasonable to correlate Church history with these thousand-year days. If I am correct then, Christ must return on or <u>before</u> Pentecost 0f 2036, or June 3, 2036, regardless of when He returns relative to the end of the dispensation. He must return before the Sabbath begins. During the millennium, the devil will be bound. God will rest. Remember, however, that if a member of the flock falls into a ditch on the Sabbath, it is lawful to put forth the effort to free him or her from their quagmire.

Taking this study to the next level, Jesus was crucified and spent three days in the grave. His resurrection was discovered early on the morning of the first day of the week.

On Pentecost, the Holy Spirit recreated at least one event of Jesus spiritually. With very little detail, we will cover that event. The Holy Spirit baptism of the church recreates Christ's burial in the tomb for three days. The Holy Spirit was buried in the body of the church on Pentecost and has been there for 2000 years. That is two days. He must spend one more day in the grave—the Sabbath. Sin will not be tolerated during the Sabbath as Christ will rule with a rod of iron. The millennium, following the tribulation, is described by Ezekiel.

For I will take you from among the nations, gather you out of all countries, and bring you into your own land. Then I will sprinkle clean water on you, and you shall be clean; I will cleanse you from all your filthiness and from all your idols. I will give you a new heart and put a new spirit within you; I will take the heart of stone out of your flesh and give you a heart of flesh. I will put My Spirit within you and cause you to walk in My statutes, and you will keep My judgments and do them. Then you shall dwell in the land that I gave to your fathers; you shall be My people, and I will be your God. I will deliver you from all your uncleanness's. I will call for the grain and multiply it and bring no famine upon you. And I will multiply the fruit of your trees and the increase of your fields, so that you need never again bear the reproach of famine among the nations. Then you will remember your evil ways and your deeds that were not good; and you will loathe yourselves in your own sight, for your iniquities and your abominations. Not for your sake do I do this," says the Lord GOD, "let it be known to you. Be ashamed and confounded for your own ways, O house of Israel!" 'Thus says the Lord GOD: "On the day that I cleanse you from all your iniquities, I will also enable you to dwell in the cities, and the ruins shall be rebuilt. The desolate land shall be tilled instead of lying desolate in the sight of all who pass by. So they will say, 'This land that was desolate has become like the garden of Eden; and the wasted, desolate, and ruined cities are now fortified and inhabited.' Then the nations which are left all around you shall know that I, the LORD, have rebuilt the ruined places and planted what was desolate. I, the LORD, have spoken it, and I will do it." (Eze 36:24-36)

The battle is not completely over, however. The devil must be loosed a short season for the final battle. After that final battle, the victory is complete. The final judgment, however, occurs after the millennium. (Rev. 20:7-15) Then we see the Holy City. (Rev. 21:1)

This illustration for the Sabbath reaffirms the timeline for the return of Christ, but the days must be shortened, so this date is "at the latest". As for the question I raised concerning specificity a few pages earlier in this chapter, I refer you to Daniel, chapter 12.

And he said, "Go your way, Daniel, for the words are closed up and sealed till the time of the end. Many shall be purified, made white, and refined, but the wicked shall do wickedly; and none of the wicked shall understand, but the wise shall understand. "And from the time that the daily sacrifice is taken away, and the abomination of desolation is set up, there shall be one thousand two hundred and ninety days. Blessed is he who waits, and comes to the one thousand three hundred and thirty-five days. (Dan 12:9-12)

The messenger delivering this prophecy to Daniel was specifically enumerating the days from the setting up of the abomination of desolation. The "appointed time" was referenced five times in the book of Daniel. One must remember that patterns are very important in Scriptures. God reinforced His instructions to Moses three times in Exodus concerning the Tabernacle that he should make it according to the "pattern" he was shown.

If God is emphatic with His people about following His established pattern, is God not also emphatic about continuing those patterns in His own dealings with mankind? Look at the number forty. This number is a number that can be given different names for its significance: trial, preparation, ministry. It rained forty days in Noah's times. Israel travelled in the wilderness forty years, during which period, unbelief, demonstrated almost at the outset of their exodus from Egypt, was destroyed. Israel essentially spent 400 (40x10) years as prisoners of Egypt. Jesus fasted forty days before beginning His ministry. After His resurrection, he taught His disciples for forty days in preparation for their ministry.

Pardon once again, my heresy. It has been said that Jesus was in His mid-thirties when He was crucified. Was not His time on earth a preparation time for Him to take His place at the right hand of the Father? In a word, Yes!

His birth year is uncertain, except that it was between 5 and 0 BC. Most think He was born in 4 BC. Some have concluded firmly that He was born in 4 BC. The year of His crucifixion is thought to have been between 30 and 36 AD. Thirty-six AD is considered the latest possible year for the crucifixion and resurrection. I would be greatly surprised to learn that His time on earth was other than forty years. From 4 B.C. to 36 A. D. is forty years. Thus, He preserves the pattern. By adding evidence to the importance of patterns (principles), the closing of this dispensation, on Pentecost of 2036 at the latest seems a little more likely.

Further Evidence

According to an article, After Earth, published in the March 2011 issue of Popular Science, there are reasons to be concerned about our life on earth. The least likely event to end this age is that of an asteroid impact, yet according to this article, in 1989 a small asteroid crossed earth's orbit a mere six hours after earth had passed that position. The impact of this asteroid would have been equivalent to the force of 1,000 nuclear bombs. That may not be enough power to destroy the earth, but it could fulfill prophecy of a great star falling to earth. (Rev. 8:10)

Another and more likely scenario is overpopulation of the earth. This same article points out that "by 2030 we will be consuming two planets' worth of natural resources annually." Add to this "that the number of droughts, earthquakes, epic rains and floods over the past decade is triple the number from the 1980s and nearly 54 times that of 1901, when this data was first collected."

Of course, science is the not the final word. Scripture is the final word, but the words of Jesus have alerted us that when we see certain signs, we should be aware that the end is near.

And you will hear of wars and rumors of wars. See that you are not troubled; for all these things must come to pass, but the end is not yet. For nation will rise against nation, and kingdom against kingdom. And there will be famines, pestilences, and earthquakes in various places. All these are the beginning of sorrows. (Mat 24:6-8)

But when you hear of wars and rumors of wars, do not be troubled; for such things must happen, but the end is not yet. For nation will rise against nation, and kingdom against kingdom. And there will be earthquakes in various places, and there will be famines and troubles. These are the beginnings of sorrows. (Mar 13:7-8)

The statistics cited in the article, After Earth, corresponds to the warnings of these Scriptures. Evidence from another source also alerts us to the reliability of God's Word.

No more shall an infant from there live but a few days, nor an old man who has not fulfilled his days; For the child shall die one hundred years old, But the sinner being one hundred years old shall be accursed." (Isa 65:)

As unlikely that this should be possible, news media have been recently reporting that through the science of stem-cell and other research, in the next twenty years people will be able to live a thousand years, so dying at one hundred years would be like dying while yet very young.

Twenty years from the date I am typing this document will be 2032. Much of the overpopulation that is now consuming our resources and preventing sufficient food production will likely have been destroyed by plagues and wars. The answer to what will keep the population from again overpopulating the earth I must, of course, leave in the hands of God.[202]

Again, news media have been reporting on hailstorms, and hailstones seem to keep getting bigger, or is that my imagination? Hailstones used to be small for the most part. Lately, the hail stones seem to have been getting larger and larger: pea size, golf ball size, baseball size, and recently pineapple size. Now people are being injured by hail breaking car windows. They could be much larger. In fact, the Bible states that they will reach over a hundred pounds during the tribulation.

And great hail from heaven fell upon men, each hailstone about the weight of a talent. Men blasphemed God because of the plague of the hail, since that plague was exceedingly great. (Rev 16:21)

Hailstones of this size would be about one hundred pounds. Of course, they are not that large yet, but they seem to be moving in that direction.

Prayerfully Judge for yourself the veracity of this chapter.

---

[202] Scientists are looking for an alternate earth or another earth-like planet. They think they have found several, the nearest discovered (at the time of this writing) being 26,000 light years from earth. To transport people there to inhabit the planet would require getting there. If we could travel at light speed, the other immediate problem is living for 26,000 years. Cryogenics could "possibly" solve that problem.

Addend: the late Steven Hawking, a brilliant scientist and confirmed atheist, has stated that the earth has only enough resources to support our population for another one thousand years. Dr. Hawking would likely be saddened to know that his prediction directly supports Bible prophecy.

But the fruit of the Spirit is love, joy, peace, longsuffering, kindness, goodness, faithfulness, gentleness, self-control. Against such there is no law. (Gal 5:22-23)

The Blood of the Innocents

Original Sin

And the woman said to the serpent, "We may eat the fruit of the trees of the garden; but of the fruit of the tree which is in the midst of the garden, God has said, 'You shall not eat it, nor shall you touch it, lest you die.'" Then the serpent said to the woman, "You will not surely die. For God knows that in the day you eat of it your eyes will be opened, and you will be like God, knowing good and evil." So when the woman saw that the tree was good for food, that it was pleasant to the eyes, and a tree desirable to make one wise, she took of its fruit and ate. She also gave to her husband with her, and he ate. Then the eyes of both of them were opened, and they knew that they were naked; and they sewed fig leaves together and made themselves coverings.

Gen 3:2-7

The first example of a payment for sin was the life of an animal that provided a covering for the sins of Adam and Eve. Whatever that life was, it was without sin. A life without the guilt of sin was sacrificed to provide a suitable covering for their nakedness, the awareness of which was evidence of their sin.

The Murder of Abel.

Now Adam knew Eve his wife, and she conceived and bore Cain, and said, "I have acquired a man from the LORD." Then she bore again, this time his brother Abel. Now Abel was a keeper of sheep, but Cain was a tiller of the ground. And in the process of time it came to pass that Cain brought an offering of the fruit of the ground to the LORD. Abel also brought of the firstborn of his flock and of their fat. And the LORD respected Abel and his offering, but He did not respect Cain and his offering. And Cain was very angry, and his countenance fell. So the LORD said to Cain, "Why are you angry? And why has your countenance fallen? If you do well, will you not be accepted? And if you do not do well, sin lies at the door. And its desire is for you, but you should rule over it." Now Cain talked with Abel his brother; and it came to pass, when they were in the field, that Cain rose up against Abel his brother and killed him.

Gen 4:1-8

As the sheep[203] that provided the covering for Adam and Eve was innocent of any evil, so Abel was innocent of sin. The righteous seed of Abel was preserved through Seth, the third son of Adam and Eve.

Eve said of Seth, "For God has appointed another seed for me instead of Abel, whom Cain killed." Gen. 4:25

Thus, the righteous seed was preserved despite the murderous intentions of Cain. This becomes the second example of the death of the innocent and preservation of

---

[203] Author choice as the Bible does not specify the animal sacrificed.

the righteous. It is also an example of the principle that "the elder shall serve the younger."

The Birth of Moses

And he said to his people, "Look, the people of the children of Israel are more and mightier than we; come, let us deal shrewdly with them, lest they multiply, and it happen, in the event of war, that they also join our enemies and fight against us, and so go up out of the land." Therefore they set taskmasters over them to afflict them with their burdens. And they built for Pharaoh supply cities, Pithom and Raamses. But the more they afflicted them, the more they multiplied and grew. And they were in dread of the children of Israel. So the Egyptians made the children of Israel serve with rigor. And they made their lives bitter with hard bondage--in mortar, in brick, and in all manner of service in the field. All their service in which they made them serve was with rigor. Then the king of Egypt spoke to the Hebrew midwives, of whom the name of one was Shiphrah and the name of the other Puah; and he said, "When you do the duties of a midwife for the Hebrew women, and see them on the birthstools, if it is a son, then you shall kill him; but if it is a daughter, then she shall live." But the midwives feared God, and did not do as the king of Egypt commanded them, but saved the male children alive. So the king of Egypt called for the midwives and said to them, "Why have you done this thing, and saved the male children alive?" And the midwives said to Pharaoh, "Because the Hebrew women are not like the Egyptian women; for they are lively and give birth before the midwives come to them." Therefore God dealt well with the midwives, and the people multiplied and grew very mighty. And so it was, because the midwives feared God, that He provided households for them. So Pharaoh commanded all his people, saying, "Every son who is born you shall cast into the river, and every daughter you shall save alive."

And a man of the house of Levi went and took as wife a daughter of Levi. So the woman conceived and bore a son. And when she saw that he was a beautiful child, she hid him three months. But when she could no longer hide him, she took an ark of bulrushes for him, daubed it with asphalt and pitch, put the child in it, and laid it in the reeds by the river's bank. And his sister stood afar off, to know what would be done to him. Then the daughter of Pharaoh came down to bathe at the river. And her maidens walked along the riverside; and when she saw the ark among the reeds, she sent her maid to get it. And when she opened it, she saw the child, and behold, the baby wept. So she had compassion on him, and said, "This is one of the Hebrews' children." Then his sister said to Pharaoh's daughter, "Shall I go and call a nurse for you from the Hebrew women, that she may nurse the child for you?" And Pharaoh's daughter said to her, "Go." So the maiden went and called the child's mother. Then Pharaoh's daughter said to her, "Take this child away and nurse him for me, and I will give you your wages." So the woman took the child and nursed him. And the child grew, and she brought him to Pharaoh's daughter, and he became her son. So she called his name Moses, saying, "Because I drew him out of the water."

Exo 1:9-2:10

Because many innocents died, Moses lived, and later led Israel to freedom.

Millenia after the first deaths of innocents, another group of innocents was murdered to prevent the will of God from being fulfilled. Take note, however, that there is a new element introduced: that of water. The first examples of innocent deaths occurred in the dispensation of blood. Water had not yet been introduced as part of salvation. We entered the water dispensation with Noah's flood. Water baptism is a type of learning of God's Word. Moses was the first teacher of God's holiness. Through him, the priesthood was established, and the laws of God introduced. It is through being buried in the understanding of God's Word that we gain overcoming power.

The innocents, we begin to understand to be substitutes for the deliverer. As the sufferings of Christ was to become a substitute for our due judgment, these innocents died that the Word of God and its power would go forth into the world. It has been established through repetition. It is incontrovertible. We have salvation through the blood of Christ. It has now been fully established, but the capstone is not yet revealed, and there will be additional examples of the deaths of innocents.

Moses is the deliverer, and he has been preserved, but the nation of Israel is still in bondage to Pharaoh. Also, God will demand restitution for the lives of the innocents of Israel. The tribes of Israel are still in bondage.

William Moore

The deliverance of Israel

God has plagued Egypt. The nation is ravaged, and a hard-headed Pharaoh still refuses to free the people of Israel, so God sends one last judgment on Israel. This judgment will be so terrible that Pharaoh will let Israel go. At the same time, God will have retribution for the deaths of the innocents when trying to kill the deliverer, Moses.

The firstborn of Egypt must die. It will be the innocents of Egypt that will provide the blood sacrifice necessary for the salvation of the nation.

Note also, that we are, at this point, in the water dispensation, so water is also necessary. When Pharaoh chases after the freed nation of Israel, they are blocked by the Red sea. They are blocked in on one side by the sea and being assailed from behind by the army of their task masters.

Moses leads Israel into the dry seabed to escape their tormentors, and their assailants chase after them when God permits. What has been a salvation for the Jews, however, was further judgment on Egypt. The army of Egypt follows them into the seabed only to see the waters quickly rise and destroy them.

Again, we see the power of baptism in that it destroys the power of the enemy to overcome God's people. That is accomplished by the grace of God and the Word of God residing in the hearts of His saints.

The Birth of the Church

For this event, I will not so much cite Biblical sources as historic, although the Bible does attest to it as well. This event is the death of Christians through persecution by the Jews and the rest of the world. Many saints were killed that we might have this salvation. Christian martyrs for two thousand years have provided the provender for the fires of persecution through which this Gospel is spread throughout the world.

This death of the innocents continues till this day and has taken a more historic position. This death of these innocents, Jesus and His disciples, introduced the fire dispensation.

The final death of the innocents

America has been a Christian nation: flawed, but Christian. The flaw has become critical. We have now sanctioned the death of children simply for the convenience of their parents. That is accomplished through abortion.

America's sanction of abortion is equivalent to the passing of our children through the fire as an offering to Satan. He is the cause of all the evil in the world and the author of abortion. Millions of children have been sacrificed for convenience. In Biblical times, the mothers made their children pass through the fire.[204]

---

[204] Not abortion, but identical results. If alive for this, it is even more horrific.

Yes, sometimes the unborn are sacrificed to preserve the life of the mother. There are likely other reasons that justify an abortion, but in most cases, it is simply a matter of convenience. It is a fulfillment of God's principals, but woe to those guilty of supporting it. God is forgiving! He forgives our sins. May God be merciful to all penitents.

YOU will, in my opinion, (assuming nominal health and reasonably young age) see the return of Jesus Christ and the Sabbath of God, the Millennium. The final death of innocents will, I expect, be in the form of persecution of Christians throughout the world. We have seen an increase in attacks on churches. I expect this will continue to increase.

There is much more that could be said about the death of the innocents, but this is sufficient for our study. Do be mindful, however, of the fact that some Politian's in America are working to outlaw the Bible. Where might it go from there?

Prophetic repetition

There is a nature in prophecy that is seemingly never spoken of. That nature is the nature of repetition. We seem to allow to slip by the fact that Prophecies can be repetitious: they build on one another or a subsequent prophecy may expand or clarify a previous prophecy. The Bible is filled with repetition. Repetition establishes principles: that is, B follows A, and B may expand on A. What repetition always does, is to more firmly establish a truth.

The wisest man on earth, aside of Christ, was Solomon. Solomon identified this principal twice in Ecclesiastes.

That which has been *is* what will be, That which *is* done is what will be done, And *there is* nothing new under the sun.

Is there anything of which it may be said, "See, this *is* new"? It has already been in ancient times before us. Ecc 1:9,10

That which is has already been, And what is to be has already been; And God requires an account of what is past. Ecc 3:15

We take from this that one prophecy may be simply a repetition of an earlier prophecy. It may also add clarification as to what to expect. Solomon built the first temple and pagans destroyed it. The Temple was rebuilt and the predecessor of THE antichrist, Antiochus Epiphanes, desecrated it. Then it was razed by the Romans. The prophecy of its desecration was foretold by Daniel.

And forces shall be mustered by him, and they shall defile the sanctuary fortress; then they shall take away the daily sacrifices, and place there the abomination of desolation.

Dan 11:31

"And from the time that the daily sacrifice is taken away, and the abomination of desolation is set up, there shall be one thousand two hundred and ninety days.

Dan 12:11

During the time of Antiochus, the temple was defiled by the sacrifice of pigs on the altar. It was destroyed shortly after the crucifixion of Christ by the Roman army. Yet, we are assured that the Temple will be rebuilt. I doubt the Shekinah glory will anoint it. That doubt is because the Holy Spirit is the Shekinah glory, and that glory is shining in the temple of the body of Christ, the Church. I am made to understand that in the last few years, Jews have been turning to Christ as never before.

When we study prophecy, we should also be familiar with history. The ancient adage is a truism, "history repeats itself." Again, what is to be has already been.

The Temple has been destroyed twice and will be destroyed one more time, at the end of this dispensation.

Further, I believe God tells us of a nuclear holocaust that will devastate the earth. I will not delve deeply into this topic as it is relatively new to me. However, I will share with you what I now think possible.

The revelator speaks of a great star falling to the earth. Of course, this could be a spiritual event identified in a literal sense. It could also be one or more nuclear explosions.

"And you, son of man, prophesy against Gog, and say, 'Thus says the Lord GOD: "Behold, I am against you, O Gog, the prince of Rosh[205], Meshech, and Tubal; and I will turn you around and lead you on, bringing you up from the **far north**, and bring you against the mountains of Israel. Then I will knock the bow out of your left hand and cause the arrows to fall out of your right hand. You shall fall upon the mountains of Israel, you and all your troops and the peoples who are with you; I will give you to birds of prey of every sort and to the beasts of the field to be devoured. You shall fall on the open field; for I have

---

[205] Russia(?)

spoken," says the Lord GOD. "And I will send fire on Magog and on those who live in security in the coastlands. Then they shall know that I am the LORD. So I will make My holy name known in the midst of My people Israel, and I will not let them profane My holy name anymore. Then the nations shall know that I am the LORD, the Holy One in Israel. Surely it is coming, and it shall be done," says the Lord GOD. "This is the day of which I have spoken. "Then those who dwell in the cities of Israel will go out and set on fire and burn the weapons, both the shields and bucklers, the bows and arrows, the javelins and spears; and they will make fires with them for seven years. They will not take wood from the field nor cut down any from the forests, because they will make fires with the weapons; and they will plunder those who plundered them, and pillage those who pillaged them," says the Lord GOD. "It will come to pass in that day that I will give Gog a burial place there in Israel, the valley of those who pass by east of the sea; and it will obstruct travelers, because there they will bury Gog and all his multitude. Therefore they will call it the Valley of Hamon Gog. For seven months the house of Israel will be burying them, in order to cleanse the land. Indeed all the people of the land will be burying, and they will gain renown for it on the day that I am glorified," says the Lord GOD. "They will set apart men regularly employed, with the help of a search party, to pass through the land and bury those bodies remaining on the ground, in order to cleanse it. At the end of seven months they will make a search. The search party will pass through the land; and when anyone sees a man's bone, he shall set up a marker by it, till the buriers have buried it in the Valley of

Hamon Gog. The name of the city will also be Hamonah. Thus they shall cleanse the land." "'And as for you, son of man, thus says the Lord GOD, 'Speak to every sort of bird and to every beast of the field: "Assemble yourselves and come; Gather together from all sides to My sacrificial meal Which I am sacrificing for you, A great sacrificial meal on the mountains of Israel, That you may eat flesh and drink blood. You shall eat the flesh of the mighty, Drink the blood of the princes of the earth, Of rams and lambs, Of goats and bulls, All of them fatlings of Bashan. You shall eat fat till you are full, And drink blood till you are drunk, At My sacrificial meal Which I am sacrificing for you. You shall be filled at My table With horses and riders, With mighty men And with all the men of war," says the Lord GOD. "I will set My glory among the nations; all the nations shall see My judgment which I have executed, and My hand which I have laid on them. So the house of Israel shall know that I am the LORD their God from that day forward. The Gentiles shall know that the house of Israel went into captivity for their iniquity; because they were unfaithful to Me, therefore I hid My face from them. I gave them into the hand of their enemies, and they all fell by the sword. According to their uncleanness and according to their transgressions I have dealt with them, and hidden My face from them." "'Therefore thus says the Lord GOD: 'Now I will bring back the captives of Jacob, and have mercy on the whole house of Israel; and I will be jealous for My holy name--after they have borne their shame, and all their unfaithfulness in which they were unfaithful to Me, when they dwelt safely in their own land and no one made them afraid. When I have brought them back from the peoples and gathered them out of their enemies' lands, and I am hallowed in them in the sight of many nations, then they shall know that I am the LORD their God, who sent them into captivity among the nations, but also brought them back to their land, and left none of them captive any longer. And I will not hide My face from them anymore; for I shall have poured out My Spirit on the house of Israel,' says the Lord GOD."

Eze 39:1-29

This prophecy speaks of Gog, and it is a popular tendency to identify Gog and Russia as one. This is a tendency to which I agree. It specifically refers to Gog as the far north. Of course, this does not prove the relationahip.

The first angel sounded: And hail and fire followed, mingled with blood, and they were thrown to the earth. And a third of the trees were burned up, and all green grass was burned up. Then the second angel sounded: And something like a great mountain burning with fire was thrown into the sea, and a third of the sea became blood. And a third of the living creatures in the sea died, and a third of the ships were destroyed. Then the third angel sounded: And a great star[206] fell from heaven, burning like a torch, and it fell on a third of the rivers and on the springs of water. The name of the star is Wormwood. A third of the waters became wormwood, and many men died from the water, because it was made bitter.

Rev 8:7-11

These prophecies could be interpreted as nuclear devastations. A star named wormwood will poison the

---

[206] Nuclear explosion(?)

waters of the earth, rivers and perhaps oceans. Nuclear warfare could affect the oceans and inland waterways in this respect. Nuclear warfare could easily explain the time needed, seven months, to gather the dead for burial.

We are speaking of Prophetic iterations. I have used very few Scriptural references to illustrate my point. Hopefully, they are adequate to inspire further study that may shed light on what, exactly, will occur. The truth is not to be hidden from believers. Prophecies and history are there to be warnings for preparation.

While speaking historically, Ezra 7, could be prophetically interpreted as to how Israel will be treated by the rest of the world after the tribulation.

Outside the Box Solution

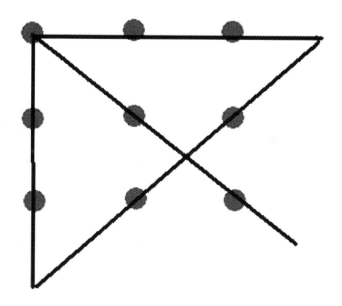

Outside the Box

Bibliography

Allman, W. (1994, May 9). Alternative Realities. *U. S. News and World Report.*

Augustine, S. (400). *The City of God.*

Brier, B. (1999). *The History of Ancient Egypt.* The Teaching Company.

Covey, S. R. (2004). *The 8th Habit.* New York: Free Press.

Covey, S. R. (n.d.). *The 7 Habits of Highly Effective Families.*

Covey, S. R. (n.d.). *The 7 Habits of Highly Effective People.*

Foxe, J. (2001). *The New Foxe's Book Of Martyrs.* Gainesville: Bridge-Logos.

Freeman, J. M. (1972). *Manners and Customs of the Bible.* Plainfield, N. J.: Logos.

Greene, B. (2003). *The Elegant Universe.* New York: Norton.

Greene, B. (2005). *The Fabric of the Cosmos.* New York: Vantage.

Hadas, M. (1956). *A History of Rome.* Garden City, N. Y.: Doubleday.

Hicks, B. (n.d.). *Precious Gems in the Tabernacle.* Jeffersonville, In: Christ Gospel Churches.

Kleist, J. A. (1948). The Epistle of Barnabas. In *Ancient Christian Writers* (pp. 37-65). Westminster, Maryland: Newman Press.

Larkin, C. (1918). *Dispensational Truth.* Rev. Clarence Larkin.

Larkin, C. (1929). *The Book of Daniel.* Philadelphia: Erwin Moyer.

McDowell, J. (2005). *More Than a Carpenter.* Carol Stream, IL: Tyndale House.

Moore. (1999). *I Must Decrease.* 1st Books.

Moore. (2007). *The Elder Shall Serve The Younger.* Xulon Press.

Morris, C. G. (1993). *Understanding Psychology.* Englewood Cliffs: Prentice Hall.

NeoTech. (1993). *Infinte Riches Trhough Cassandra's Secret.* Las Vegas: Zon.

Pink, A. W. (1974). *Gleanings in Exodus.* Chicago: Moody Press.

Price, R. (2005). *The Temple and Bible Prophecy.* Eugene, Oregon: Harvest House.

Producers@morethandreams.org. (2006). *Mohammed* (Vols. DVD video, 46 minutes). morethandreams.org.

Rana, F. (2008). *The Cell's Design.* Grand Rapids: Baker Books.

Rees, M. (1999). *Just Six Numbers.* New York: Basic Books.

Riess, A. T. (2004, February). The Expanding Universe: From Slowdown to Speed Up. *Scientific American.*

Rohl, D. (2003). *From Eden To Exilt.* London: Arrow Books.

Ross, H. (2001). *The Creator and the Cosmos.* Colorado Springs: NavPress.

Ruffin, C. B. (1991). *Padre Pio: The True Story.* Huntington, Indiana: Our Sunday Visitor.

Schroeder, G. (1992). *Genesis and the Big Bang.* New York: Bantam.

Schroeder, G. (2001). *The Hidden Face Of God*. New York: The Free Press.

Schroeder, G. L. (1997). *The Science of God*. New York: The Free Press.

Sheik. (1999). *I Dared to call Him Father*. New York: McGraw Hill.

Shiff, P. (1901). *A Select Library of the Nicene and Post-Nicene Fathers of the Christian Church, Vol. IV, St. Augustine: The Writings Against the Manichaeans and Against the Donatists*. New York.

Smith), H. W. (1875). *The Christian's Secret of a Happy Life*. London: Willard Tract Society.

Talk, d. (1999). Jesus Freaks. Bloomington, Mn: Bethany House.

Talk, d. (2003). Jesus Freaks Vol II. Minneapolis: Bethany House.

Trochu, A. F. (1985). *Saint Bernadette Soubirous*. Rockford, Illinois: Tan Books and Publishers, Inc.

Whiston, W. (1974). *Works of FlaviusJosephus*. Grand Rapids, Michigan: Baker Book House.

Printed in the United States
By Bookmasters